Friedrich Hölderlin

Eduard Mörike

SELECTED POEMS

The Farewell
29
The Poet's
Vocation
33

suborn
35

GERMAN LITERARY CLASSICS
IN TRANSLATION

General Editor: KENNETH J. NORTHCOTT

Georg Büchner
LEONCE AND LENA; LENZ; WOYZECK
Translated by Michael Hamburger

Friedrich Hölderlin and Eduard Mörike
SELECTED POEMS
Translated by Christopher Middleton

J. M. R. Lenz
THE TUTOR *and* THE SOLDIERS
Translated by William E. Yuill

Gotthold Ephraim Lessing
MINNA VON BARNHELM
Translated by Kenneth J. Northcott

Friedrich von Schiller
WILHELM TELL
Translated by William F. Mainland

Friedrich Hölderlin
Eduard Mörike

SELECTED POEMS

Translated
and with an
Introduction
by
CHRISTOPHER
MIDDLETON

The University of Chicago Press
Chicago and London

The University of Chicago Press, Chicago 60637
The University of Chicago Press, Ltd., London

International Standard Book Number (clothbound): 0–226–34933–0
Library of Congress Catalog Card Number: 72–79570

CONTENTS

PREFACE

Quantities of scholarly commentary have grown up around Hölderlin and Mörike during the past quarter-century. In Hölderlin's case this has sometimes meant that his ideas and poetics have been studied more closely than his practices as a poet. The most perceptive readings of actual poems by either poet are often isolated studies in Germanistic journals or in collections of miscellaneous essays. My main concern in preparing this book was to place some poems by each poet in the open (original and translation) for the delight and instruction of the reader with or without knowledge of German, with or without guidance from someone more specialized. For reasons of space I had to exclude poems written by Hölderlin before 1797 and (with one exception) after 1806. Of the long elegies, only one is included ("Bread and Wine"); others, like "The Archipelago," as well as poems written before and after the decade of this selection, can be read in Michael Hamburger's Bollingen and Penguin editions (see bibliography). The Mörike selection spans forty years. Here, too, limitations of space, combined with translator's perplexity, prevented me from including famous longer poems such as "Der alte Turmhahn" and the narratives "Märchen vom sicheren Mann" and "Idylle vom Bodensee." I was not able to translate more than one of Mörike's ballads. All the same, I believe that both selections include essential works by each poet, and that they are not unbalanced.

In the introduction I have not examined "ideas" to any great extent. Ideas are crucial in Hölderlin's case, less so in Mörike's. One may argue about Hölderlin's actual contribution to the philosophical system of Idealism. In his discussions with Hegel and Schelling, in Tübingen, Stuttgart, and

Nürtingen (1790–98), his searching intelligence may well have been the catalyst which brought the historic formula of triadic process—thesis, antithesis, synthesis. But ideas are elements in an intellectual context of which a poem is a transformation. A poem may be nourished by an idea, but it has a life of its own. Supporting philosophical insight (until one has assimilated all pertinent data) is ancillary rather than central to the experience of a poem as a poem. If one finds Hölderlin becoming obscure, it may be that he has arrived in a domain where language itself lends no support. Still, one may turn for one's own support to the intellectual context—the Eleatics, Rousseau, Hemsterhuis, Herder, Schiller—and to Hölderlin's letters and theoretical writings. But other writers have devoted space to his ideas; and given the limits of this book I have concentrated more on the poems for their own sakes. Readers are referred to Hamburger, Salzberger, and Benn (see bibliography) for discussion of ideas. There are many more analytic and complicated discussions in German.

As a recent study of the whole epoch, H. G. Schenk's *The Mind of the European Romantics* (Doubleday-Anchor, 1970) is sprightly and informative. Since some knowledge of the pastoral tradition is helpful, I mention William E. McCulloh's *Longus* (Twayne, 1970) as an intelligent guide to that field.

I wish to thank Michael Hamburger, pioneer among English Hölderlin translators, and Christoph Meckel for their help with certain words and constructions in Hölderlin. To Edwin Watkins I owe thanks for help with Hölderlin's classical measures. The students of a Mörike seminar in Austin (summer 1971) also alerted me to matters I would have missed. We approached the "musical" components of Mörike's poems, to start with, by listening to Hugo Wolf's settings. We also played some Greek folk dances for the scintillations of dactyl and trochee, plus one or two dances with fast and slow adoneus measures. Encouragement also came from other sources and connections. The interest in Hölderlin of the Brazilian concrete poets was recently shown when Haroldo de Campos published his version of "The Titans" in a Rio de Janeiro newspaper. Serbian and Croatian poets have translated Hölderlin, not to mention the French ones. Marina Svetaieva inscribed some lines by Hölderlin in her own copy of her book *Remeslo* (1923). During the mid-1920s, Osip Mandelstam was reading Mörike in Armenia. In the tiny Swabian village of Ochsenwang, two years ago, a lady of eighty recited to me, eloquently and by heart, passages from letters which the curate Mörike had written from there in 1832, in the same room where he lived with his starling. Notwithstanding the poisons of busy manunkind, the pure source possibly still flows, bringing the original information.

UNSYSTEMATIC INTRODUCTION

I

It should not be supposed that the two German poets repre-
sented in this book have a great deal in common. Their
birthplaces are less than a day's walk apart; but when Mörike
was born in 1804, Hölderlin was thirty-four years old and
almost insane. By the time Mörike went to the Tübingen
theological college—the *Stift*—where Hölderlin had been a
student more than thirty years before, the age of revolution
and wars in which Hölderlin had come to his maturity was a
thing of the past and a period of reaction had set in, with
Württemberg no longer a dukedom but a kingdom. Hölderlin's
poems, like Blake's, are visionary works from an era of deep
social turbulence, of violence, injustice, and lofty aspiration.
Mörike's poems have, by and large, a less apocalyptic social
context; and even though they do have some visionary
qualities, these qualities are worked into filigree structures
rather than monumental ones. Yet the two poets do have
their roots in the same region and the same society. And both,
for all their differences of character, are heirs to the cultural
traditions of that region (which had once been a center of
medieval poetry), lovers of its physical landscape, and living
voices from its bygone times. Both, too, are poets of the
pastoral tradition going back to Greek prototypes; and often
their metrics are, oddest of all, Greco-Alemannic. It is as if
some spirit, which moves and speaks in rhythms, had floated
from its older Mediterranean moorings to settle for a time in
the surround of small towns, hills, rivers, and breezy wood-
lands, the crumpled green terrain which was the Swabia
known to Hölderlin and Mörike two thousand years later.

Here again there are distinctions. Hölderlin is heroic, and

he translated Pindar and Sophocles (accenting in the latter the "Asiatic" components). Mörike is not heroic in the least. He is more intent on the everyday incident, without grandeur: he translated the Sicilian proto-idyllist Theocritus, but also (among other Greek and Latin poets) Catullus and Horace as models of precise *parlando* tone. (Actually Mörike for the most part refurbished existing translations.) Both poets make antique elements new. Neither is merely bookish in his relation to his classics. Greek or Latin poetry explored and defined modes of consciousness on which civilization, for good or ill, continuously depends; and when Hölderlin or Mörike looks back, or takes the step back, into the past, it is a creative act of commitment to civilized values, an act which brings peculiar tensions into the sense of the present. Hölderlin, like Nietzsche later, was prepossessed by the magnitude of the Greek intelligence. Mörike, set chronologically between Hölderlin and Nietzsche, is suspicious about ideas of magnitude, with their drift toward preposterousness. A master of condensation, he is deepest when he senses the universe as an organism living by measure, as a matter of proportion, modulating itself in the subtlest perceptions and the tiniest forms. But this sense of measure is not less Greek than the idea of magnitude; and it also betokens some kind of kinship between Mörike and such artists of the infinitesimal as Giacometti and Erik Satie.

Some of the differences between Hölderlin and Mörike can be gauged from Mörike's feelings about the older poet. He must have seen Hölderlin, a madman in his fifties, walking about in Tübingen in 1822, before he actually met him. When he did meet him in July 1823 (probably introduced by his friend Wilhelm Waiblinger), he took with him another friend, Rudolf Lohbauer, and a young artist called Johann Georg Schreiner. Schreiner's and Lohbauer's joint sketch of Hölderlin, balding slightly, with a long wispy sideburn, a straight and rather fleshy nose, the head bowed forward, and a muscular left hand with palm to the fore, indicates that Mörike was curious enough about Hölderlin to initiate a portrait, but hardly that he was in awe of him.[1] At about this

1. In the summer of 1826 Mörike took Schreiner to see Hölderlin again, and afterwards Schreiner made a second sketch from memory.

time he immersed himself in Hölderlin's novel *Hyperion* (1797–99). He read it with rapture, together with another friend, Johannes Mährlen, sprawling among cowslips and maybugs in a field on the outskirts of Tübingen. But in May 1832, reminding Mährlen of this in a letter, he wrote: "Ultimately the whole thing is a touching caricature, single lovely lyrical passages, incomparably true, fearfully transposed into an action. . . . One feels ravished, a god's fingers suddenly touching the tenderest fibers of one's soul, powerfully uplifted, and then again so sick, pusillanimous, hypochondriacal, and miserable, that every trace is expunged of the actual province of all poetry, including tragic poetry. . . . One is dejected, for it is half a work of art, which, if it had been thought out with more principle and consideration, could so easily have been a whole one." In February 1843, five months before Hölderlin's death, Mörike was invited by the poet's sister to look through a basketful of manuscripts at Nürtingen. While he was doing so, servant girls would come into the room and do a little knitting: "That kind of diversion was necessary," he wrote to Wilhelm Hartlaub, "otherwise one might almost have gone clean out of one's mind amid such wreckage." He found much to wonder at in the basket, manuscripts dense with corrections, the Sophocles translations, letters from friends, a letter or two possibly from "the hand of the lady we know as Diotima," also galleys of *Hyperion*; but he could not see any sense at all in some of the writing—"utterly confused stuff."

It was not until Hellingrath's edition began to appear a few years before the First World War that another generation of readers was enabled to study some of these manuscript texts (the cautious selections of 1826 and 1846 had long been out of print). Only after the Second World War did Friedrich Beissner's edition appear, clarifying every obscure reading and lacuna, as far as they can be clarified. Mörike, who came to be regarded as a Hölderlin connoisseur, and who owned several

---

Much later Mörike remarked on Hölderlin's typical gesture shown in this sketch: pointing a demonstrative forefinger (letter to Wilhelm Hensen, 13 May 1873, *Unveröffentlichte Briefe*, ed. F. Seebaß, 2d ed. [Stuttgart, 1945], 465).

manuscripts himself, saw Hölderlin as a poet whose break-
down was prefigured already in some of his best writing, as in
Hyperion. We have no idea what he might have thought
about the last completed hymns, or about "The Rhine" and
"Patmos." Conventional as it may have been, there was
nothing smug about his view of Hölderlin (most writers of the
mid-century simply ignored him). Mörike himself was a poet
who was subjected to deep psychic shocks in his twenties,
who knew about the demonic, and who was later plagued by
illnesses needing, it seemed, homeopathic treatment. He, too,
could never quite come to terms with the Swabian clerical
establishment, a power which had strained Hölderlin as well,
rebellious as he was, under the sense of obligation to become a
clergyman. They were both eccentric and inspired poets; both,
to say the least, were difficult men.

II

Hölderlin was of medium height, well built, and gray-eyed.
His hair was brown, his complexion fair. In the portrait by
Franz Karl Hiemer, Hölderlin is wearing a white wig, the
hair covering his ears and collar. The forehead is broad and
high, the eyes are set well apart, lower and upper lids well
marked, and the root of the nose is spatulate. The shape of
the face is oval, but undulant volumes run from the fairly
high cheekbones to the squarish chin. A fine, bowlike curve
marks the ridge of the upper lip; the lower lip is rounded and
sensuous, seemingly supported by a little arched fold of
shadow. Hiemer's portrait was thought by Hölderlin's sister
to be not a good likeness; probably it idealizes the face. But
though scholars have missed in it requisite traces of "manly
pride," the expression mirrors Hölderlin's luminous sensi-
bility. He is smiling a little, and looking straight at you; yet he
seems also shy, not certain about the world he is looking at,
tender toward it, but wondering what it is. There is an almost
girlish grace in the features; or, with his face at this angle, he
has the look of a nocturnal animal, not tame, caught in a flash
of light. It is a face which looks outward, while all the time it
is sending coded signals back inward. Other portraits also
show the unusual depth of his head, from brow to the back of

the skull. The broad left shoulder slopes at an angle of forty-five degrees to the back and head, the head being thus poised upright but off center. Hölderlin liked to dress well. The visible upper body is clad in a velveteen jacket of a sea-green color, with vertical ribbings. The shirt is white, open-collared, and a series of folds and pleats descends as far as the second jacket buttonhole.

This young man can ride, swim, and fence; an exact contemporary of Beethoven, he is also an excellent pianist and flautist. He knows Hebrew, Greek, and Latin, also some French. He is reading Kant, and has read some Plato; a few months from now he will be reading Leibniz and Spinoza. He was sixth in his graduating class at the *Klosterschule* of Maulbronn, with an *A* in "Poetry (also Greek)." He is a close friend of Hegel at the Tübingen *Stift*. In a month's time he will meet the third seminal mind of Idealism—Schelling, a new student, only fifteen years old. It is one year after the outbreak of the French revolution. Specifically: on the morning of 9 September 1790 this Hölderlin is standing in a platoon of about twenty students, drawn up in three lines, in the examination hall of the *Stift*, a paneled room, for the building dates from the sixteenth century. Each student carries in his hand a pamphlet: the theses on "The Psalms and Acts of the Apostles," propounded by Professor Schnurrer. And each in turn has to deliver a defense of this or that proposition, probably in Latin. Schnurrer is sure of his students; he says "—I am having my theses defended, that is to say—I'm defending them myself." These procedures are boring and normal. The *Stift* has stringent rules. Four months after the Bastille was stormed (July 1789), Duke Karl Eugen, despotic ruler of the Duchy of Württemberg and regent of the *Stift*, had insisted that discipline be even stricter. Hölderlin has been there now for a year, and from the beginning he had wanted out—to study law rather than theology, to escape from "the dejection forced upon body and soul" by "mistreatment . . . pressures and contempt" (letter to his mother, November 1789). On the other hand he is writing poems, and he has good friends, Neuffer and Magenau. They read Klopstock and Schiller together, and drink Rhine wine, which Hölderlin

finds "electrically healing for the soul." They recite their
poems and discuss them, sometimes in the small garden house
at the inn called "The Lamb" on the Österberg. Hölderlin's
poems are hymns in Schiller's manner, grand in tone,
sumptuously rhymed, ápostrophes to the freedom and love
which his Greeks brought to bear on the world and with
which the French revolutionaries are now regenerating
Europe. In September 1791, three of these poems appear in
Gotthold Friedrich Stäudlin's *Musenalmanach für das Jahr
1792*; and Stäudlin is a friend of Christian Friedrich Schubart,
the libertarian apostle of Klopstock. Hölderlin also has to preach
sometimes. Toward the end of March 1791 he is determined
to preach from the heart, for he feels that sincerity must
replace convention in society, so that "everyone should be
what he really is." During Hölderlin's student years at
Tübingen—a minor university, with only a few hundred
students, half of them in the college of theology—Duke Karl
Eugen is perpetually seeing that stricter rules are applied.
Hölderlin's father died in 1772, when the poet was two years
old; and when he was nine his stepfather died. His image of
authority was a mixed one. The loving stepfather who died
was a different character from the totalitarian Karl Eugen
presiding from afar over the *Stift*. Two of his constant ques-
tions were: Under what provocation does a loving God punish
man?—and: What is to be done when divine and human
planes of being cease to connect? There is some ambivalence
in his rebellion against authority throughout his life. In
September 1806, when he is being bundled into the coach that
will take him from Homburg to the Autenrieth clinic in
Tübingen, he shouts in rage and fright: "I'm not a Jacobin!"
—believing that they are arresting him as a revolutionary
sympathizer.

In February 1792 he writes to his sister in Nürtingen: "We
must give our country and the world an example to show that
we are not created and disposed to let others play an arbitrary
game with us." The same month brings the coalition of
Austria and Prussia against France. In May 1793, a radical
democrat called Wetzel (soon to write a powerful nihilistic
book called *Die Nachtwachen des Bonaventura*, "The Vigils of

Bonaventura") runs away from the *Stift*. One afternoon a month later, a haggard Hölderlin declaims to a visiting poet, Friedrich Matthison, his "Ode to the Genius of Courage." He is by now working on his novel *Hyperion*; and his despair about the revolution is voiced when, after the assassination of Marat late in July 1793, he writes a letter condemning that "atrocious tyrant" and all the other anti-Girondist "violators of the people." (A year later, August 1794, he is glad when Robespierre is executed.) Moved afresh by Schiller's lofty-minded Marquis Posa (in *Don Carlos*), he writes to his step-brother early in September 1793: "My love is mankind, the generations of centuries to come. . . . Freedom must come one day, and virtue will flourish better in the holy and warming light of freedom, than in the icy zone of despotism. . . . This is the holy aim of my wishes and doings: that in our time I may quicken the seeds that shall ripen in a future time." When Hegel left the *Stift* that September, Hölderlin's last words to him were "Reich Gottes!" ("May God's Kingdom come!").

The successive deaths of his two fathers had not left Hölderlin's family destitute. His mother's grief must have cast a pall over much of Hölderlin's childhood. But financially the family (a highly respected one) was still well off, and despite the total of eight deaths among relatives during the first nine years of Hölderlin's life, the kinship system peculiar to Württemberg society kept family feeling intact. He even had a small patrimony. As firstborn son of such a family, and as *Magister* from the *Stift*, he was accepted when he left Tübingen as tutor in the household of Schiller's friend Charlotte von Kalb (Schiller, too, was a Swabian). This was at Waltershausen in Thuringia, where Hölderlin spent the first nine months of 1794 in the seclusion of the von Kalb family manor. There were three choices open to a young Württemberger who had attended *Klosterschule* and *Stift*: he went into the church (itself a socially powerful system), or he received a short-term traveling scholarship, or he became a tutor in a household of the *haute bourgeoisie*. There was always pressure, from the Württemberg Protestant consistory, in favor of the clerical profession; possibly, too, Hölderlin's mother had taken a vow, on the death of her first husband, that her son Friedrich Christoph would become a servant of God, or of the consistory. "Servant of God" Hölderlin was inclined to be, of his own accord. But in his own way. The service of God in a salaried profession within a church which was the spiritual arm of an authoritarian political system seemed to him a form of sacrilege. Waltershausen, followed by about eight months with his nine-year-old pupil in Jena, was only the first stage in Hölderlin's itinerary as a tutor. Thereafter he went to the Gontards in Frankfurt am Main (1796–September 1798); and after a subsequent period of twenty months (September 1798–May 1800) in Homburg, where he wrote and rewrote his *Empedocles* tragedy and was attempting to live by his pen, supported meagerly by family funds, he went for four months to Hauptwil in Switzerland (December 1800–April 1801). Finally, late in 1801, he traveled by coach to Lyon and from there about 350 miles on foot across central and southwestern France to Bordeaux, where he stayed as tutor in the German consul's household for about three months. Then abruptly he left Bordeaux, and traveled (much of the way probably on foot) via Paris and Strasbourg to Stuttgart. That journey of 1802 took almost three months, and little is known about it. Returning to Stuttgart in June, he appeared among friends looking "deathly pale, very thin, with hollow wild eyes, long hair and a beard, and dressed like a beggar" (Matthison). He stood there and simply said, when he saw Matthison: "Hölderlin." Yet by October 1802 he had recovered. He went to Regensburg with his friend Isaak von Sinclair, who as a jurist was involved in settling some territorial disputes. Sinclair reported that he had never seen Hölderlin "more full of soul and intelligence." In Regensburg, Hölderlin talked at some length with Friedrich, ruler of the state of Homburg-Hessen, a religious man and a benign authoritarian (see notes to "Patmos"). During the last months of that year he was at work in Nürtingen on his poem "Patmos," which he dedicated to the Landgraf Friedrich.

Looking back now six years from 1802, we see Hölderlin freshly arrived in Frankfurt in late December 1795. His meeting with Susette Gontard, the wife of his employer, marked a turning point in his life.[2] While he had been in Jena (1794–95), he had been immersed in speculative philosophy. He had seen Schiller not infrequently, but little of Goethe. He had found his high pedagogical ideals frustrated by the backward boy whose tutor he was. The philosophizing had wearied him: he would rise at about 5 A.M., making coffee, smoke his pipe, and read unendingly, later attending Fichte's lectures. The Fichtean system starts at a point where Kant drew a limit. Hölderlin found Fichte's strenuous ethical image of man congenial, but his epistemology was of a kind to trap the self-reflexive consciousness inside its own functionings and verbalisms. Knowledge of objects is not knowledge of conditions in consciousness which we project upon objects: but here the balance shifts from objects, in favor of "pure" subjectivity. Another step and it would seem that "God" is subjective. Self-knowledge: a labyrinth of reflexion in which all the objective beauty and glory ascribed to "God"—or qualities ascribed to any mode of being which is "Not-I"—become shadows rather than substance. Possibly one of the most radical thoughts of the Goethe era was the thought that the human mind projects its own contents, including values, upon the world: that man shapes the world in his image. It was a revolutionary thought if you translated it into social concepts, even though it was antithetic to the Marxist concept of history, in which the objective socioeconomic nexus is the world-shaping factor, not any Fichtean internally ramifying ego. Hölderlin fled from Jena with the nightbirds of this titanic egoism darkening his vision of things. Then at last he arrives in Frankfurt, and early in 1796 he sees Susette Gontard. Her presence tells him that the beauty and intelligence which the Greeks had found to be features of God, are truly and intrinsically "objective," out there, in others, for any to behold, if they have the love with which to see aright. She

2. Her letters to Hölderlin, some of which Mörike had seen in 1843, were not published until 1921, when the identity of Hölderlin's "Diotima" was established. He derived this name for her from Plato's *Symposium*, where Diotima (which means "Justice of God") is the priestess of Love, of whom Socrates speaks. See "The Farewell" and "If from the distance . . ."

is incarnation—of harmony, peace, the ultimate heart's desire.

Susette Gontard was twenty-seven at the time, one year older than Hölderlin. Her husband, Jakob Friedrich, was her second cousin; he was five years older than she, and they had four children. She had already been married for ten years. Herr Gontard was a textiles magnate and banker, who put business first, but a cultivated man for all that. Six months after Hölderlin meets the Gontards, French armies invade the Frankfurt region, and Hölderlin goes with Susette and her children northward, to Cassel and Bad Driburg, where they spend the summer, returning to Frankfurt when the troubles have passed. But they hardly pass. Württemberg is occupied by the French in 1796; in October that year Hölderlin hears from a friend in Paris, Johann Gottfried Ebel, that things look bad in France, the revolution is going wrong. In March 1798 the French besiege Mainz. What had first seemed like a French movement to bring liberty and regeneration to France as an example for other peoples under the yoke of absolutism, has now become a military operation to impose nationalist France by violence on the rest of Europe. Austria is defeated in December 1800. Hopes of better times rise again with the Treaty of Lunéville, February 1801, the occasion of Hölderlin's recently discovered cryptic and massive "Celebration of Peace." I note these details because there is a tendency to isolate Hölderlin's lofty idealism and his relationship with Susette Gontard, his Diotima, from this constant turbulence and terror. Yet I would not argue that the physical pressures of events "explain" anything, least of all the determination he showed to translate the social revolution of the times into a spiritual one, realized in poetry. The pressures were still mounting. When Hölderlin walked through France, pistol in pocket, during the winter 1801–2, crossing the mountains of the Massif Central into Périgord, passing not far from that womb (unknown to anyone) of culture in Europe, Lascaux, it must have been for him like walking through the wild interior space of a volcano.[3] Susette was far behind: within six

3. The English agriculturalist Arthur Young had traveled in this region only twelve years before: see his *Travels in France and Italy*

months, after nursing her children through measles, weakened
by tuberculosis, she herself was dead. Forty years later and six
months before his own death Hölderlin was asked about her,
and he replied: "Ah, my Diotima. Don't speak to me about
my Diotima. Thirteen sons she bore me. One is Pope, another
is the Sultan, the third is Emperor of Russia," then suddenly
he broke out in his Swabian dialect: "Ont wisset Se, wies no
ganga ischt? Närret isch se worde, närret, närret, närret! (And
do you know what happened to her? She went mad, she did,
mad, mad, mad)."

III

After this rapid sketch of Hölderlin—in which there are
inevitably gaps and missing depths[4]—we should now dwell for
a moment on some characteristic points in a poem of his
Homburg period (1798–1800). I wish also to raise certain issues
that are involved in translating Hölderlin. Reading him, one
is faced with poetic language of a highly incandescent kind.
The particles in these lustrous structures of language are active
in peculiar ways. If there is any common ground between
Hölderlin and Goethe it is this: for both poets every life
experience is a linguistic experience.[5] *Logos* and *mythos* are
not fixed stars any more (as they still had been, with a few
variations, in the Baroque period). With his unique feeling for
language, the poet as artificer expresses "soul" as language;
and this "soul" is conscious of being in a time world, subject
to fluctuations ("moods"). This new sense of the internality
of language in space and time makes the poet not so much an

During the Years 1787, 1788, and 1789 (London: Everyman Library,
1927), especially the vivid descriptions of the mountainous Auvergne
region (June 1787, pp. 24–27, and August 1789, pp. 190–98).

4. Readers with German are referred to *Hölderlin: eine Chronik
in Text und Bild*, ed. Adolf Beck and Paul Raabe (Frankfurt am
Main, 1970), especially the chronicle (pp. 7–110) by Adolf Beck and
Karl-Gert Kribben. Stansfield, Hamburger, and Salzberger can also
be consulted (see Bibliography). Some of the notes to poems in the
selection contain other biographical details.

5. Rudolf Kassner, "On Goethe's Greatness and his Fortune,"
translated by this writer, *Delos* 5 (1970): 74–97 (original in Kassner's
Umgang der Jahre [Erlenbach-Zürich, 1949]).

imitator (as he was in any relatively fixed world of the *logos*) as an inaugurator, who has a hand in the continuous work of creation. The ensuing exploration of what we might call "positive irrationality" marked as crucial a point in the life of the Western poetic mind as the exploration later, by such writers as Gogol, Dostoevsky, and Kafka, of negative irrationality, the bane of our own century. Hence the passion animating Hölderlin's view of history, not merely as a series of happenings, but as the rhythmical realization of an eschatological plan (the "divine economy" of the Swabian Pietists) which moves through dark night to the day of apocalypse. (Mörike no longer sees history in this way.) Hence, too, the lack of any spare words in Hölderlin's mature poetry, and the essentiality of his syntax. Consider the telescoped and telescopic cola of the first sentence in "Patmos": "Nah ist / Und schwer zu fassen der Gott" (literally: "Near is and hard to grasp the God"). It sometimes looks as if, in some of the last fragments (like the one with the editorial title "Like seacoasts . . ."), Hölderlin is converting the involutions of German syntax into concentrated forms resembling Chinese ideograms. Certainly it is poetry departing from plain linear progression, or, to put it picturesquely, poetry as a field of vision crossed and recrossed by whirlwinds of fire. That, perhaps, is how Hölderlin experienced "ideas": they crossed his mind like whirlwinds of formal sensation. One thus has to be careful when one asks what is the true axis of a particular word in its context, or what is its function in that context. One can intuit the radius of a word's connotations, but one is hard put to define that radius. One also has to allow for the fact that connotations valid then may not be perceptible (or translatable) now.

In stanza 2 of the poem "Heidelberg" (text on p. 20) comes the phrase with the word *tönt* in it. The bridge "sounds." Hölderlin wrote *tönt* in his first draft (1798), changed it to *rauscht* (a faint dull roar, or a murmur), and finally in 1800 he restored *tönt*. Mörike, who admired the poem especially and copied a text for his friend Hartlaub from an unpublished manuscript in March 1847, commended *tönt* for its "fine feeling." It is probable that Hölderlin had in mind here not the noise on the bridge but the vibrating of the arch of the bridge under the transient weight of wagons and people.[6] In 1800 this vibration would have connoted, for him and for Hegel, a trembling of matter as it becomes animated (= ensouled) and edges toward immateriality (like the sounding of a cello string).[7] Hölderlin's sense of such musical values was acute. It develops as he composes in his later hymns intricate fugal structures. This vibrance of the material object is not connoted for many contemporary readers by the word *sounds*, which can do little more than denote a vague noise. *Vibrates* would be wrong, because no sound is explicit in the word; besides, *tönt* does not say *vibrates*.

With the above connotation, *tönt* occurs in a rhythmic verbal pattern which projects a complete image of a segment of world where sky and earth, height and depth, water and land, motion and stillness, meet. English can follow the lexical directions but hardly the rhythmic and tonal organization of such an image. Opposites coincide in a specific place, graphically presented. Moreover, opposites are integrated in the image; and this integration epitomizes that vibrant oneness of all being which for the young pantheistic Hölderlin was signified so resonantly by the Greek phrases ἐν και παν (hen kai pan = the one and all), and ἐν διαφερον ἑαυτῳ (hen diapheron heautō = the one differentiated in itself [Heraclitus]). Hölderlin refers to the latter as the "essence of beauty" in his novel *Hyperion* (vol. 1, 1797).[8] This dialectical consonance of a whole poetic image, epitome of a cosmos, is the context to which *tönt* relates as microcosm to macrocosm. The

6. He first passed through Heidelberg when he was eighteen, on 3 June 1788, was there again in June 1795, probably in December 1795, and again in late May or early June 1800. The bridge was built in 1786–88.

7. Hegel called this vibrance "die ideelle Seelenhaftigkeit" ("ideal soul-quality"): see his *Ästhetik* (Stuttgart, 1928), 3:124. My source: Emil Staiger, *Meisterwerke deutscher Sprache* (Zürich-Berlin, 1943), 15, essay on "Heidelberg."

8. Hyperion's nineteenth letter to Bellarmin. The *hen kai pan* phrase was supposedly written on a placard hung on Hölderlin's wall during one period in Tübingen. Brecht, as a refugee near Svendborg in Denmark during the 1930s, had on his wall an antithetic sign: "Die Wahrheit ist konkret" ("Truth is concrete").

poem need not be read thus in the context of the metaphysics peculiar to incipient Idealism; but that context does bear on it, as ideas about cosmic circularity and the *pneuma* in Renaissance geometry bear on John Donne's "Valediction: Forbidding Mourning."

But then "Heidelberg" is introduced as an "artless song." The marvel is that the supposedly "artless" poem projects (without irony) into a supposedly "objective" world a kind of order which is for Hölderlin intrinsic to "beauty." The poem is a field in which subject and object are, for an infinite moment, one. In the "song," it might seem, nature spontaneously reveals her intricate and varied order as beauty in vibrance. The text is language imbued with the vibrance which for Hölderlin is also revealed in the "aether," *Aither*, air's luminous vesture of the divine (as again in the late fragment "Greece"). This is a clue to the structural relation in stanza 2 between the bird (of air above) and the vibrant sounding bridge (below). However vehement his language may become, Hölderlin goes about transforming chance into pattern. I mention this only in passing: one element in his grand vision of reality as a harmonic system operating in history is the old Platonic doctrine of the "world soul."

The angle of vision keeps changing. Stanza 3: into the mountainous distance. Stanza 4: toward the rushing river. Stanza 5: to the streams pouring into the river and to the image of the town reflecting in the waves (low-angle perspective). The English "jockeying over" here might be objected to: it sidesteps the original *bebte aus* = "tremble out of"—which means that the town's image shimmers to the wave surface as if it had been in the water's depth. This upward trembling is a central detail in the pattern of up-and-down motions and it is magnified in what follows. The up-down shift of stanza 2 (bird-bridge) recurs in stanza 6— gigantic fort, torn to the ground. Again it recurs in stanza 7— sun pouring down. Again at the juncture of 7 and 8—forests rustle down across the fort. The lowest point is reached last: the *Unter* of the last line leading, after a kaleidoscopic shift of detail, into the present-tense repose of *ruhn*.

This interanimation of motion and repose, upward and

downward, outward and inward, is realized also in th
of the poem. Briefly, in the modulations back and forth
between the pitches of front and back vowels (*i–a–u*). Com-
pared with the original phonic structure, the translation is
pitched about three intervals too high in the lower registers.
Also the phonics of the translation do not alternate enough
between thrust and suavity, such as occurs in the original in
stanzas 5–6. Still, the translation does conserve a scene in
which "nature" is a constellation of forces. The order of
nature is still animated, even if some of the animating
sound-vibrance is lost.

   While translating one has to observe how the original parts
of speech function. The rhythmic and phonic design of the
original is such that the contours of things come to seem fluid,
because everything is happening. Such animation, in the
stories of Hölderlin's contemporary Heinrich von Kleist, can
lead to a kind of syntax in which things are almost obliterated
—they become eddies in the whirl of action. Not so here. The
present participles ("Heidelberg," stanzas 3, 4, 7, 8) are parts
of this wavering design. Likewise the ten intransitive verbs:
denoting actions unimpeded by objects, but related as in a
field of force. Yet every "thing" is in plain view for the mind's
eye, everything is *anschaulich*. Is there a kinship between this
sense of the visible world and that of Rilke with his world of
"pure relation" in the *Sonnets to Orpheus* (1922)? One should
read Rilke's poem "To Hölderlin" (1914). Parts of speech can
be translated attentively; but their kinds of activity in this
kind of stanza (asclepiadic) often depend on the inflections of
German which English lacks.

   The sequence of tenses also shares in the vibrance. "Heidel-
berg" begins with a present-tense assertion, and it moves at
once into the *möchte*, which has a future projection (adum-
brating the song to come). Stanza 2 has two intransitive verbs
in the present, and one reflexive verb. Stanzas 3–7 shift into
the preterite, with a split pluperfect and a present tense in
stanza 5. Stanza 8 begins in the preterite but ends in the
present (both verbs intransitive). The scene in the poem is
recollected. Stanza 2 invokes the town's presence by framing
it in the present tense. Once the presence is established, a

specific recollected moment is evoked in the preterite (stanzas 3–4). In stanza 5, a still remoter past is recalled with the pluperfect but it is framed in the quasi-mythic present (*wirft*). Yet in 6 the "time" is both closer than the pluperfect and remoter than that present, for the tense is still preterite. With the two present participles of 7 (*alternd, verjüngend*), time is gathering again for a shift into the present. But it does not arrive there until the very last word: *ruhn*. This is a fully realized pattern of fusion in memory between what was and what is. Mörike is also intent on such patterns. It is memory radiantly sensing active pattern in time, memory contesting mortality. What is far in space or remote in time becomes living presence without being abstracted from the fluctuations of time. Here, as in many poems, Hölderlin speaks not to fellow humans but to the presences entrancing his imagination: earth, river, sky, or gods. This is not merely a nod to the convention in the ode ("apostrophe") which generically requires such a form of address. Hölderlin refreshes the convention, for he has or desires a profound intimate relation to the "thou" he addresses. This meaning of deep memory comes to the fore in his poem "Remembrance" (1803). In Mörike, too, one finds a fondness for speaking to things. Old-fashioned as it may sound, such speech is permeated with the feeling of an intimate creative relationship.

Both the vibrance and the intimacy in Hölderlin's whole image in "Heidelberg" might remind some people of Van Gogh's later paintings, with their "luminous currents of force." At least, Hölderlin and Van Gogh have sometimes been loosely associated (perhaps as artists who both "burned themselves out" in the south of France, though that notion rests on a false chronology of Hölderlin's last poems). Here there is none of Van Gogh's torrid ferocity, in which we see, as Artaud said, "a slow fertile nightmare being elucidated little by little."[9] Either way, what we see in "Heidelberg" is not nature naked. The poem is a sequence of images of nature as she was felt to be. In Hölderlin's poetics of transfiguration, the lyric poem is precisely this: "the continuous metaphor of a

9. *Artaud Anthology*, edited by Jack Hirshman, 2d ed. (San Francisco, 1965), 151.

feeling."[10] And the quality of the feeling here, though apparently mouth to mouth with an actual scene, is still in Hölderlin's sense "ideal." Spontaneous feeling, enshrined in memory, is refined by the transforming imagination, which crystallizes out in words that "come into being, like flowers" ("Bread and Wine" V). Early drafts of this poem are dated 1798–99, and the final draft was written during the summer 1800. During this period Hölderlin was wrestling with problems of a transition in style, from the odes to the hymns. This entailed a hard look at what he called "the ice-cold history of common day," as well as self-criticism on account of his "overhasty" idealizing tendency to overlook concrete infinitesimals and aspire to a purely intellectual harmony.[11] More relevant to Hölderlin than any loose Van Gogh analogy I find Osip Mandelstam's observation, that in Dante as at the basis of the waltz we can find "the purely European passion for periodic wavering movements, that same intent listening to the wave, which runs through all our theory of light and

10. *Sämtliche Werke* (Grosse Stuttgarter Ausgabe, see Bibliography) 4:266.
11. Letter to Neuffer, 12 November 1798. This and other relevant texts are discussed by Peter Szondi, *Hölderlin-Studien* (Frankfurt am Main, 1967), 105ff., especially 111. See also Michael Hamburger's introduction to his Penguin selection, 17ff. In the letter to Neuffer, Hölderlin wrote (*Sämtliche Werke* 6:290): "I am afraid of being disturbed by reality in the inward communion with which I gladly attach myself to something else; I am afraid to chill the warm life in me with the ice-cold history of common day, and this fear springs from my having been more sensitively receptive than others to any destructive thing which befell me, ever since my youth, and this sensitivity seems to be rooted in my being not firmly and indestructibly organized enough in relation to the experiences which I have had to undergo" (translation from *The Poet's Vocation*, 15, see Bibliography). In his fragment "A Word about the *Iliad*," from the same period, Hölderlin commends the .type of person who has integrated his faculties into a harmonious whole, but he goes on: "Sometimes we are tempted to think that, while he can feel the whole spirit of things, he averts his eyes overmuch from particulars; and that, while others do not see the wood for the trees, he forgets the trees on account of the wood; also that, although he has soul, he is not exactly reasonable, and is thus not understandable to others" (*Sämtliche Werke* 4:226).

sound, all our theory of matter, all our poetry and all our music."[12]

IV

I am going to approach Mörike's poetry now in a rather different way. I have been suggesting that "Heidelberg" can be read as an epitome of a world view at a certain stage in Hölderlin's meteoric development. That view is a physiognomical one: the visible world is fraught with a temporal drama of transcendent ideas. This becomes the great tragic vision of Hölderlin's later hymns (as "The Rhine" and "Patmos"), where visible objects and events are intricately interconnected as elements in a grand cosmic theater, where all is substance and all is metaphor. The "world" is like a face: poetic vision divines an ideal structure which its flitting expressions, or transformations, embody in space and time. Rimbaud is still far off. The transformations for Hölderlin are not those of an ego which has imposed on itself the task of "disorientation" or "hallucination," with a view to exploring an Africa of the mind where ultimate secrets may be wrested from the psyche. Hölderlin is on the threshold of this, as his *Empedocles* versions show; he also goes in terror of the bad nexus of narcissism and hubris. But his dwelling proper is another domain: poetry as ontology. Mörike's method is another possibility: a poetry transfiguring everyday situations. Even in his custom of writing little occasional poems to go with gifts or greetings we can find a strange and original desire to poeticize the most ordinary things in life. The danger here was that you might end up with mere "background" poetry, and a great number of nineteenth-century German poems are just that: *Trivialpoesie*. Yet in Mörike's poems, including many of his occasional ones, there is a delicacy and good artistic sense which obviate that particular danger. I want to approach his work via a comparison between his poem "Urach Revisited" (text on pp. 136–40), written in May 1827 when he was twenty-three, and Wordsworth's "Lines Composed a Few Miles above Tintern

12. Osip Mandelstam, "Talking about Dante," trans. Clarence Brown, *Delos* 6 (1971): 87–88.

Abbey," dated 13 July 1798 when Wordsworth was twenty-eight. This will lead into some general thoughts on Mörike's artistry, and on his sense of self in time.

Both Wordsworth's poem and Mörike's concern a relationship between the poet and nature.[13] For both poets, earlier experience of nature in a specific place meant spontaneous enjoyment of communion with her. This is explicit in Wordsworth. Mörike does not declare that such communion was the case, but it is the gist of his stanzas 1–6. Wordsworth tempers his evocation of the old days with allusion to the "coarser pleasures" he then knew, but he does gently commend the "animal" which he then was: "For nature then . . . / To me was all in all." In both poems the poet looks into the foreground of a time five years ago. From the later standpoint in time, the older communion is absent. More or less directly, too, each of the poems bears in its own way on an age-old traumatic point in the evolution of human consciousness: that point in man's remote background when he broke with nature and opted for culture (or drifted into it). Anagogically, both poems are about a view of "paradise." Wordsworth claims that he has kept his paradise by internalizing and sublimating it (lines 22ff.). He has no wish to go back in time. Mörike feels that he has lost his paradise, and he does wish to go back in time. For him, then and now do not have the internal continuity which for Wordsworth is assured by his being reflexive —his reflexiveness.

This area of reflexiveness is where the ways divide. Wordsworth is content, even complacent, in the reflexive attitude which he has achieved. It is loftier, more sublime, and more embracing. He has a stronger sense of self, and the maturer eye is "made quiet by the power / Of harmony," so that "We see into the life of things." His reflexive internalizing of the landscape is "abundant recompense" for any loss. Now he can view nature as "the anchor of my purest thoughts." Not so Mörike in "Urach Revisited." He voices anguish at being shut out from nature in her immediacy. He attempts, bodily and mentally, to penetrate nature's monologue (heard in the

13. For Wordsworth I have used the Modern Library edition, *Selected Poetry*, ed. Mark van Doren (New York, 1950), 103–8.

sounds of the torrent). He fails. The spirit of nature does audibly speak, but her speech is an enigmatic monologue. Nature cannot "rise out of her own enigma." The poet's alienation from nature in space is then paralleled by his alienation from his own past boyhood (internal time). He cannot (stanzas 7–9) relive the boy he has outgrown, or his companionship with the friend he had. The boy he was, and whom he still resembles, cannot be reinhabited. Mörike does not explain this impediment, he does not elaborate on the intervening mental change as Wordsworth does. He says that nature excludes him and that his past is lost. He does not say that some recompense comes from increased reflexiveness.

Wordsworth elaborates on his change of mind, from "nature" to "culture." He becomes more and more absorbed in the self he has developed. He says (lines 75–76): "I cannot paint / What then I was," but he does then boldly evoke what nature was—torrent and rock, mountain and wood, which were "to me / An appetite." Mörike, contrariwise, with a few graphic strokes presents both the boy he was and simultaneously the scene he loved. In Wordsworth's poem, the actual scene now gradually sinks from sight. The reflexive "I" overshadows its objects, the values of reflection loom ever larger, while objects of perception dwindle. Wordsworth addresses his sister as fellow ecstatic (younger than he is) who shall in time also have a mind which is "a mansion for all lovely forms." But he sternly admonishes her to "remember me, / And these my exhortations." More and more like Polonius he becomes, indulging his self-importance, presuming to a wisdom won from contemplating nature's formal charms. Mörike does woo his self-image, the boy he was; he does experience a narcissistic moment (end of stanza 9). But this is a desperate moment, and a fortunate one, for the impossibility of reunion leaves him wide open to a fresh flow of impressions from outside (unlike Wordsworth). His sensibility is freed from the thralldom of retrospective self-love by the sight of thunder approaching. Mörike does not strike an egotistical-sublime posture here or anywhere else. Now he actually witnesses the revelation of cosmic elements in action; he feels his whole being spring back to life—"ethereally tensed"—as the storm approaches. The sound and spectacle of the thunder then present the drama of a new communion, in which the place is felt to be a present focus of his "powers," and is celebrated as a "wondrous nest of my love." As an "I" the poet has almost disappeared: the personal pronoun modulates into its possessive forms, while thunder and Urach become the real agents. The vision here of nature's transcendent dynamic impulsions is the antithesis of Wordsworth's reflexive self-absorption and his beholding nature as an "anchor." Wordsworth's conclusion suggests a terminal stillness. Mörike's appeal to the *genius loci*, the "angel" of the place, suggests a fresh release of psychic energy, even a rebirth.

These contrasts occur throughout in terms of language. Wordsworth is ruminant. Only at the outset, briefly in the middle, and at end does he focus a few present details of the landscape. Otherwise he patrols the mental scene engendered in his memory. Mörike's language scans and evokes persistently actions present and past. Crisply it records from moment to moment the past and present impacts of these actions on his feeling. And, as so often in his work, the feelings are mixed ones—bitter and sweet, delight and torment. This mixed feeling was one of his innovations in the language of the German lyric. As the scenes change he moves, body and mind, in and out among the distinct features of the scene. Not a murmur about the nature of the changes in his mind during the five-year interim. As for the question of "culture" breaking with "nature" (a crucial theme in Schiller and Hölderlin), one might say that here we have two linguistically different versions of the cultural enterprise. In Wordsworth there is the devious transformation of experience into reflexive moral tone—with sanctity as an extreme possible development. In Mörike there is the transformation of active sensibility, with the utmost immediacy, into art—the art of what he called, thirty-six years later, the "sensing spirit." In Schiller's famous terms, Wordsworth is *sentimentalisch* and Mörike *naiv*. Mörike receives the smile, Wordsworth the frown, from Leopardi with his anti-"sentimental" and pro-Greek distinction: "The Romantics do not realize that if these feelings are awakened by *naked* nature, it is necessary, in order to reawaken them, to imitate nature's *nakedness*, and to transpose into poetry those simple and innocent objects which by their own strength alone, and *unawares*, produce that effect upon our spirit, just as they are, and neither more nor less" (Leopardi's italics).[14]

Two considerations follow: (1) We may disagree in a qualified way with the view, fairly widespread during the 1950s, that Mörike lacked a Goethean capacity for living to the limits of consciousness in the fullness of the present moment. Memory and desire do concern him, but he is not in a quasi-Romantic way lacking in "presence of mind." There are many other poems, from every period of his work, which speak just as strongly against this view of him ("To an Aeolian Harp," "Plague of the Forest," "On a Lamp," "Think now, O Soul"). The freshness of Mörike's language is due not least to the tensions it explores and sustains: between the moment-to-moment life of his sentient mind, and the variety of immediate concrete externals. This type of tension entails a sense of the past as a time pattern which feeling can refine and imagination restore at any moment. Everything depends here on the ways in which language enacts a series of psychic transformations. Likewise Mörike's treatment of classical Greek measures—a past beyond the personal past—is much fresher and freer than anything to be found in the work of *passéiste* poets like Platen. The crossweaving of time patterns consorts with the crossweaving of moods, mentioned above. The new thing he brought into German poetry was his crystal gaze into the heart of these patterns.

(2) Mörike as a poet is not one of the hyperreflexive minds found far and wide during the Romantic epoch in Europe. This does not mean that he was not complicated as a human being, far from it. On one level it is a question of his having avoided the auto-intoxication which plagued Europeans of his age. On another level it is a question of artistry. His artistry does not permit rumination for its own sake. "He thought in

14. From the *Zibaldone* (I, 21–23, dated *c*. 1817–18), in Giacomo Leopardi, *Selected Prose and Poetry*, ed. and trans. Iris Origo and John Heath-Stubbs (New York: Signet Classics, 1966), 81–82.

images," said his biographer Harry Maync. To adapt T. S. Eliot's remark about Henry James: The texture of his mind was too fine to be violated by an idea. Abstraction does not float loose in his poems; it is enshrined in the mode of perception which, as it unfolds, structures the linguistic physiognomy of any utterance. Mörike's syntax and prosody are the living flesh of any such abstraction. His "thought" is present in patterns of vowels and consonants, down to the very phonemic atoms of which the poem is a constellation. This can be seen in the grammar of lines 3–4 in stanza 5 of "Urach Revisited," also in stanza 10, with the repetition of the phrase "habe seinen Lauf" ("let all things take their course," grammatical repetition marking the brink of narcissistic stagnation). Likewise in 1863 Mörike's Erinna does not, at the end of her poem, versify the idea that she does not want to have Sappho mourning for her too soon: Erinna says that she will sacrifice her hairnet, which is graphically present, so that Sappho shall not have to cut off a curl. One can call this poetry physiognomic or, in Brecht's sense, gestic: when such linguistic events occur as textures of sound or as delicately fashioned rhythmical turns, they are integral moves in the dance of language as it voices the dynamics of actual sensory experience. The resonant and athletic containedness of his poems distinguishes him sharply from Novalis (1772–1801). Like many poets who lived in the wake of the French Revolution and amid the shaking of the foundations of Christian Europe, Novalis and Mörike were both deeply cognizant of a presence, in the human world, of "powers" transcending finite consciousness (Mörike was also an expert on ghosts). But whereas Novalis is intent on the metaphoric significations of things, on an algebra of metaphor, Mörike is intent on things as compact quiddities, having singular qualities of vibrance in sensation and emotion. One might say of him what Grillparzer said of Lope de Vega: "Lope de Vega makes no comparisons, but almost every one of his expressions has a sensuous force, and the image is not ornament but the thing itself." [15]

15. Franz Grillparzer, *Sämtliche Werke*, ed. August Sauer (Vienna, 1937), vol. 1, part 15, p. 215.

To broaden this view of Mörike as a poet who feels in terms of structures, I approach again the question of time in his poems. The crossweaving of past and present tenses makes him a poet of singular interest in the nineteenth century. Conventionally he is regarded as a poet who "escaped" into the idyll, who lived a secluded (*Biedermeier*) sort of life, some of it as a country parson, and who shrank from historical issues which Heine was so sharp about (even Lenau wrote urgent poems on public themes). But one should take a closer look. The nineteenth century, it is said, deified history. History was the whole process which sweeps everyone willynilly along. Its laws could be discovered scientifically, or at least interpreted knowingly. Outside of sequential historical process and the march of technical progress with its social transformations, little had weight: *ex deo machina*. Germany, it has also been said, got the worst of it. All this arising as the old absolutes slowly eroded, including that political absolutism against which Hölderlin had leveled his grand veto: "No power on earth should be monarchical." Mörike had a mind for other concerns. He was not ill informed about current events, indeed they excited him; nor did the great popular and liberal movements of the day leave him unmoved. But as an artist he had other concerns. Like Hölderlin, he turned against the "times." Not, it is true, with a sort of defiant, utopian despair, but in horror at their violence (in 1834) and because he was averse (in the 1840s) to the impurity in motive and work which political gesticulation was bringing into poetry.[16]

16. Letter to F. T. Vischer, 20 January 1834: "After the violent events of recent times, I still brood and glow in a sort of feverish commotion under a damp, ice-cold blanket that I have pulled over myself . . ." Letter to Wilhelm Hartlaub, May 14 1839: "These people [the political poets] think the Lord God himself couldn't help marveling at them when they fling into his beard their bitter cosmic reflexions, as if from horseback. Yet how cosy they are in their skins! Their mustache wax and a sop thrown them by some reviewer are more dear to them than Warsaw, Missolonghi, and Byron into the bargain" (*Briefe*, ed. F. Seebaß [Tübingen n.d.], 404, 476). As early as ca. 1826–28, Mörike wrote a poem called "Night Visions" ("Nachtgesichte"), in which history is a nightmare from which we are trying to awaken: a Mediterranean panorama, where Napoleon

Even allowing for changes that do occur as Mörike's work proceeds—the shift from more rhapsodic to more "objective" expression—the time textures in his poems, early or late, tempt one to think that for him time was far too personal, psychic, even sacred, to be crassly generalized into "history." If one goes a little further, it begins to seem that his sense of the interleaving and crossweaving of time levels (normally perceived in sequence) as experienced at certain moments, is also a sense of life as a process in which certain fundamental types of event keep recurring. He may sense these recurrences in nature, as the elements of air, earth, fire, water. Or more often he will seize on moments of collision between the two focal areas of elemental activity: nature and the psyche. His lyrics, ballads, and his prose frequently explore those sunken psychic areas where demons, creative or destructive elementals, seem to dwell.

At these moments of collision a fusion occurs and the psyche transcends change. Nature's enigma itself induces a flash of insight, and the psyche is then self-aware on a deep level where recurrence is the law of presence. Not that change does not occur, but change as the be-all and end-all of things is seen as an illusion put upon us by a psychic failure, a lack of feeling, a loss of vision. (He did read Schopenhauer, but not before March 1862.) The critique of progress—that necessary myth of his century—implied here brings Mörike a little closer to Nietzsche than one might have suspected, or than Nietzsche would have liked: in his polemical mood of 1875 Nietzsche found Mörike lacking in lucidity and his "music" altogether piffling.[17] It also brings Mörike fairly close to

---

appears as a monstrous phantom. The poem ends in a burst of "horrible laughter" as the dreaming poet wakes up.

17. *Nietzsche Werke: Kritische Gesamtausgabe*, ed. Giorgio Colli and Mazzino Montinari (Berlin, 1967), vol. 1, section 4, p. 204. Nietzsche adds: "I can only put up with poets who have, among other things, thoughts, poets like Pindar and Leopardi." He does not mention Hölderlin here, though he had thought highly of him before (1861). Nietzsche's note was written just after Mörike's death; he was objecting to current claims that Mörike was "the greatest German lyric poet."

Hölderlin again, for Hölderlin's "gods" are eternally recur-
rent, as ultimate modes of being whose positive and negative
activities enter the fabric of history.

Yet there are differences to be watched. Mörike has a more
pastoral than historical vision of good and evil. And he is not
an iconoclast made desperate by the death of God. For him, the
"lyric moment" of collision and fusion occurs when past and
present mingle in the webs of perception where memory, not
destiny, is the spider. In that moment, what is felt to be the
case is an eternity forever refreshing things and souls. Mark
well, once again, that the result is not grand expostulation,
declamation, or gesticulation. Infinitesimals of ordinary life
and language are knit into concrete patterns which voice the
sense of illumination as it bears on actual mundane situations.
Mörike often starts a poem with a casual "The other day
when . . ." or "In such and such a place . . ." What he was
doing was hardening the contours and varying the range of the
old Romantic seraphic tone by purging that tone of its vapors.[18]
One has to watch for hints, piths and gists, for he is a poet of
"classical restraint." This kind of undertone, with vistas of
implication, can be found even in a minor poem like "At the
Church of Mary among the Hills" (1842). At the end there
is the astounding (but casual) image of light as a "hundredfold
flute"—and then comes the enigmatic epithet attached to the
day that will be refreshed: the selfsame day ("Des gleichen
Tages"). Around this ruined church he perceives a nature

18. How he was doing this in the later 1820s can be seen if one
compares the dithyrambic poem "Im Freien" ("Outdoors," ca. 1824,
not published in his lifetime and not in this collection) with "Besuch
in Urach," and "Auf eine Lampe." "Im Freien" reads like a sketch
for the Urach poem and may show some influence from Hölderlin,
certainly from Goethe's poems of the early 1770s. The older (Roman-
tic) lyrical identification of subject and object disappears. It has been
said that Mörike brought a new perspective into the German lyric,
at a time when "realism" was developing in German fiction. With
him, the lyric subjectivity is humbler, cognizant of its limits vis-à-vis
the object world, and sensible to the distances between self and thing,
word and thing. See Heinz Schlaffer, *Lyrik im Realismus: Studien
über Raum und Zeit in den Gedichten Mörikes, der Droste und
Liliencron* (Bonn, 1966), 112.

varied and without monotony, but somehow changeless. Here
the selfsame day keeps coming around. How can this be? It is
because nobody goes there; the church is "alone" (stanza 1).
Change is the illusion put upon humans, and put about by
them wherever they go, in their state of alienation from
nature. We are back among the motifs of "Urach Revisited,"
but the spiral of Mörike's development is now rounding a
bend where the atmospherics are most delicate, and where
unobtrusive words catch the signals that come from silence.

The beautiful thing, too, in his perspectives of the 1840s,
has that inexhaustible radiant separateness which nature
enjoys ("On a Lamp"). A blade of grass breathes a cryptic
message ("From the Churchyard"). By the 1860s—"Pictures
from Bebenhausen"—he is again intent on the elastic relation
(of intimacy and over the distance) between nature as a source
of life and those structures which the "sensing spirit" brings
from that source, and which we call "tower" rather than
"crystal," artifact rather than natural phenomenon. Briefly,
Mörike does not ignore actual time, nor does he extrapolate
history from the life process. But time in the poetic process, a
kind of purified time, he tends to see in a way that reminds us
of Plato's "moving image of eternity," or of Blake's "time is
the mercy of eternity." For, in the last analysis, this time is
felt as music, with the circling harmonic structures of music.
Further, all the brilliant time-life which is the formal figura-
tion of eternity is surrounded by an ultimate circle of un-
fathomable primeval darkness. However cosy he may become,
Mörike does not forget this. In his miniature folk epic
"Märchen vom sicheren Mann" ("The Tale of the Certain
Man"), a micromyth of creation and redemption, this darkness
is there as a presence before any presence came into time. He
touches on this circle of ultimate darkness, too, in his poem
"To Wilhelm Hartlaub." Here he comes to one of the doubts
experienced by most thoughtful writers during the nineteenth
century: Is what we call "reality" an aesthetic construct? Are
there agencies which erode the frameworks of our constructs
and topple us into an abyss where unmeaning reigns supreme?
Mörike is, however, a poet not of terror but of wonder.
Wonder is the one mood which he stubbornly sustains, in the

midst of his pragmatical century, as the source of his sense of what is real.

The reader could begin his own explorations with the poems which contain the circle image, explicit or hinted: "Divine Reminiscence," "Corinna"; or which have circularity as their structuring principle in sound or syntax: "The Beautiful Beech Tree," "On a Lamp." [19] From these he could pass to "Song for Two in the Night," in which (as in the above titles) the time sense appears in terms of measure, as the medium of musical (or sacred) time. [20] And for the moment of collision and fusion he could look to the poems in which there is a lightning flash, or a spark, or a sudden ray of light: "Urach Revisited," "The Forsaken Girl," "To Wilhelm Hartlaub," "Divine Reminiscence," "New Love," "Think now, O soul," and "Erinna to Sappho." The motifs of time, music, measure, and the sudden flash of illumination are structural constants in Mörike's work.

V

Johann Georg Schreiner's pencil portrait of Mörike (1824) shows a young man with fair, wavy hair and a broad brow. The upper face, including the jutting nose, is fairly massive in relation to the lower part, mouth and chin, which are molded delicately. The chin is rounded and has a cleft; the mouth lines are sinuous rather than full, with faint dimples at the corners. The eyes, which were blue, are watchful but not large. In other portraits they look out from behind flimsy glasses. It looks as if they might have had a ring of darker blue around the iris. The head tilts forward a little. Faint arcs of shadow under the eyes suggest a slight fatigue, even suffering. At the time of the portrait, Mörike was not yet twenty;

19. "Auf eine Christblume" (not translated) of 1841 is of special interest here, for its sound patterns and exquisite imagery of concentric circles (of nature and spirit). Bibliography.

20. Cf. "Inschrift auf eine Uhr mit den drei Horen" (1846, not translated). The salutory effect of church bells at dawn, in "Daybreak," may have to do with their being for Mörike signals of sacred time.

possibly it was made during his mysterious liaison with Maria Meyer.[21]

Eduard Mörike came to the Tübingen *Stift* from the Urach *Klosterschule* in 1822. He was born on September 8, 1804, the third child of a large Ludwigsburg family. His father, Karl Friedrich, a cultivated man with North German forebears, and a busy doctor, had had a stroke in 1815, which left him partly paralyzed. In an autobiographical sketch of 1834, Mörike recalls the occasion on which his father pulled him between his knees and tried to say something but could not find the words. Nine months before the father's death in 1817, the five brothers drew up a contract of loyalty to one another. It is signed by Carl Eberhard (b. 1797), Eduard, August (b. 1807), Ludwig (or Louis, b. 1811), and Adolph (b. 1813): the signatures become more and more childish as the list descends.[22] Eduard kept the terms of this contract all his life. His brothers were eccentric people: Carl was imprisoned for political activities in 1831 (he also wrote music); Louis, an estates manager, was often in debt; and the unfortunate Adolph disappeared in the early 1840s, turning up again in 1859 after blank years in America and India. Eduard's poverty was due not least to his having repeatedly to pay the debts of Carl and Louis, borrowing money usually from friends, or from a publisher. His sisters Luise (b. 1798) and Klara (b. 1816) were quite different. The death of Luise in 1827, following August's sudden death in 1824, was a terrible blow to Eduard. Klara became his adored companion; his dependence on her led to the strange ménage à trois in which his two "sisters," Klara and Margarethe von Speeth (b. 1818, whom he married in 1851) were not always on the best of terms. Klara was a sprightly and practical person, often delightfully funny, and there was nothing queer about her brother's fondness for her. Margarethe was a Catholic; as wife of a retired Protestant clergyman she was regarded by her relatives as a sinner, whereas she seems to have been quite a prude.

21. See note on the "Peregrina" cycle.
22. Each signature is followed by a symbol. Eduard's symbol (he was then thirteen) is a lyre, written as a Greek *psi* [(ψ)].

Mörike's life did bog down in small and large complications as it went on; yet the "external events" remain clear cut.

He was no great scholar, either at Urach or at Tübingen, but he could read Greek and Latin, knew some French, probably some English, and he read widely in his own way. His power of imaginative invention was out of this world, and it was combined with an earthy clear-headedness—it is not surprising that one of his favorite authors was the eighteenth-century polymath Georg Christoph Lichtenberg. His friend Ludwig Bauer records vocal improvisations by Mörike, lasting for hours, in which his fantasy figures, each with a special voice, would perform all kinds of exploits. Bauer once visited the curate Mörike at Plattenhardt in 1828 (one of his ten curacies during the years 1826–33), and wrote about the visit in a letter:

Night came on, the moon was shining in the sky and evening bells ringing, when, behold, the Trusty Man awoke, perhaps in even greater splendour than in the most brilliant of his earlier periods. He began with charming reflexions about the stars, because he could not get at them, he called the sun a rubicund old geezer (*Rautstrunsel*—dialect), the moon—a useless (*Unnaitig*, dialect for *unnötig*) tin plate. Then he sang a song in such a dreadful, gurgling (*wasserorgelnd*) style, ornamenting it with rustic trills, that it nearly drove me crazy.[23]

The unsettled life of a curate disagreed with Mörike, so much that he asked for leave late in 1827 and spent most of the next year wandering about, or staying in Stuttgart, thinking to become a professional writer. But that trade got the worst of him too, and by January 1829 he is a curate again, believing that the church might after all leave him more peace and time than any other profession. In August 1829 he became engaged to Luise Rau, a parson's beautiful daughter. The letters he wrote to her are creations of troubadour love, luminous with details of his world and of the volatile states of

23. Quoted from Margaret Mare, *Eduard Mörike*, 34–35 (see Bibliography), with Miss Mare's inserted notes. This is recommended as a detailed and reasonable biography.

his mind. He was also now writing his novel *Maler Nolten*, which was published in 1832. The engagement came to an end in 1833: there were features in the novel which offended Luise and her mother (her father was dead); besides, Mörike did not seem to be getting along in life at all. One legend says that at the time of the break Mörike threatened Luise with a knife—which seems quite out of character, but he was beside himself. Soon after this, however, he did receive a parish of his own; and at the end of July 1834 he moved with his mother and sister to the village of Cleversulzbach, a few miles northeast of Heilbronn. Much has been made of his nine years here. His first commentators and readers thought of him as an arcadian parson-poet who would patrol his little garden in dressing gown and slippers, delighting in the trees and flowers. Heine remarked icily (1838): "People assure me that a most excellent poet of the Swabian school is Herr Mörike, who recently came to light, but who hasn't appeared yet (in print, that is). I am told that he sings not only of maybugs, but even of larks and thrushes, which is, to be sure, most praise-worthy."[24] Eight years before this, Mörike had written to Johannes Mährlen: "The parcel you sent me contained packing paper with some of Heine's wishywashy political stuff printed on it. A great disgust took hold of me."[25]

The early 1830s are years of upheaval in Paris and in Poland, and of frightful political oppression in many parts of Germany. It is Büchner's decade, a decade during which liberal plans are made and frustrated, and it begins the massive German emigration to the U.S.A. in the 1840s. Mörike's brother Karl is imprisoned in 1831 for distributing political pamphlets; while still a precarious curate, Mörike himself is investigated, to his great alarm. Installed at Cleversulzbach,

24. *Heines Werke*, ed. E. Elster (Leipzig: Meyers Klassiker-Ausgaben, n.d.), vol. 7, pp. 328ff. The first edition of Mörike's poems did appear that year (1838).

25. 11 February 1830 (*Briefe*, ed. F. Seebaß [Tübingen, n.d.], 189). Later, Mörike made the curious statement that Heine was a poet to his fingertips, but that he could not live with him for fifteen minutes "because his whole being is a lie" (to Theodor Storm, in conversation, 1855; see *Briefe*, ed. Werner Zemp [Zürich, 1949], 403).

he finds the parsonage a cold house. From 1834 on, he complains of rheumatism, colds, intestinal troubles, sore throat. The rheumatism attacks his spine, and there are times when he cannot walk. The throat infection hampers his delivery of the weekly sermon; and he is averse to preaching, in any case. He asks for a supply of sermons from a friend who is also a clergyman. He has to have assistance from curates (perhaps one of them appears in "To Longus"). The round of the seasons, the arcadian peace, are pleasures halved by vexations of many kinds, not excluding the cloddishness of the peasants. The famous Cleversulzbach idyll, "Der alte Turmhahn," was only begun there; all but twenty lines of it was written years later in retrospect. But Mörike was at least able to look after his ailing mother, to whom he eventually gave a grave close to that of Schiller's mother in the village churchyard. He carefully noted in letters to Justinus Kerner the activities of the parsonage poltergeist, Rabausch by name (Mörike nicknamed him "the old mole"). And he revised the method of registering births, marriages, and deaths in the parish so well that his work was shown to the king of Prussia and Württemberg, Friedrich Wilhelm IV, as a model that might be generally adopted. In 1843, on grounds of ill health, and two years after his mother's death, Mörike was given indefinite leave with a small pension. He moved with his sister Klara to Wermutshausen for the winter 1843–44, staying there with his friend Wilhelm Hartlaub.

There follows a period in the towns of Schwäbisch-Hall (1844), where Mörike collected fossils, and Mergentheim (1845–51). The later Mergentheim years were punctuated by spells of illness and brief stays in other places, including Egelshofen on Lake Constance. In April 1845, Mörike and Klara took lodgings in the household of a retired military gentleman, Oberstleutnant von Speeth, and his wife. Their daughter Margarethe was put in Mörike's trust when the colonel died, and the curious triangular relation which dominated Mörike's later years had begun. Margarethe was twenty-seven when he met her. At Egelshofen in 1851 (the year in which he married Margarethe) he thought of opening a small private school for girls, with Klara and Margarethe as his assistants. He also thought he might become the king's librarian. But in the autumn of that year he accepted (after first refusing) an appointment at the large and respectable girls' school in Stuttgart, the *Katharinenstift*. In order to finance the move, he had to borrow money from two sources: it was no more than $200 in present values, but the fact is that Mörike was poor now, as later. When he died, though he was not unknown as a poet "for the happy few," with an honorary doctorate and the Bavarian Order of Maximilian, his total estate was worth about 400 Gulden (about $1,000).

He taught at the *Katharinenstift*, living in Stuttgart, for fifteen years. It is a period which overlaps with Gottfried Keller's employment as City Clerk in Zürich. Once a week, Mörike would read Shakespeare to his pupils (in the Schlegel-Tieck translation) and talk about the plays. Also he had the audacity to read and discuss Goethe, and to defend Goethe's pagan sensuality—abominated by the educational establishment of the time, though Karl Wolff, the school principal, was a less orthodox person than most, and a good friend and patron to Mörike.[26] Later, he lectured on the medieval *Nibelungenlied*. During this period he wrote few important poems; but several prose works of a singular legendary character are dated in the early 1850s, his story about Mozart was published in 1855, and his Theocritus and Anacreon retranslations appeared in 1855 and 1864. Now, too, he was reading a number of philosophers: Spinoza and Hegel (1859), and Schopenhauer (1862). Letters of 1867–68 (after his retirement) refer also to the Swabian visionary *Theosoph*, Friedrich Christoph Oetinger (1702–82), whom Mörike had probably read in Cleversulzbach. The year before he retired (again for reasons of health), Turgenev visited him, and it is strange that this Russian novelist, one of the foremost mid-century analysts of nihilism, knew "Der

26. It is worth noting that the great French entomologist Jean-Henri Fabre (1823–1915) was driven out of Avignon University in the 1870s by the Catholic establishment, for giving "sex lectures" at evening classes for young ladies and others. In fact he was giving the most searching and eloquent lectures on pollination and insect life, and some of his findings were crucial for the ecology of French viniculture.

alte Turmhahn" by heart. In November the same year (1865) another Russian, Queen Olga of Württemberg, sat in the front row at one of Mörike's classes and listened attentively while doing some crochet work.

Mörike was much loved as a teacher. His charisma was indeed a living source for friendships far and wide, as the two solid volumes of his letters show. He was, for all that, a touchy person. After noticing in his new friend Hermann Kurz in 1838 a tendency to glibness ("etwas Süffisantes"), he dropped the familiar *du* and fairly soon dropped Kurz. His good friend and correspondent Justinus Kerner of Weinsberg, the eminent physician, poet, and parapsychologist, who had once attended the mad Hölderlin in Tübingen, was also dropped when he voiced doubt about Mörike's sincerity as regards his pastoral duties at Cleversulzbach (1843). Yet great stretches of time during the middle and later years of Mörike's life were taken up by the writing of letters, to keep friendships fresh, to advise poets (like Karl Mayer, who enjoyed about fifteen years of careful advice), and to cope with family problems, including the harassing affairs of the family von Speeth.[27]

Mörike's last years are not tragic, but they are sad. His rheumatic pains return, his wife is often ill, he has a bad cough, which increases the rheumatic pains. That is how it is during the last two years. During the early and middle 1860s his health is tolerable. He takes his daughters, Fanny (b. 1855) and Marie (b. 1857), for walks in rustic parts of Stuttgart. His letters recount small happenings on these walks, a matter of peaches, a question of grapes, a meeting with a lizard, and what this or that child said. He lives with Margarethe, Klara,

27. The letters, which have never been translated, are remarkable. They abound in vivid details of daily life, encounters with people and animals, thoughts on reading, reflections on events, and (not least) ravishing dreams. They also show Mörike's tendency to "think in images": he visualizes Leibniz's monads as frog spawn, and of Schelling's *Urgrund* (metaphysical basis of reality) he wrote: "Our thoughts, when they try to grapple with Schellings *Urgrund*, are like two drills penetrating a plank from opposite sides and meeting in the dark. Then they slowly withdraw and back in the daylight tell one another what prodigies they met on their travels" (21 May 1832, to Johannes Mährlen, in *Briefe*, ed. F. Seebaß, 342–43).

and his daughters in a few modest rooms, and they take in two
French lodgers. He begins the revision of *Maler Nolten*, a work
never completed. He writes "occasional" poems to accompany
events or greetings, or as thank offerings. There is a special
new friendship with the artist Moriz von Schwind (1804–71),
who lives in Munich. And for two years, 1867–69, the family
lives at Lorch, a village where Mörike takes pottery lessons and
incises little poems on the pots he makes. He also makes
sketches of village and domestic scenes, as he has done since
the 1820s (earlier sketches are often grotesque). Then they
return to Stuttgart. Margarethe and Klara sometimes quarrel;
Marie is extremely frail (she died in 1876), and the time comes
when Fanny wants to marry an unsuitable young man.
Finally in the spring and summer of 1874 there are crises. In
July Mörike leaves his wife and takes Klara to the Hartlaubs
at Stöckenburg. He wanders now from place to place—
Bebenhausen, Fellbach, Lorch, Nürtingen—with little to
encourage him but a few friends, like Louise and Friedrich
Walther. Not until two weeks before his death did Margarethe
come to him for a formal reconciliation. On his birthday in
1874, while sitting in the garden at Stöckenburg, he heard in
the air a harplike musical chord; nobody else heard it, and he
said: "It means me. This is my last birthday." [28] In November
he and Klara moved back to Stuttgart. He endured more
pains through the spring, and on June 4, 1875, he quietly died.

Some reflections, to conclude, on Mörike's life in his time.
It was a life lived in its details, even more so than most; and
to such details a sketch like this can do no justice. But was this
life, against certain appearances, a paradigm of the life of the
century? It began with a surge of imaginative energy, within
limits of political unfreedom (the Carlsbad Decrees and their
consequences). It passed through middle years of inward

28. This is documented in Harry Maync's biography (1902; 5th
ed., 1947), in Mare, and elsewhere. The sounds are called *Ster-
beklänge*. It was said by Jakob Boehme's friend and biographer,
Abraham von Frankenberg, that Boehme heard them just before he
died, in 1624 (Victor Weiss, *Die Gnosis Jakob Boehmes* [Zürich,
1955], 16), though what Boehme heard was singing.

stabilization and external unrest—the revolutions of 1848, a period when Mörike had no idea where to go. And it ended in melancholy, with a dark internal despair, relieved only by a few thrusts from the old creative drive. Perhaps this secluded life did figure forth the changing features of the times. The second half of the century finds a number of German writers sharing a certain mood. There is a sense of satiety; the external world, to Mörike as to Gottfried Keller, seems solid and permanent. They observe objects with intently serious and loving care: people, buildings, old books and new ones, rooms, manuscripts, and clocks. This grave gaze was not entirely a symptom of decrepitude; indeed, it was deeply civilized. But not only was the century growing old; also—after decades of lessons in history and massive tomes from such historians as Haller, Ranke, Menzel, Treitschke, and Burckhardt—Europe knew in its bones that it was an old civilization. Nietzsche, at least, detected symptoms of senility here. It is not just a question of literary style, "poetic realism" as literary historians call it. Mörike's letters of the 1850s and 1860s are permeated with a sense of things in this world as permanent entities, saturated with value and solid life, among which he is at home, if anywhere, and by which he is framed. Or is it that his mind was going out to things, wanting to collect them into its shelter, somehow divining their deeper impermanence on the brink of an abyss which opened in the twentieth century? Nor is this sense of things confined to writers like Mörike and Keller. Baudelaire's story "Fanfarlo" and Gérard de Nerval's "Sylvie" are studded with objects, so intently observed that they seem to glow with spirit: clocks, houses, sofas, old desks and chests, kitchenware. An ordered, domesticated world.

Nietzsche supposed that this superstructure had rotten foundations, in guilt, largely unconscious, in "slave morality," and hypocrisy—the entropic remnants of a lost turbulence of the kind that shapes a culture. Perhaps Mörike's last years were "depressed," much as depression is visible in the later pictures of him, or in pictures of Keller and Adalbert Stifter: the sag-jawed, pouchy faces of ancient harlequins. This is not the ugly opulence of late nineteenth-century German architecture. It is more akin to Brahms's overloaded orchestra, to the brooding sadness of his orchestral music (these men are absolutely not Wagnerian). One thing is different with Mörike: he did in later years thoughtfully profess belief in a beyond, the beyond which had always fascinated him, with its spirits and gulfs of starlight and magical coincidences. And for all its distant look, his face, as observed at the time by Isolde Kurz, could quite suddenly become radiant, as if it were a mask put on by "a smiling Ariel." Perhaps, too, it is parochial to see the breakdown of his marriage in a naïve Freudian way, as a result of the triangular relation, with the two women as rival "mothers" and Mörike as the "child." The sickness on all sides during his last years, the nervous tensions, the griefs and wanderings, might have had their roots deep down in the state of European culture at large. Two ancient factors of civilization as known till then are felt to be disappearing: the sense of the sacred, and the sense of harmony. Both Hölderlin's poems and Mörike's catch the rays of that sunset. Both poets battle to maintain, by redefining or relocating, those senses as powers in reason which help people not to be brutal. But steadily things darken with some fearful guilt. Europe sickens with bad conscience, hoarding its grievances, failing to give back to life its due. This was Nietzsche's version of guilt in *The Genealogy of Morals* (1887). Since then, the abyss has opened; compounding bad conscience with false consciousness we misdirect experience in ways unimaginable to nineteenth-century people. Too much has happened for the guilt to be banished by either antidote—libidinal zest and intelligent proud probity—commended by Nietzsche in his last writings.

Friedrich Hölderlin

DA ICH EIN KNABE WAR . . .

Da ich ein Knabe war,
   Rettet' ein Gott mich oft
      Vom Geschrei und der Rute der Menschen,
     Da spielt ich sicher und gut
       Mit den Blumen des Hains,
         Und die Lüftchen des Himmels
        Spielten mit mir.

Und die du das Herz
Der Pflanzen erfreust,
Wenn sie entgegen dir
Die zarten Arme strecken,

So hast du mein Herz erfreut,
Vater Helios! und, wie Endymion,
War ich dein Liebling,
Heilige Luna!

O all ihr treuen
Freundlichen Götter!
Daß ihr wüßtet,
Wie euch meine Seele geliebt!

Zwar damals rief ich noch nicht
Euch mit Namen, auch ihr
Nanntet mich nie, wie die Menschen sich nennen,
Als kennten sie sich.

Doch kannt ich euch besser,
Als ich je die Menschen gekannt,
Ich verstand die Stille des Aethers,
Der Menschen Worte verstand ich nie.

Mich erzog der Wohllaut
Des säuselnden Hains
Und lieben lernt ich
Unter den Blumen.

Im Arme der Götter wuchs ich groß.

(1797 or 1798)

WHEN I WAS A BOY ...

When I was a boy
　A god rescued me often
　　From shouts and whips of men,
　　　It was then that I played
　　　　Safely and well with woodland flowers
　　　　And the winds of heaven
　　　　　Played with me.

And as you delight
The hearts of plants,
When to you they extend
Their delicate arms,

So you delighted my heart,
Father Helios, and like Endymion
I was your darling,
Sacred Moon!

O all you faithful
Friendly gods!
If only you knew
How my soul loved you.

True, in those days I did not
Call you by name, and you
Never called me as men do, as if
They knew one another, with names.

Yet I knew you better
Than I ever knew men,
I understood air, its stillness,
Never the language of men.

The whispering woodland's
Harmony taught me,
And I learned to love
Among the flowers.

I grew tall in the arms of the gods.

HYPERIONS SCHICKSALSLIED

Ihr wandelt droben im Licht
  Auf weichem Boden, selige Genien!
    Glänzende Götterlüfte
     Rühren euch leicht,
      Wie die Finger der Künstlerin
      Heilige Saiten.

Schicksallos, wie der schlafende
  Säugling, atmen die Himmlischen;
  Keusch bewahrt
   In bescheidener Knospe,
    Blühet ewig
     Ihnen der Geist,
      Und die seligen Augen
      Blicken in stiller
      Ewiger Klarheit.

Doch uns ist gegeben,
  Auf keiner Stätte zu ruhn,
  Es schwinden, es fallen
   Die leidenden Menschen
    Blindlings von einer
    Stunde zur andern,
      Wie Wasser von Klippe
      Zu Klippe geworfen,
       Jahr lang ins Ungewisse hinab.

(End of 1797?)

HYPERION'S SONG OF FATE

You walk up there in the light
  On floors like velvet, blissful spirits.
    Shining winds divine
      Touch you lightly
        As a harper touches holy
          Strings with her fingers.

Fateless as babes asleep
  They breathe, the celestials.
    Chastely kept
      In a simple bud,
        For them the spirit
          Flowers eternal,
            And in bliss their eyes
              Gaze in eternal
                Calm clarity.

But to us it is given
  To find no resting place,
    We faint, we fall,
      Suffering, human,
        Blindly from one
          To the next moment
            Like water flung
              From rock to rock down
                Long years into uncertainty.

DIE KÜRZE

„Warum bist du so kurz? liebst du, wie vormals, denn
   Nun nicht mehr den Gesang? fandst du, als Jüngling, doch,
      In den Tagen der Hoffnung,
         Wenn du sangest, das Ende nie!"

Wie mein Glück ist mein Lied.—Willst du im Abendrot
   Froh dich baden? hinweg ists! und die Erde ist kalt,
      Und der Vogel der Nacht schwirrt
         Unbequem vor das Auge dir.

(1798)

BREVITY

Why make it so short? Have you lost your old liking
  For song? Why, in days of hope, when young,
    You sang and sang,
      There scarce was an end of it.

My song is short as my luck was. Who'd go
  Gaily swimming at sundown? It's gone, earth's cold,
    And the annoying nightbird
      Flits close, blocking your vision.

DEM SONNENGOTT

Wo bist du? trunken dämmert die Seele mir
  Von aller deiner Wonne; denn eben ists,
    Daß ich gesehn, wie, müde seiner
      Fahrt, der entzückende Götterjüngling

Die jungen Locken badet' im Goldgewölk;
  Und jetzt noch blickt mein Auge von selbst nach ihm;
    Doch fern ist er zu frommen Völkern,
      Die ihn noch ehren, hinweggegangen.

Dich lieb ich, Erde! trauerst du doch mit mir!
  Und unsre Trauer wandelt, wie Kinderschmerz,
    In Schlummer sich, und wie die Winde
      Flattern und flüstern im Saitenspiele,

Bis ihm des Meisters Finger den schönern Ton
  Entlockt, so spielen Nebel und Träum um uns,
    Bis der Beliebte wiederkömmt und
      Leben und Geist sich in uns entzündet.

(1798)

TO THE SUNGOD

Where are you? Drunken my darkening soul reels
   At all your rapture; for, but a moment since,
      I saw the young enchanting god,
         Tired after his day's travel,

Bathe in the golden cloud his boyish curls;
   And still now my helpless eye pursues him,
      But gone he is, and far, to peoples
         Living in piety, who still revere him.

Earth, I love you! For with me you are grieving,
   And, like hurt done to a child, our sorrow
      Changes to sleep, and as the winds
         Flutter and whisper among the strings

Of a musical instrument, till the master charms
   The lovelier tone from it, swirling dream and mist
      Around us play till our lover return
         And life and the spirit catch fire in us.

AN DIE PARZEN

Nur Einen Sommer gönnt, ihr Gewaltigen!
   Und einen Herbst zu reifem Gesange mir,
      Daß williger mein Herz, vom süßen
         Spiele gesättiget, dann mir sterbe.

Die Seele, der im Leben ihr göttlich Recht
   Nicht ward, sie ruht auch drunten im Orkus nicht;
      Doch ist mir einst das Heilge, das am
         Herzen mir liegt, das Gedicht, gelungen,

Willkommen dann, o Stille der Schattenwelt!
   Zufrieden bin ich, wenn auch mein Saitenspiel
      Mich nicht hinab geleitet; Einmal
         Lebt ich, wie Götter, und mehr bedarfs nicht.

(1798)

TO THE FATES

Grant me a single summer, you lords of all,
  A single autumn, for the fullgrown song,
    So that, with such sweet playing sated,
      Then my heart may die more willing.

The soul, in life robbed of its godly right,
  Rests not, even in Orcus down below;
    Yet should I once achieve my heart's
      First holy concern, the poem,

Welcome then, O stillness of the shadow world!
  Even if down I go without my
    Music, I shall be satisfied; once
      Like gods I shall have lived, more I need not.

DER MENSCH

Kaum sproßten aus den Wassern, o Erde, dir
  Der jungen Berge Gipfel und dufteten
    Lustatmend, immergrüner Haine
      Voll, in des Ozeans grauer Wildnis

Die ersten holden Inseln; und freudig sah
  Des Sonnengottes Auge die Neulinge,
    Die Pflanzen, seiner ewgen Jugend
      Lächelnde Kinder, aus dir geboren.

Da auf der Inseln schönster, wo immerhin
  Den Hain in zarter Ruhe die Luft umfloß,
    Lag unter Trauben einst, nach lauer
      Nacht, in der dämmernden Morgenstunde

Geboren, Mutter Erde! dein schönstes Kind;—
  Und auf zum Vater Helios sieht bekannt
    Der Knab, und wacht und wählt, die süßen
      Beere versuchend, die heilge Rebe

Zur Amme sich; und bald ist er groß; ihn scheun
  Die Tiere, denn ein anderer ist, wie sie,
    Der Mensch; nicht dir und nicht dem Vater
      Gleicht er, denn kühn ist in ihm und einzig

Des Vaters hohe Seele mit deiner Lust,
  O Erd! und deiner Trauer von je vereint;
    Der Göttermutter, der Natur, der
      Allesumfassenden möcht er gleichen!

Ach! darum treibt ihn, Erde! vom Herzen dir
  Sein Übermut, und deine Geschenke sind
    Umsonst und deine zarten Bande;
      Sucht er ein Besseres doch, der Wilde!

Von seines Ufers duftender Wiese muß
  Ins blütenlose Wasser hinaus der Mensch,
    Und glänzt auch, wie die Sternenacht, von
      Goldenen Früchten sein Hain, doch gräbt er

MAN

Scarce had the young peaks begun, O earth,
  To burgeon from your waters, and from the gray
    Ocean wilderness the first islands,
      Dense with evergreen woods, to waft

Fragrant breaths of pleasure; and the sungod's eye
  Gazed with joy upon the new arriving
    Plants, radiant children of his
      Eternal youth, and your offspring.

Then on the fairest island, round whose woods
  Calm and delicate air constantly flowed,
    Lay, after a warm night,
      Born under grapes at break of day,

O mother earth, your fairest child; and up he looks,
  The boy, to his father Helios, him he knows,
    And he wakes and takes, tasting the sweet
      Berries one by one, the holy

Vine as nurse; soon he is tall; the animals
  Shun him, for he is different, man, resembling
    Neither his father nor yourself,
      For in his being, from the start,

His father's sheer soul uniquely blent,
  And daringly, with your delight, O earth, and sorrow:
    His will it is to be like nature,
      The mother of gods, and all-embracing.

Ah! hence from your heart's reach his exuberance
  Drives him, earth, your gifts and tender trammels
    Are all for nought; wild he is
      And something better is what he looks for.

Leaving his fragrant meadow inland, man
  Must set forth on blossomless deep waters;
    And though his orchard shine with fruit,
      Gold like the night of stars, he digs his

Sich Höhlen in den Bergen und späht im Schacht,
   Von seines Vaters heiterem Lichte fern,
      Dem Sonnengott auch ungetreu, der
         Knechte nicht liebt und der Sorge spottet.

Denn freier atmen Vögel des Walds, wenn schon
   Des Menschen Brust sich herrlicher hebt, und der
      Die dunkle Zukunft sieht, er muß auch
         Sehen den Tod und allein ihn fürchten.

Und Waffen wider alle, die atmen, trägt
   In ewigbangem Stolze der Mensch; im Zwist
      Verzehrt er sich und seines Friedens
         Blume, die zärtliche, blüht nicht lange.

Ist er von allen Lebensgenossen nicht
   Der seligste? Doch tiefer und reißender
      Ergreift das Schicksal, allausgleichend,
         Auch die entzündbare Brust dem Starken.

(1798)

Tunnels in the hills, and scans the shaft, aloof
  From his father's calm light, and more,
    Disloyal to the sungod, who bears no love
      For slavish men and mocks care.

For forest birds more freely breathe, although
  Man's heart more gloriously soars aloft,
    And he, seeing the future, dark,
      Must see death and alone fear it.

And in persistent fright and pride man wields
  Weapons against all that breathes; in feuds
    He burns his life out, and his peace,
      Fragile, flowers but little time.

Of all his fellow beings, man, is he not
  Most full of bliss? So fate, balancing all,
    Ever more deep and rushing, grips
      Yet his strong inflammable heart.

MEIN EIGENTUM

In seiner Fülle ruhet der Herbsttag nun,
  Geläutert ist die Traub und der Hain ist rot
    Vom Obst, wenn schon der holden Blüten
      Manche der Erde zum Danke fielen.

Und rings im Felde, wo ich den Pfad hinaus,
  Den stillen, wandle, ist den Zufriedenen
    Ihr Gut gereift und viel der frohen
      Mühe gewähret der Reichtum ihnen.

Vom Himmel blicket zu den Geschäftigen
  Durch ihre Bäume milde das Licht herab,
    Die Freude teilend, denn es wuchs durch
      Hände der Menschen allein die Frucht nicht.

Und leuchtest du, o Goldenes, auch mir, und wehst
  Auch du mir wieder, Lüftchen, als segnetest
    Du eine Freude mir, wie einst, und
      Irrst, wie um Glückliche, mir am Busen?

Einst war ichs, doch wie Rosen, vergänglich war
  Das fromme Leben, ach! und es mahnen noch,
    Die blühend mir geblieben sind, die
      Holden Gestirne zu oft mich dessen.

Beglückt, wer, ruhig liebend ein frommes Weib,
  Am eignen Herd in rühmlicher Heimat lebt,
    Es leuchtet über festem Boden
      Schöner dem sicheren Mann sein Himmel.

Denn, wie die Pflanze, wurzelt auf eignem Grund
  Sie nicht, verglüht die Seele des Sterblichen,
    Der mit dem Tageslichte nur, ein
      Armer, auf heiliger Erde wandelt.

Zu mächtig, ach! ihr himmlischen Höhen, zieht
  Ihr mich empor, bei Stürmen, am heitern Tag
    Fühl ich verzehrend euch im Busen
      Wechseln, ihr wandelnden Götterkräfte.

MY POSSESSION

The autumn day rests in its fullness now,
  Grapes gleam pure and the orchard is red
    With fruit, though to the earth a few
      Fair blossoms fell as a thanksgiving.

And out in the country, where I walk a peaceful
  Path, crops are ripe to the satisfaction
    Of men who own them; blithe toil,
      Plenteous too, this wealth is bringing.

From heaven the light looks mildly down and through
  Their trees upon the busy people, sharing
    Their joy, for the fruits ripened
      Not by handiwork of people only.

And do you shine also for me, O golden light?
  Breeze, do you blow my way again, blessing
    As once you did, a joy of mine,
      And flutter my heart as for the fortunate?

Fortune was mine once, yet that gentle life
  Was fleeting like the rose, ah! and the sweet
    Blossoming stars that remain to me
      Tell me of this, and all too often.

Fortune is his who, loving his gentle wife,
  Lives in his home at peace and in an honored land;
    That much the lovelier, for his safe being
      On sure terrain, his heaven shines.

For, like a plant, if it has sunk no root
  In ground of its own, the mortal soul must wither,
    Man being poor and daylight all
      That moves with him on the holy earth.

Too potent, ah! you haul me, heavenly altitudes,
  Upward, battering gales on a calm day—
    And I feel you chop and change, consuming
      Me in my depths, you powers divine!

17

Doch heute laß mich stille den trauten Pfad
   Zum Haine gehn, dem golden die Wipfel schmückt
     Sein sterbend Laub, und kränzt auch mir die
       Stirne, ihr holden Erinnerungen!

Und daß mir auch, zu retten mein sterblich Herz,
   Wie andern eine bleibende Stätte sei,
     Und heimatlos die Seele mir nicht
       Über das Leben hinweg sich sehne,

Sei du, Gesang, mein freundlich Asyl! sei du,
   Beglückender! mit sorgender Liebe mir
     Gepflegt, der Garten, wo ich, wandelnd
       Unter den Blüten, den immerjungen,

In sichrer Einfalt wohne, wenn draußen mir
   Mit ihren Wellen allen die mächtge Zeit,
     Die Wandelbare, fern rauscht und die
       Stillere Sonne mein Wirken fördert.

Ihr segnet gütig über den Sterblichen,
   Ihr Himmelskräfte! jedem sein Eigentum,
     O segnet meines auch, und daß zu
       Frühe die Parze den Traum nicht ende.

(Autumn 1799)

But let me walk today the quiet familiar path
    To the orchard where leaves that are dying crown
        Every tree with gold; sweet memories,
            Weave for my brow a garland also.

And that, like others, I too may find a place
    To abide and save my mortal heart in, lest
        My soul, unhoused, clean gone
            Above what's living, pine away,

Be you, O song, my welcoming refuge, bringer
    Of my felicity, the garden kempt
        With careful love, where underneath
            Ageless blossoms I shall walk,

Living in sure simplicity, and hear the surge
    Of potent changeful time that roars far off
        With all its waves, and the calmer sun
            Helps everything I do to prosper.

O heavenly powers who bless, benign, above
    All mortal things, each mortal's own possession,
        Bless also mine, and let not fate
            Bring too soon to the dream an ending.

HEIDELBERG

Lange lieb ich dich schon, möchte dich, mir zur Lust,
    Mutter nennen, und dir schenken ein kunstlos Lied,
        Du, der Vaterlandsstädte
           Ländlichschönste, so viel ich sah.

Wie der Vogel des Walds über die Gipfel fliegt,
    Schwingt sich über den Strom, wo er vorbei dir glänzt,
        Leicht und kräftig die Brücke,
           Die von Wagen und Menschen tönt.

Wie von Göttern gesandt, fesselt' ein Zauber einst
    Auf die Brücke mich an, da ich vorüber ging,
        Und herein in die Berge
           Mir die reizende Ferne schien,

Und der Jüngling, der Strom, fort in die Ebne zog,
    Traurigfroh, wie das Herz, wenn es, sich selbst zu schön,
        Liebend unterzugehen,
           In die Fluten der Zeit sich wirft.

Quellen hattest du ihm, hattest dem Flüchtigen
    Kühle Schatten geschenkt, und die Gestade sahn
        All ihm nach, und es bebte
           Aus den Wellen ihr lieblich Bild.

Aber schwer in das Tal hing die gigantische,
    Schicksalskundige Burg nieder bis auf den Grund,
        Von den Wettern zerrissen;
           Doch die ewige Sonne goß

Ihr verjüngendes Licht über das alternde
    Riesenbild, und umher grünte lebendiger
        Efeu; freundliche Wälder
           Rauschten über die Burg herab.

Sträuche blühten herab, bis wo im heitern Tal,
    An dem Hügel gelehnt, oder dem Ufer hold,
        Deine fröhlichen Gassen
           Unter duftenden Gärten ruhn.

(Early summer 1800; drafts ca. 1798–99)

HEIDELBERG

Long have I loved you and for my own delight
  Would call you mother, give you an artless song,
    You, of all the towns in our country
      The loveliest that ever I saw.

As the forest bird crosses the peaks in flight,
  Over the river shimmering past you floats
    Airy and strong the bridge,
      Humming with sounds of traffic and people.

Once, as if it were sent by gods, enchantment
  Seized me as I was passing over the bridge
    And the distance with its allure
      Shone into the mountainscape,

And that strong youth, the river, was rushing on down
  To the plain, sorrowing-glad, like the heart that overflows
    With beauty and hurls itself,
      To die of love, into the floods of time.

You had fed him with streams, the fugitive, given him
  Cool shadow, and all the shores looked on
    As he followed his way, their image
      Sweetly jockeying over the waves.

But into the valley hung heavy the vast
  And fate-acquainted fort, by lightnings torn
    To the ground it stood on; yet
      Eternal sun still poured

Its freshening light across the giant and aging
  Thing, and all around was green with ivy,
    Living; friendly woodlands ran
      Murmurous down across the fort.

Bushes flowered all down the slope to where,
  In the vale serene, with hills to prop them, shores
    For them to cling to, your small streets
      Mid fragrant garden bowers repose.

DER NECKAR

In deinen Tälern wachte mein Herz mir auf
Zum Leben, deine Wellen umspielten mich,
   Und all der holden Hügel, die dich
     Wanderer! kennen, ist keiner fremd mir.

Auf ihren Gipfeln löste des Himmels Luft
Mir oft der Knechtschaft Schmerzen; und aus dem Tal,
   Wie Leben aus dem Freudebecher,
     Glänzte die bläuliche Silberwelle.

Der Berge Quellen eilten hinab zu dir,
Mit ihnen auch mein Herz und du nahmst uns mit,
   Zum stillerhabnen Rhein, zu seinen
     Städten hinunter und lustgen Inseln.

Noch dünkt die Welt mir schön, und das Aug entflieht
Verlangend nach den Reizen der Erde mir,
   Zum goldenen Paktol, zu Smyrnas
     Ufer, zu Ilions Wald. Auch möcht ich

Bei Sunium oft landen, den stummen Pfad
Nach deinen Säulen fragen, Olympion!
   Noch eh der Sturmwind und das Alter
     Hin in den Schutt der Athenertempel

Und ihrer Gottesbilder auch dich begräbt,
Denn lang schon einsam stehst du, o Stolz der Welt,
   Die nicht mehr ist. Und o ihr schönen
     Inseln Ioniens! wo die Meerluft

Die heißen Ufer kühlt und den Lorbeerwald
Durchsäuselt, wenn die Sonne den Weinstock wärmt,
   Ach! wo ein goldner Herbst dem armen
     Volk in Gesänge die Seufzer wandelt,

Wenn sein Granatbaum reift, wenn aus grüner Nacht
Die Pomeranze blinkt, und der Mastixbaum
   Von Harze träuft und Pauk und Cymbel
     Zum labyrinthischen Tanze klingen.

THE NECKAR

In your valleys my heart awoke to life,
   Your ripples played around me, and to none
      Of the sweet hills which know you, wanderer,
         To none of them am I a stranger.

On their summits the air from heaven would often
   Melt my pains of servitude; from the valley
      Shone the bluish silvery ripple,
         Like life itself from the cup of joy.

Streams from the mountains ran down into you,
   So did my heart, and away you carried us
      To the quiet sublime Rhine and to its
         Cities below and happy islands.

Still I think the world beautiful, and gaze
   Rapt-eyed and far to distant charms of earth,
      Golden Pactolus, shores of Smyrna,
         Ilium's woodland. I would like

Often to land at Sounium, I'd ask the silent
   Path about your columns, O Olympia,
      Before tempestuous winds and age
         Bury you down among the tumbled

Stones and temple statues of the Athenians, for alone
   Long years you have stood, pride of a world
      Which is no more. And you, beautiful
         Ionian islands, where the sea wind

Cools the hot coast and whispers as it runs
   Through laurel, when the sun is warming the vine,
      Ah! and where a golden autumn turns
         The sighs of poor folk into song,

When pomegranates ripen, when from green night
   The orange gleams and the mastic tree drips
      Its resin and the drum and cymbal
         Sound for labyrinthine dancing.

Zu euch, ihr Inseln! bringt mich vielleicht, zu euch
Mein Schutzgott einst; doch weicht mir aus treuem Sinn
Auch da mein Neckar nicht mit seinen
Lieblichen Wiesen und Uferweiden.

(Summer 1800)

To you, islands, to you he shall bring me, my
    Guardian god, one day, perhaps; but even then
      I shall be true in mind to my Neckar,
        Its pleasant fields and willows by the water.

LEBENSLAUF

Größers wolltest auch du, aber die Liebe zwingt
  All uns nieder, das Leid beuget gewaltiger,
    Doch es kehret umsonst nicht
      Unser Bogen, woher er kommt.

Aufwärts oder hinab! herrschet in heilger Nacht,
  Wo die stumme Natur werdende Tage sinnt,
    Herrscht im schiefesten Orkus
      Nicht ein Grades, ein Recht noch auch?

Dies erfuhr ich. Denn nie, sterblichen Meistern gleich,
  Habt ihr Himmlischen, ihr Alleserhaltenden,
    Daß ich wüßte, mit Vorsicht
      Mich des ebenen Pfads geführt.

Alles prüfe der Mensch, sagen die Himmlischen,
  Daß er, kräftig genährt, danken für Alles lern,
    Und verstehe die Freiheit,
      Aufzubrechen, wohin er will.

(Summer 1800)

A LIFE'S COURSE

You too wanted greater things, but love thrusts
    Everyone down, and sorrow bows us yet more,
        Though not in vain does our parabola
           Return from whence it came.

Upward and on, or down! Is nothing straight,
    Nothing right, in holy darkness where
        Dumb nature plots the days to come,
           Or on the steepest slope of hell?

This have I learned. For never, as mortal masters do,
    Have you heavenly powers, sustainers of all,
        To my knowledge ever with caution
           Led me along a level path.

Let man test everything, say they, the heavenly powers,
    And learn, from that strong food, to give thanks
        For all things, understanding the freedom
           To get up and go, wherever he will.

DER ABSCHIED

Zweite Fassung

Trennen wollten wir uns? wähnten es gut und klug?
　Da wirs taten, warum schröckte, wie Mord, die Tat?
　　Ach! wir kennen uns wenig,
　　　Denn es waltet ein Gott in uns.

Den verraten? ach ihn, welcher uns alles erst,
　Sinn und Leben erschuf, ihn, den beseelenden
　　Schutzgott unserer Liebe,
　　　Dies, dies Eine vermag ich nicht.

Aber anderen Fehl denket der Weltsinn sich,
　Andern ehernen Dienst übt er und anders Recht,
　　Und es listet die Seele
　　　Tag für Tag der Gebrauch uns ab.

Wohl! ich wußt es zuvor. Seit die gewurzelte
　Ungestalte, die Furcht Götter und Menschen trennt,
　　Muß, mit Blut sie zu sühnen,
　　　Muß der Liebenden Herz vergehn.

Laß mich schweigen! o laß nimmer von nun an mich
　Dieses Tödliche sehn, daß ich im Frieden doch
　　Hin ins Einsame ziehe,
　　　Und noch unser der Abschied sei!

Reich die Schale mir selbst, daß ich des rettenden
　Heilgen Giftes genug, daß ich des Lethetranks
　　Mit die trinke, daß alles,
　　　Haß und Liebe, vergessen sei!

Hingehn will ich. Vielleicht seh ich in langer Zeit
　Diotima! dich hier. Aber verblutet ist
　　Dann das Wünschen und friedlich
　　　Gleich den Seligen, fremde gehn

Wir umher, ein Gespräch führet uns ab und auf,
　Sinnend, zögernd, doch itzt mahnt die Vergessenen
　　Hier die Stelle des Abschieds,
　　　Es erwarmet ein Herz in uns,

28

THE FAREWELL

Second version

Did we intend to part, thinking it good and wise?
  Why did the act once done shock us like murder? Ah,
    Little we understand
      Ourselves, for a god is in us.

Fail him? Ah, fail the one who for us created
  All meaning and all life, into our love
    Put life and soul, guarding it,
      This one thing I cannot do.

But meaning a different fault the world's intent
  Practises a different task, hard, different laws;
    Custom and habit snaffle
      Day by day the soul from us.

So be it. I knew as much. Since ever rooted
  Malformity, fear, cleft gods and men apart,
    Must with blood to atone them
      Mortal hearts in love pass on.

Do not have me speak, let me never again behold
  This deadly thing, that I may make my way in peace,
    At least, into solitude,
      And let this parting be our own.

Hand me the cup yourself, that I with you may drink
  The holy bane, enough, the saving draft, and drink
    Lethe's oblivion, that we may both
      Forget the hate and the love also.

I go, willing. Long hence, perhaps, Diotima, I
  Shall see you here. But wishes will have bled away,
    And all at peace, like souls
      Of the departed, we shall walk about,

Strangers, conversation leading us up and down,
  Pensive, hesitant, though now the place of our farewell
    Reminds us, who shall be forgotten,
      A heart grows warm in us,

29

Staunend seh ich dich an, Stimmen und süßen Sang,
  Wie aus voriger Zeit, hör ich und Saitenspiel,
    Und die Lilie duftet
      Golden über dem Bach uns auf.

(Summer 1800)

I look at you with wonder, voices I hear and sweet
   Song as from a time gone by, and music of strings,
      And the lily wafts to us,
         Golden, its fragrance above the stream.

DICHTERBERUF

Des Ganges Ufer hörten des Freudengotts
    Triumph, als allerobernd vom Indus her
        Der junge Bacchus kam, mit heilgem
            Weine vom Schlafe Völker weckend.

Und du, des Tages Engel! erweckst sie nicht,
    Die jetzt noch schlafen? gib die Gesetze, gib
        Uns Leben, siege, Meister, du nur
            Hast der Eroberung Recht, wie Bacchus.

Nicht, was wohl sonst des Menschen Geschick und Sorg
    Im Haus und unter offenem Himmel ist,
        Wenn edler, denn das Wild, der Mann sich
            Wehret und nährt! denn es gilt ein anders,

Zu Sorg und Dienst den Dichtenden anvertraut!
    Der Höchste, der ists, dem wir geeignet sind,
        Daß näher, immerneu besungen
            Ihn die befreundete Brust vernehme.

Und dennoch, o ihr Himmlischen all, und all
    Ihr Quellen und ihr Ufer und Hain' und Höhn,
        Wo wunderbar zuerst, als du die
            Locken ergriffen, und unvergeßlich

Der unverhoffte Genius über uns
    Der schöpferische, göttliche kam, daß stumm
        Der Sinn uns ward und, wie vom
            Strahle gerührt, das Gebein erbebte,

Ihr ruhelosen Taten in weiter Welt!
    Ihr Schicksalstag', ihr reißenden, wenn der Gott
        Stillsinnend lenkt, wohin zorntrunken
            Ihn die gigantischen Rosse bringen,

Euch sollten wir verschweigen, und wenn in uns
    Vom stetigstillen Jahre der Wohllaut tönt,
        So sollt es klingen, gleich als hätte
            Mutig und müßig ein Kind des Meisters

THE POET'S VOCATION

Shores of Ganges heard the paean for the god
  Of joy when Bacchus came, conquering all,
    Young, from the Indus, with holy wine
      Rousing the peoples from their slumber.

And you, angel of our time, shall you arouse them too,
  The peoples unawakened? Give the laws,
    Give life to us, conquer, you alone,
      As Bacchus once, have right of conquest.

Not the thing that is man's care and skill,
  Inside a house or underneath the sky,
    Though a man fends and feeds more nobly
      Than animals do. Something else

Is put in the poet's trust and care to serve.
  To the highest lord, to him it is, we own,
    That, being sung ever anew, him
      Friendly hearts may sense more clearly.

Nevertheless, O all you heavenly gods
  And all you streams and shores, hilltops and woods,
    Where first, when by the hair one of you
      Seized us and the unhoped-for spirit

Unforgettably came, astonishing, down
  Upon us, godlike and creative, dumbfounding
    The mind, every bone shook
      As if struck by lightning—should we not,

You deeds rampaging out in the wide world,
  You days of destiny, fast and furious, when the god goes,
    Keeping his counsel, wherever the rage-drunk
      Gigantic horses happen to take him—

Should we not speak of you? And when from the calm
  And constant year harmony sounds in us, should
    It ring as if in idle caprice
      Some child had dared to touch for fun

Geweihte, reine Saiten im Scherz gerührt?
　　Und darum hast du, Dichter! des Orients
　　　　Propheten und den Griechensang und
　　　　　　Neulich die Donner gehört, damit du

Den Geist zu Diensten brauchst und die Gegenwart
　　Des Guten übereilest, in Spott, und den Albernen
　　　　Verleugnest, herzlos, und zum Spiele
　　　　　　Feil, wie gefangenes Wild, ihn treibest?

Bis aufgereizt vom Stachel im Grimme der
　　Des Ursprungs sich erinnert und ruft, daß selbst
　　　　Der Meister kommt, dann unter heißen
　　　　　　Todesgeschossen entseelt dich lässet.

Zu lang ist alles Göttliche dienstbar schon
　　Und alle Himmelskräfte verscherzt, verbraucht
　　　　Die Gütigen, zur Lust, danklos, ein
　　　　　　Schlaues Geschlecht und zu kennen wähnt es,

Wenn ihnen der Erhabne den Acker baut,
　　Das Tagslicht und den Donnerer, und es späht
　　　　Das Sehrohr wohl sie all und zählt und
　　　　　　Nennet mit Namen des Himmels Sterne.

Der Vater aber decket mit heilger Nacht,
　　Damit wir bleiben mögen, die Augen zu.
　　　　Nicht liebt er Wildes! Doch es zwinget
　　　　　　Nimmer die weite Gewalt den Himmel.

Noch ists auch gut, zu weise zu sein. Ihn kennt
　　Der Dank. Doch nicht behält er es leicht allein,
　　　　Und gern gesellt, damit verstehn sie
　　　　　　Helfen, zu anderen sich ein Dichter.

Furchtlos bleibt aber, so er es muß, der Mann
　　Einsam vor Gott, es schützet die Einfalt ihn,
　　　　Und keiner Waffen brauchts und keiner
　　　　　　Listen, so lange, bis Gottes Fehl hilft.

(1800–1801)

The master's consecrated and pure strings?
  Was it for this you heard the prophets of the East
    And Greek song and lately, poet,
      Voices of thunder? Was it for this—

To press the spirit into service, burst in upon
  The presence of the good, deriding it, heartless
    Disavow simplicity itself and make it
      Play for a fee like a beast captive?

Until the selfsame spirit, goaded to a rage,
  Cries out, remembering its source, and the master
    Hurling his hot darts comes
      And leaves you flat, a soul extinguished.

Too long all things divine have been put to use,
  Heavenly powers trifled away, mercies
    Squandered for sport, thankless, a
      Generation of schemers, and it presumes,

When the most sublime lord tills their fields,
  To know daylight and the thunderer, all these
    The telescope scans and quantifies
      And names with names the heaven's stars.

And yet with holy night the father will veil
  Our eyes, that still we may not perish. Untamed
    Excess he loves not. Power
      Expands but cannot suborn heaven.

Nor is it good to be too knowing. Gratitude
  Knows him. Yet to keep and contain it alone
    Is a hard burden, others the poet
      Gladly joins who help understanding.

Fearless yet, if he must, man stands, and lonely
  Before God, simplicity protects him, no
    Weapon he needs, nor subterfuge
      Till God's being not there helps him.

35

BROT UND WEIN

An Heinze

I

Rings um ruhet die Stadt; still wird die erleuchtete Gasse,
    Und, mit Fackeln geschmückt, rauschen die Wagen hinweg.
Satt gehn heim von Freuden des Tags zu ruhen die Menschen,
    Und Gewinn und Verlust wäget ein sinniges Haupt
Wohlzufrieden zu Haus; leer steht von Trauben und Blumen,
    Und von Werken der Hand ruht der geschäftige Markt.
Aber das Saitenspiel tönt fern aus Gärten; vielleicht, daß
    Dort ein Liebendes spielt oder ein einsamer Mann
Ferner Freunde gedenkt und der Jugendzeit; und die Brunnen
    Immerquillend und frisch rauschen an duftendem Beet.
Still in dämmriger Luft ertönen geläutete Glocken,
    Und der Stunden gedenk rufet ein Wächter die Zahl.
Jetzt auch kommet ein Wehn und regt die Gipfel des Hains auf,
    Sieh! und das Schattenbild unserer Erde, der Mond,
Kommet geheim nun auch; die Schwärmerische, die Nacht kommt,
    Voll mit Sternen und wohl wenig bekümmert um uns,
Glänzt die Erstaunende dort, die Fremdlingin unter den Menschen,
    Über Gebirgeshöhn traurig und prächtig herauf.

II

Wunderbar ist die Gunst der Hocherhabnen und niemand
    Weiß, von wannen und was einem geschiehet von ihr.
So bewegt sie die Welt und die hoffende Seele der Menschen,
    Selbst kein Weiser versteht, was sie bereitet, denn so
Will es der oberste Gott, der sehr dich liebet, und darum
    Ist noch lieber, wie sie, dir der besonnene Tag.
Aber zuweilen liebt auch klares Auge den Schatten
    Und versuchet zu Lust, eh es die Not ist, den Schlaf,
Oder es blickt auch gern ein treuer Mann in die Nacht hin,
    Ja, es ziemet sich, ihr Kränze zu weihn und Gesang,
Weil den Irrenden sie geheiliget ist und den Toten,
    Selber aber besteht, ewig, in freiestem Geist.
Aber sie muß uns auch, daß in der zaudernden Weile,
    Daß im Finstern für uns einiges Haltbare sei,

BREAD AND WINE

For Heinse

I

The town around is hushed, the little street in the lamplight
  Quietens and the twinkling wagons rumble away.
People filled with joys of the day go home to their rest,
  Pensive heads are content to be weighing profit and loss,
Under a homely roof; and emptied of flowers and grapes
  The market, busy before, rests from manual toil.
But music of strings floats from distant gardens, perhaps
  It is a lover playing, perhaps some lonely man
Thinking of absent friends and the time of his youth; and fountains,
  Flowing as ever and fresh, sprinkle a flower bed.
Bells toll quiet in the dusky air, and a watchman
  Heeding the hours that pass, calls what o'clock it is.
Now a rushing of wind has excited the treetops too,
  Look, and the moon comes, shadow image of earth,
Secretly into the sky; the dreamer is coming, night
  Brimming with stars and caring doubtless little for us;
There in her wonder she gleams, rising, strange among humans,
  Sad and splendid above the crests of mountain and hill.

II

Marvelous favors she brings, the night sublime, and nobody
  Knows whence they may come, or what her doing may be.
Thus she bestirs the world and the hopeful souls of men;
  Even the wise cannot tell what she may hold in store,
For such is his will, the highest god, who loves you, wherefore
  Better than her you love the conscient solar day.
But sometimes even an eye that is clear may long for shadow
  And may willingly venture, before it is needful, to sleep.
Or to gaze at the night may please a man who is loyal and true,
  Yes, to dedicate song and garlands to her is good,
For she is sacred to souls that are lost and to the dead
  Though in herself she persists in the freest spirit of all.
Yet for the time of our doubt and hesitant waiting,
  That in the dark we may grasp something solid at least,

37

BROT UND WEIN *(continued)*

Uns die Vergessenheit und das Heiligtrunkene gönnen,
　Gönnen das strömende Wort, das, wie die Liebenden, sei,
Schlummerlos, und vollern Pokal und kühneres Leben,
　Heilig Gedächtnis auch, wachend zu bleiben bei Nacht.

III

Auch verbergen umsonst das Herz im Busen, umsonst nur
　Halten den Mut noch wir, Meister und Knaben, denn wer
Möcht es hindern und wer möcht uns die Freude verbieten?
　Göttliches Feuer auch treibet, bei Tag und bei Nacht,
Aufzubrechen. So komm! daß wir das Offene schauen,
　Daß ein Eigenes wir suchen, so weit es auch ist.
Fest bleibt Eins; es sei um Mittag oder es gehe
　Bis in die Mitternacht, immer bestehet ein Maß,
Allen gemein, doch jeglichem auch ist eignes beschieden,
　Dahin gehet und kommt jeder, wohin er es kann.
Drum! und spotten des Spotts mag gern frohlockender Wahnsinn,
　Wenn er in heiliger Nacht plötzlich die Sänger ergreift.
Drum an den Isthmos komm! dorthin, wo das offene Meer rauscht
　Am Parnaß und der Schnee delphische Felsen umglänzt,
Dort ins Land des Olymps, dort auf die Höhe Cithärons,
　Unter die Fichten dort, unter die Trauben, von wo
Thebe drunten und Ismenos rauscht im Lande des Kadmos,
　Dorther kommt und zurück deutet der kommende Gott.

IV

Seliges Griechenland! du Haus der Himmlischen alle,
　Also ist wahr, was einst wir in der Jugend gehört?
Festlicher Saal! der Boden ist Meer! und Tische die Berge,
　Wahrlich zu einzigem Brauche vor alters gebaut!
Aber die Thronen, wo? die Tempel, und wo die Gefäße,
　Wo mit Nektar gefüllt, Göttern zu Lust der Gesang?
Wo, wo leuchten sie denn, die fernhintreffenden Sprüche?
　Delphi schlummert und wo tönet das große Geschick?

She must grant us oblivion, rapture drunken and holy,
  Grant us the flowing word, which, like lovers, may be
Wakeful ever, and fuller the cup and life more daring,
  Holy remembrance too, keeping our watch through the night.

III

Also for nothing it is we hide our hearts, for nothing
  Keep, masters and pupils alike, our courage up.
For who would intend suppression, who would forbid us joy?
  The fire divine impels us too, by day and by night,
To get up and go. So come, let us scan the open spaces,
  Search for the thing that is ours, however distant it is.
One thing is certain: whether at high noon or lasting
  Into the middle of night, there is a measure applies
For all, but to each is assigned a property special to him,
  Whence he issues and whither he goes, as best he can.
That's how it is, and folly exults to deride derision
  Once that folly has seized the poet in holy night.
So come to the Isthmus, come where the ocean below Parnassus
  Murmurs and sparkling snow mantles the Delphic rocks,
Come to the slopes of Olympus and up to the peak of Kithaeron,
  Among the pines and among the vineyards whence appear
Murmuring Thebe and Ismenos below in the country of Kadmos:
  The god approaches from there, and points back, showing the
      way.

IV

O happy Greece, dwelling of all the heavenly powers,
  So they are true, the tales told to us in our youth.
Festive mansion, your floor is the sea, the mountains your tables,
  Built long since, if the truth were told, for a single use.
But where are the thrones, where the temples, where are the jugs
  Brimming with nectar and where the songs that delighted the
      gods?
Where is their radiance now, those oracles darting afar?
  Delphi sleeps, and where does the clamor of destiny sound?

Wo ist das schnelle? wo brichts, allgegenwärtigen Glücks voll,
  Donnernd aus heiterer Luft über die Augen herein?
Vater Aether! so riefs und flog von Zunge zu Zunge
  Tausendfach, es ertrug keiner das Leben allein;
Ausgeteilet erfreut solch Gut und getauschet, mit Fremden,
  Wirds ein Jubel, es wächst schlafend des Wortes Gewalt:
Vater! heiter! und hallt, so weit es gehet, das uralt
  Zeichen, von Eltern geerbt, treffend und schaffend hinab.
Denn so kehren die Himmlischen ein, tiefschütternd gelangt so
  Aus den Schatten herab unter die Menschen ihr Tag.

V

Unempfunden kommen sie erst, es streben entgegen
  Ihnen die Kinder, zu hell kommet, zu blendend das Glück,
Und es scheut sie der Mensch, kaum weiß zu sagen ein Halbgott,
  Wer mit Namen sie sind, die mit den Gaben ihm nahn.
Aber der Mut von ihnen ist groß, es füllen das Herz ihm
  Ihre Freuden und kaum weiß er zu brauchen das Gut,
Schafft, verschwendet und fast ward ihm Unheiliges heilig,
  Das er mit segnender Hand törig und gütig berührt.
Möglichst dulden die Himmlischen dies; dann aber in Wahrheit
  Kommen sie selbst und gewohnt werden die Menschen
          des Glücks
Und des Tags und zu schaun die Offenbaren, das Antlitz
  Derer, welche, schon längst Eines und Alles genannt,
Tief die verschwiegene Brust mit freier Genüge gefüllet,
  Und zuerst und allein alles Verlangen beglückt;
So ist der Mensch; wenn da ist das Gut, und es sorget mit Gaben
  Selber ein Gott für ihn, kennet und sieht er es nicht.
Tragen muß er, zuvor; nun aber nennt er sein Liebstes,
  Nun, nun müssen dafür Worte, wie Blumen, entstehn.

VI

Und nun denkt er zu ehren in Ernst die seligen Götter,
  Wirklich und wahrhaft muß alles verkünden ihr Lob.

Where is the lightning speed, where the ubiquitous luck
   Thunder flashes around, out of a sky that is clear?
"Father of Air!" they shouted, from tongue to tongue the words
   Multiplying their sense, life was not borne alone;
Such a benefit, shared, is a joy, and exchanged with others
   Becomes a rapture, the word's energy growing in sleep:
"Father Serene!" the primordial symbol spreads to the limit,
   Down from parent to son, creative, hitting the mark.
For that is the way the heavenly powers house among men:
   Comes, shaking their roots, out of the shadows, their day.

V

First when they come, they are not felt, rushing to meet them
   Children are dazzled, their luck a blinding light as it comes,
And men shun them, even a demigod hardly can tell
   By what names they are called as they approach with their gifts.
But courage in plenty they bring to man, filling his heart
   With joys, and he hardly knows how to make use of their goods;
Working, wasting, almost he calls unholy things holy,
   Blessing them all with a touch, in a foolish and friendly way.
The heavenly ones take little offence; but then they come
   In truth as they are and men soon take their luck as it comes,
The sun by day and the gods revealed are familiar sights
   Shaping the countenance which, by ancients named "one and
        all,"
Has filled to the brim with free satisfaction the reticent heart,
   And first and alone is the source of gratified desire.
Man's nature is such: when the good is there and a god
   Himself is the giver, the gifts are out of sight and of mind.
First he must learn to endure; but now he names what he loves,
   Now, now must the words come into being, like flowers.

VI

And now he intends for the blithe gods all serious honor,
   All things announcing their praise, everything real and true.

Nichts darf schauen das Licht, was nicht den Hohen gefället,
  Vor den Aether gebührt Müßigversuchendes nicht.
Drum in der Gegenwart der Himmlischen würdig zu stehen,
  Richten in herrlichen Ordnungen Völker sich auf
Untereinander und baun die schönen Tempel und Städte
  Fest und edel, sie gehn über Gestaden empor—
Aber wo sind sie? wo blühn die Bekannten, die Kronen des Festes?
  Thebe welkt und Athen; rauschen die Waffen nicht mehr
In Olympia, nicht die goldnen Wagen des Kampfspiels,
  Und bekränzen sich denn nimmer die Schiffe Korinths?
Warum schweigen auch sie, die alten heilgen Theater?
  Warum freuet sich denn nicht der geweihete Tanz?
Warum zeichnet, wie sonst, die Stirne des Mannes ein Gott nicht,
  Drückt den Stempel, wie sonst, nicht dem Getroffenen auf?
Oder er kam auch selbst und nahm des Menschen Gestalt an
  Und vollendet' und schloß tröstend das himmlische Fest.

VII

Aber Freund! wir kommen zu spät. Zwar leben die Götter,
  Aber über dem Haupt droben in anderer Welt.
Endlos wirken sie da und scheinens wenig zu achten,
  Ob wir leben, so sehr schonen die Himmlischen uns.
Denn nicht immer vermag ein schwaches Gefäß sie zu fassen,
  Nur zu Zeiten erträgt göttliche Fülle der Mensch.
Traum von ihnen ist drauf das Leben. Aber das Irrsal
  Hilft, wie Schlummer, und stark machet die Not und die Nacht,
Bis daß Helden genug in der ehernen Wiege gewachsen,
  Herzen an Kraft, wie sonst, ähnlich den Himmlischen sind.
Donnernd kommen sie drauf. Indessen dünket mir öfters
  Besser zu schlafen, wie so ohne Genossen zu sein,
So zu harren, und was zu tun indes und zu sagen,
  Weiß ich nicht, und wozu Dichter in dürftiger Zeit.
Aber sie sind, sagst du, wie des Weingotts heilige Priester,
  Welche von Lande zu Land zogen in heiliger Nacht.

Nothing that means no pleasure for them may be brought to light,
　　Idle attemptings are not for the lofty gods of the air.
Therefore to stand in the holy presence aright and with dignity,
　　Peoples join and arise in glorious orders, linked
Level to level; beautiful temples and cities they build,
　　Solid and noble, which tower up from the shore of the sea—
Yet where are they? Where have they gone, the familiar blossoming
　　Crowns of the feast? Thebes withers and Athens; no more
The clatter of arms in Olympia, golden chariots racing,
　　And what of the garlands they hung on the Corinthian ships?
Why are they silent, even the ancient holy theaters?
　　Why has the joy disappeared out of the sacred dance?
Why does a god no longer, as once, on the brow of a man
　　Stamp his mark to declare: this is the target I choose.
Or a god himself came with the form and features of manhood,
　　Bringing the heavenly feast comfortingly to an end.

VII

Surely, friend, we have come too late. The gods are alive,
　　Yes, but yonder, up there, in another world overhead.
There they are endlessly active and seem not greatly to care
　　If we are living or not, such is their lenience.
For a fragile vessel is rarely able to hold them in:
　　Only at times can man cope with the fullness of God.
So life has become a dream about them. Nevertheless,
　　Error can help, like sleep, night and distress give strength,
Till heroes enough have grown, in this obdurate cradle, to stature,
　　And hearts as once have a strength matching the heavenly
　　　　　　powers.
Then they will come, with thunder. But for the present, I think,
　　Sleep may be better than life lived without comrades like this,
Waiting and always waiting; and what's to be done and be said
　　I do not know, or the object of poets in desolate times.
But, as you say, they are like the sacred priests of the winegod,
　　Who from country to country traveled in sacred night.

VIII

Nämlich, als vor einiger Zeit, uns dünket sie lange,
  Aufwärts stiegen sie all, welche das Leben beglückt,
Als der Vater gewandt sein Angesicht von den Menschen,
  Und das Trauern mit Recht über der Erde begann,
Als erschienen zuletzt ein stiller Genius, himmlisch
  Tröstend, welcher des Tags Ende verkündet' und schwand,
Ließ zum Zeichen, daß einst er da gewesen und wieder
  Käme, der himmlische Chor einige Gaben zurück,
Derer menschlich, wie sonst, wir uns zu freuen vermöchten,
  Denn zur Freude, mit Geist, wurde das Größre zu groß
Unter den Menschen und noch, noch fehlen die Starken zu höchsten
  Freuden, aber es lebt stille noch einiger Dank.
Brot ist der Erde Frucht, doch ists vom Lichte gesegnet,
  Und vom donnernden Gott kommet die Freude des Weins.
Darum denken wir auch dabei der Himmlischen, die sonst
  Da gewesen und die kehren in richtiger Zeit,
Darum singen sie auch mit Ernst, die Sänger, den Weingott
  Und nicht eitel erdacht tönet dem Alten das Lob.

IX

Ja! sie sagen mit Recht, er söhne den Tag mit der Nacht aus,
  Führe des Himmels Gestirn ewig hinunter, hinauf,
Allzeit froh, wie das Laub der immergrünenden Fichte,
  Das er liebt, und der Kranz, den er von Efeu gewählt,
Weil er bleibet und selbst die Spur der entflohenen Götter
  Götterlosen hinab unter das Finstere bringt.
Was der Alten Gesang von Kindern Gottes geweissagt,
  Siehe! wir sind es, wir; Frucht von Hesperien ists!
Wunderbar und genau ists als an Menschen erfüllet,
  Glaube, wer es geprüft! aber so vieles geschieht,
Keines wirket, denn wir sind herzlos, Schatten, bis unser
  Vater Aether erkannt jeden und allen gehört.
Aber indessen kommt als Fackelschwinger des Höchsten
  Sohn, der Syrier, unter die Schatten herab.

44

BREAD AND WINE *(continued)*

VIII

For it is so, that when they ascended, all who had brought
    Luck into life—it seems longer ago than it is—
And when the father averted his face from the world of man
    And a veil of sorrow was spread, rightly, over the earth,
When at the last a quiet spirit appeared with heavenly
    Solace, announcing the end, and vanished out of our sight,
Then as a sign that he had been here and thought to return,
    Gifts, a few, were bestowed on men by the heavenly choir,
Such as we can enjoy, in our human and usual way,
    For joy in the spirit was now, as a greater thing, too much
For men to endure, and still, still there are none with strength
    Enough for the highest joys, though somewhat of gratitude lives.
Bread is the fruit of earth, yet is blessed by the heavenly light,
    And from the thundering god flows the joy of the vine.
These, therefore, put us in mind of the gods, who once
    Were here and shall return, whenever the time is right.
Therefore they mean it in earnest, the poets who sing of the
        winegod,
    And no empty intent sounds in their praise of the past.

IX

Yes, it is rightly said that he reconciles day with the night,
    And it is he who conducts the eternal wheeling of stars,
Always joyous he is, like the evergreen needles of pine
    Of which he is fond, and the wreath of ivy he chose for his sign,
Because he is constant, bringing the vestige of gods that have fled
    Down to the darkness in which godless humanity dwells.
Songs of old had prophesied much about Children of God,
    And look, we are they; it is we—fruit of the Hesperides!
All the things foretold came wondrously true, but of men,
    See how it is, and believe! but in the crush of events
Nothing results, for we are heartless, shadows, unless
    We own to our Father of Air, and he is of each and of all.
Yet for the present his son is among us, bearing the torch
    Down where the shadows abound, the Syrian lighting his trail.

Selige Weise sehns; ein Lächeln aus der gefangnen
    Seele leuchtet, dem Licht tauet ihr Auge noch auf.
Sanfter träumet und schläft in Armen der Erde der Titan,
    Selbst der neidische, selbst Cerberus trinket und schläft.

(Winter 1800–1801)

The wise can see it, happy, and from the soul in its prison
    A smile escapes with a shine, eyes melt to the light.
The Titan asleep in earth's embrace, his dream becomes sweeter;
    Even the jealous guard, Cerberus, drinks and sleeps.

DER RHEIN

An Isaak von Sinclair

Im dunkeln Efeu saß ich, an der Pforte
Des Waldes, eben, da der goldene Mittag,
Den Quell besuchend, herunterkam
Von Treppen des Alpengebirgs,
Das mir die göttlichgebaute,
Die Burg der Himmlischen heißt
Nach alter Meinung, wo aber
Geheim noch manches entschieden
Zu Menschen gelanget; von da
Vernahm ich ohne Vermuten
Ein Schicksal, denn noch kaum
War mir im warmen Schatten
Sich manches beredend, die Seele
Italia zu geschweift
Und fernhin an die Küsten Moreas.

Jetzt aber, drin im Gebirg,
Tief unter den silbernen Gipfeln
Und unter fröhlichem Grün,
Wo die Wälder schauernd zu ihm,
Und der Felsen Häupter übereinander
Hinabschaun, taglang, dort
Im kältesten Abgrund hört
Ich um Erlösung jammern
Den Jüngling, es hörten ihn, wie er tobt',
Und die Mutter Erd anklagt',
Und den Donnerer, der ihn gezeuget,
Erbarmend die Eltern, doch
Die Sterblichen flohn von dem Ort,
Denn furchtbar war, da lichtlos er
In den Fesseln sich wälzte,
Das Rasen des Halbgotts.

Die Stimme wars des edelsten der Ströme,
Des freigeborenen Rheins,

THE RHINE

For Isaak von Sinclair

At the forest's gate I sat among
Dark ivy as the golden noon
Came down visiting the stream, from off
The Alps, their mountain staircase, built
By powers divine, God's Castle as
I call it, in accord
With old opinion, where devolves
To man yet many a thing
Decided in secret; thence
Came to my mind, against expectation,
A destiny, for my soul
Telling itself of this and that in the warm shade
Now was drifting toward Italy
And beyond, to the far coasts of Morea.

But now, in the mountains' midst, deep
Down below the silver peaks, and among
Delighting green, where the forests,
Tremulous, and piled crag heads gaze
All day down at him, there
In the coldest abyss I heard
The stripling moan for liberation,
In floundering rage accuse earth,
His mother, and the thunderer who
Begot him, and they heard him also,
His parents, pitying, yet
Mortals fled the place, for it was terrible,
With him in his chained dark torsions,
The frenzy of the demigod.

It was the voice of the most noble river,
The freeborn Rhine,

Und anderes hoffte der, als droben von den Brüdern,
Dem Tessin und dem Rhodanus,
Er schied und wandern wollt, und ungeduldig ihn
Nach Asia trieb die königliche Seele.
Doch unverständig ist
Das Wünschen vor dem Schicksal.
Die Blindesten aber
Sind Göttersöhne. Denn es kennet der Mensch
Sein Haus und dem Tier ward, wo
Es bauen solle, doch jenen ist
Der Fehl, daß sie nicht wissen wohin
In die unerfahrne Seele gegeben.

Ein Rätsel ist Reinentsprungenes. Auch
Der Gesang kaum darf es enthüllen. Denn
Wie du anfingst, wirst du bleiben,
So viel auch wirket die Not,
Und die Zucht, das meiste nämlich
Vermag die Geburt,
Und der Lichtstrahl, der
Dem Neugebornen begegnet.
Wo aber ist einer,
Um frei zu bleiben
Sein Leben lang, und des Herzens Wunsch
Allein zu erfüllen, so
Aus günstigen Höhn, wie der Rhein,
Und so aus heiligem Schoße
Glücklich geboren, wie jener?

Drum ist ein Jauchzen sein Wort.
Nicht liebt er, wie andere Kinder,
In Wickelbanden zu weinen;
Denn wo die Ufer zuerst
An die Seit ihm schleichen, die krummen,
Und durstig umwindend ihn,
Den Unbedachten, zu ziehn
Und wohl zu behüten begehren

And as he parted up there from his brothers,
Ticino and Rhodanus, his hopes
Were elsewhere, he meant to travel,
And his royal soul drove him, with impatience,
Toward Asia. But to desire a thing
In destiny's teeth is not prudent.
Yet the blindest of all are
The sons of gods. For man
Knows his house, where to build
Occurs to the animals, but to their soul
Without experience is given the defect
That they know not where to go.

   A riddle it is, whatever
Springs from the pure source. Even song
May hardly reveal it. For
As you began so you remain.
And though compulsions leave their mark,
And upbringing, birth performs
The most, and the ray of light encountering
The newborn being. But where is the man
Who can stay free
As long as he lives, and alone
Accomplish his heart's desire
From heights auspicious as the Rhine's,
And born from a womb as holy
With such fortune as his?

   Therefore his speech is a shout of joy.
He does not weep and whine
In swaddling clothes like other infants;
For though the shores at first, crooked,
Sidle up to him and coiling
Thirstily are keen to guide him, unawares,
Twixt their teeth and coddle him there, with a laugh
He rends those snakes to tatters, plunges on,

Im eigenen Zahne, lachend
Zerreißt er die Schlangen und stürzt
Mit der Beut und wenn in der Eil
Ein Größerer ihn nicht zähmt,
Ihn wachsen läßt, wie der Blitz, muß er
Die Erde spalten, und wie Bezauberte fliehn
Die Wälder ihm nach und zusammensinkend die Berge.

Ein Gott will aber sparen den Söhnen
Das eilende Leben und lächelt,
Wenn unenthaltsam, aber gehemmt
Von heiligen Alpen, ihm
In der Tiefe, wie jener, zürnen die Ströme.
In solcher Esse wird dann
Auch alles Lautre geschmiedet,
Und schön ists, wie er drauf,
Nachdem er die Berge verlassen,
Stillwandelnd sich im deutschen Lande
Begnüget und das Sehnen stillt
Im guten Geschäfte, wenn er das Land baut,
Der Vater Rhein, und liebe Kinder nährt
In Städten, die er gegründet.

Doch nimmer, nimmer vergißt ers.
Denn eher muß die Wohnung vergehn,
Und die Satzung und zum Unbild werden
Der Tag der Menschen, ehe vergessen
Ein solcher dürfte den Ursprung
Und die reine Stimme der Jugend.
Wer war es, der zuerst
Die Liebesbande verderbt
Und Stricke von ihnen gemacht hat?
Dann haben des eigenen Rechts
Und gewiß des himmlischen Feuers
Gespottet die Trotzigen, dann erst
Die sterblichen Pfade verachtend
Verwegnes erwählt
Und den Göttern gleich zu werden getrachtet.

Bearing his catch, and if in his haste some
Greater one than he does not tame him,
Nor make him grow, he must split the earth
Like lightning, and the forests hurtle
After him, bewitched, and mountains subsiding.

   But a god desires to save his sons
From flitting life, and he smiles
When without restraint, but hemmed in
By holy Alps, the rivers
Rage at him in the depths as this one does.
In such a furnace then
All things freed of dross are shaped
And beauty comes thereafter, when
Leaving the mountains he meanders
Quietly through German lands, content,
And slakes his cravings
In wholesome commerce, in husbandry,
Father Rhine, feeding his beloved
Children in towns that he has founded.

   Yet never will he forget, never,
For sooner shall man's dwelling perish,
His laws and his light of day become
Monstrous, than such a one
Forget his origin
And the pure voice of his youth.
Who first tainted the ties
Of love and made
Traps of them? In consequence
Defiant rebels made a mock
Of their own rights and, for sure,
Of heavenly fire, and then
Scorning the ways of mortals
Chose arrogance and ventured
To become the peers of gods.

Es haben aber an eigner
Unsterblichkeit die Götter genug, und bedürfen
Die Himmlischen eines Dings,
So sinds Heroen und Menschen
Und Sterbliche sonst. Denn weil
Die Seligsten nichts fühlen von selbst,
Muß wohl, wenn solches zu sagen
Erlaubt ist, in der Götter Namen
Teilnehmend fühlen ein Andrer,
Den brauchen sie; jedoch ihr Gericht
Ist, daß sein eigenes Haus
Zerbreche der und das Liebste
Wie den Feind schelt und sich Vater und Kind
Begrabe unter den Trümmern,
Wenn einer, wie sie, sein will und nicht
Ungleiches dulden, der Schwärmer.

Drum wohl ihm, welcher fand
Ein wohlbeschiedenes Schicksal,
Wo noch der Wanderungen
Und süß der Leiden Erinnerung
Aufrauscht am sichern Gestade,
Daß da und dorthin gern
Er sehn mag bis an die Grenzen,
Die bei der Geburt ihm Gott
Zum Aufenthalte gezeichnet.
Dann ruht er, seligbescheiden,
Denn alles, was er gewollt,
Das Himmlische, von selber umfängt
Es unbezwungen, lächelnd
Jetzt, da er ruhet, den Kühnen.

Halbgötter denk ich jetzt
Und kennen muß ich die Teuern,
Weil oft ihr Leben so
Die sehnende Brust mir beweget.
Wem aber, wie, Rousseau, dir,

But the gods have enough
Immortality of their own, and if there be
One thing the celestials need
It is heroes and men
And mortals generally. For since
The serenest beings feel nothing at all,
There must come, if to speak
Thus is permitted, another who feels
On their behalf, him
They use and need; but their deposition
Is that he shall destroy
His own house, curse what he loves most
As his enemy, and under the rubble
Bury his father and his child,
If he should seek to be like them and not
Allow inequality, the wild dreamer.

Hence fortune is his who found
A right destiny his own,
Where the surge of wayfaring memories
With sweet recall of hardship known
Whispers on a certain shore,
His gaze may thus extend around
To the limits
Drawn at his birth
By God for his dwelling.
Then he shall come to rest, lowly and
Serene, for all his heart desired,
The heaven he wished for, it is there, effortlessly
Surrounding him, the adventurer,
And smiles at him, now that his quiet has come.

Demigods now I'm thinking of,
And must know them, the dears, because
Their lives have so much stirred
My heart, and often.
Yet to a man, Rousseau, like you,

Unüberwindlich die Seele,
Die starkausdauernde, ward,
Und sicherer Sinn
Und süße Gabe zu hören,
Zu reden so, daß er aus heiliger Fülle
Wie der Weingott, törig göttlich
Und gesetzlos sie, die Sprache der Reinesten, gibt
Verständlich den Guten, aber mit Recht
Die Achtungslosen mit Blindheit schlägt,
Die entweihenden Knechte, wie nenn ich den Fremden?

  Die Söhne der Erde sind, wie die Mutter,
Alliebend, so empfangen sie auch
Mühlos, die Glücklichen, Alles.
Drum überraschet es auch
Und schröckt den sterblichen Mann,
Wenn er den Himmel, den
Er mit den liebenden Armen
Sich auf die Schultern gehäuft,
Und die Last der Freude bedenket;
Dann scheint ihm oft das Beste,
Fast ganz vergessen da,
Wo der Strahl nicht brennt,
Im Schatten des Walds
Am Bielersee in frischer Grüne zu sein,
Und sorglosarm an Tönen,
Anfängern gleich, bei Nachtigallen zu lernen.

  Und herrlich ists, aus heiligem Schlafe dann
Erstehen und, aus Waldes Kühle
Erwachend, abends nun
Dem milderen Licht entgegenzugehn,
Wenn, der die Berge gebaut
Und den Pfad der Ströme gezeichnet,
Nachdem er lächelnd auch
Der Menschen geschäftiges Leben,
Das othemarme, wie Segel

Whose never daunted soul
Persevered, became invincible,
With certitude of mind
And a sweet gift of listening so,
And speaking, that from holy plenitude
Like the winegod in his folly divine
And all against the rules he gives it,
The language of essences,
That the good may understand, yet strikes
Blind all who do not care and desecrating
Slaves, how shall I speak of the stranger?

    The sons of earth, their love comprehends
All, as does their mother's, whence their luck is,
And no effort, likewise all to receive.
And it comes to mortal man as a surprise,
Startling him, when he thinks
Of the heaven that he, with loving arms,
Heaped on his back,
And of the burden of joy;
Often it seems then the best thing
To be there, virtually forgotten,
Where the sun's ray does not burn
In the forest shade
By Lake Bienne among fresh green foliage,
And to be learning, with song notes
Happily indigent, like beginners, from nightingales.

    And it is glorious to be standing up then
From holy sleep and waking
Out of the forest cool, to walk
Toward the gentler light in the evening,
When he who built the mountains
And who designed the courses of streams,
Now done with guiding the short-
Breathed busy lives of men with a smile,

Mit seinen Lüften gelenkt hat,
Auch ruht und zu der Schülerin jetzt,
Der Bildner, Gutes mehr
Denn Böses findend,
Zur heutigen Erde der Tag sich neiget.—

    Dann feiern das Brautfest Menschen und Götter,
Es feiern die Lebenden all,
Und ausgeglichen
Ist eine Weile das Schicksal.
Und die Flüchtlinge suchen die Herberg,
Und süßen Schlummer die Tapfern,
Die Liebenden aber
Sind, was sie waren, sie sind
Zu Hause, wo die Blume sich freuet
Unschädlicher Glut und die finsteren Bäume
Der Geist umsäuselt, aber die Unversöhnten
Sind umgewandelt und eilen
Die Hände sich ehe zu reichen,
Bevor das freundliche Licht
Hinuntergeht und die Nacht kommt.

    Doch einigen eilt
Dies schnell vorüber, andere
Behalten es länger.
Die ewigen Götter sind
Voll Lebens allzeit; bis in den Tod
Kann aber ein Mensch auch
Im Gedächtnis doch das Beste behalten,
Und dann erlebt er das Höchste.
Nur hat ein jeder sein Maß.
Denn schwer ist zu tragen
Das Unglück, aber schwerer das Glück.
Ein Weiser aber vermocht es
Vom Mittag bis in die Mitternacht,
Und bis der Morgen erglänzte,
Beim Gastmahl helle zu bleiben.

Filling them like sails with his winds,
Leans, the artificer, toward his pupil,
Finding more good
Than evil, he, the day,
Leaning toward the earth which is today.—

Then men and gods their nuptials celebrate,
All living creatures celebrate
And equilibrium for a time
Makes destinies level,
And fugitives seek a resting place,
And sweet slumber is sought by the brave,
But lovers are
Just what they were, they are
At home where the flower enjoys
Innocuous heat and the spirit rustles
Round dark trees, but enemies are
Transformed and rush
To clasp one another's hands
Before the friendly light descending
Vanishes and the night comes.

Yet some there are
This quickly passes by, others
Retain it longer. At
All times the eternal gods
Are full of life; but into death
Even a man can keep
Stored in memory the best,
And then ultimate experience is his.
Each man has, nonetheless, his measure.
For misfortune is hard
To endure, but fortune even harder.
But at the banquet one wise man
From noon through midnight and until
The gleam of morning came could keep
A steady lucid mind.

Dir mag auf heißem Pfade unter Tannen oder
Im Dunkel des Eichwalds gehüllt
In Stahl, mein Sinclair! Gott erscheinen oder
In Wolken, du kennst ihn, da du kennest, jugendlich,
Des Guten Kraft, und nimmer ist dir
Verborgen das Lächeln des Herrschers
Bei Tage, wenn
Es fieberhaft und angekettet das
Lebendige scheinet oder auch
Bei Nacht, wenn alles gemischt
Ist ordnungslos und wiederkehrt
Uralte Verwirrung.

(Spring–summer 1801)

To you, on the hot path under pines, or
In the dark of the oak forest hidden
In the steel blade, Sinclair, my friend,
God may appear, or in clouds, you know him,
Having a young cognizance of
The power of good; and the master of men,
His smile is never
Concealed from you, by day
When the vivid world seems
Febrile or shackled, nor yet
By night, when all is blent
And orderless, and age-old
Confusion comes again.

VULKAN

Jetzt komm und hülle, freundlicher Feuergeist,
    Den zarten Sinn der Frauen in Wolken ein,
      In goldne Träum und schütze sie, die
        Blühende Ruhe der Immerguten.

Dem Manne laß sein Sinnen, und sein Geschäft,
    Und seiner Kerze Schein, und den künftgen Tag
      Gefallen, laß des Unmuts ihm, der
        Häßlichen Sorge zu viel nicht werden,

Wenn jetzt der immerzürnende Boreas,
    Mein Erbfeind, über Nacht mit dem Frost das Land
      Befällt, und spät, zur Schlummerstunde,
        Spottend der Menschen, sein schröcklich Lied singt,

Und unsrer Städte Mauren und unsern Zaun,
    Den fleißig wir gesetzt, und den stillen Hain
      Zerreißt, und selber im Gesang die
        Seele mir störet, der Allverderber,

Und rastlos tobend über den sanften Strom
    Sein schwarz Gewölk ausschüttet, daß weit umher
      Das Tal gärt, und, wie fallend Laub, vom
        Berstenden Hügel herab der Fels fällt.

Wohl frömmer ist, denn andre Lebendige,
    Der Mensch; doch zürnt es draußen, gehöret der
      Auch eigner sich, und sinnt und ruht in
        Sicherer Hütte, der Freigeborne.

Und immer wohnt der freundlichen Genien
    Noch Einer gerne segnend mit ihm, und wenn
      Sie zürnten all, die ungelehrgen
        Geniuskräfte, doch liebt die Liebe.

(1802–3)

VULCAN

Come, friendly spirit of fire, and wrap
  In cloud the sensitive minds of women,
    Swathe them in golden dreams and shield
      Their flowerlike peace, they are all kindness.

And men, let them take pleasure in planning and trade,
  Candlelight, day that is still to come,
    Let not vexation be too much,
      Let ugly care be not multiplied,

When now the north wind, always angering, my
  Arch-enemy, blows attacking the land
    With frost overnight, and late, at sleeptime,
      Sings, deriding men, his terrible song,

Makes havoc with town walls and the fence we rigged
  With much toil, ripping the quiet orchard apart,
    Troubles me, even in the middle of
      A poem, Boreas spoiling it all,

And in wild rampage spills over the gentle stream
  His black cloud, the valley swirls and
    Seethes with it, big rocks like leaves
      Plummeting down as a hill bursts open.

Yes, man is religious, more so than any
  Other being; yet when hell breaks loose
    Outside, he sits tight indoors, more his own man
      Than ever, thinking, safe, and born free.

And one friendly spirit always does like
  To live with him, and bless him; let them rage,
    All the untutored spirit powers:
      Love still is and still does love.

BLÖDIGKEIT

Sind denn dir nicht bekannt viele Lebendigen?
  Geht auf Wahrem dein Fuß nicht, wie auf Teppichen?
    Drum, mein Genius! tritt nur
      Bar ins Leben, und sorge nicht!

Was geschiehet, es sei alles gelegen dir!
  Sei zur Freude gereimt, oder was könnte denn
    Dich beleidigen, Herz, was
      Da begegnen, wohin du sollst?

Denn, seit Himmlischen gleich Menschen, ein einsam Wild,
  Und die Himmlischen selbst führet, der Einkehr zu,
    Der Gesang und der Fürsten
      Chor, nach Arten, so waren auch

Wir, die Zungen des Volks, gerne bei Lebenden,
  Wo sich vieles gesellt, freudig und jedem gleich,
    Jedem offen, so ist ja
      Unser Vater, des Himmels Gott,

Der den denkenden Tag Armen und Reichen gönnt,
  Der, zur Wende der Zeit, uns die Entschlafenden
    Aufgerichtet an goldnen
      Gängelbanden, wie Kinder, hält.

Gut auch sind und geschickt einem zu etwas wir,
  Wenn wir kommen, mit Kunst, und von den Himmlischen
    Einen bringen. Doch selber
      Bringen schickliche Hände wir.

(1802–3)

BEING DIFFIDENT

Are not many living creatures known to you?
  Do you not walk on truth, as on a carpet?
    So go, my inspiration, naked simply
      Out into life and have no care.

Come what may, let it be good and right for you.
  Be consonant with joy, what then could ever
    Hurt you, heart? At journey's end
      What find in opposition?

For, since gods and men were lonely animals once,
  And song and the choir of princes, each its own way,
    Brought the gods to communion,
      So, as tongues of the people, we

Have liked to be in the land of the living, where
  Things come together much, with joy, the same for all,
    Available to all, and so
      Our father, heaven's god, it is

Who to poor and rich does grant the thoughtful day,
  Who, at the turn of time, as we awaken, holds us
    Upright, like children, by
      His golden leading strings.

And good we are, with a mission meant for someone
  When we come, with art, bringing a certain one
    Of the gods. Ourselves, it is
      Proper and honest hands we bring.

GANYMED

Was schläfst du, Bergsohn, liegest in Unmut, schief,
Und frierst am kahlen Ufer, Gedultiger!
    Denkst nicht der Gnade du, wenns an den
        Tischen die Himmlischen sonst gedürstet?

Kennst drunten du vom Vater die Boten nicht,
Nicht in der Kluft der Lüfte geschärfter Spiel?
    Trifft nicht das Wort dich, das voll alten
        Geists ein gewanderter Mann dir sendet?

Schon tönets aber ihm in der Brust. Tief quillts,
Wie damals, als hoch oben im Fels er schlief,
    Ihm auf. Im Zorne reinigt aber
        Sich der Gefesselte nun, nun eilt er,

Der Linkische; der spottet der Schlacken nun,
Und nimmt und bricht und wirft die Zerbrochenen
    Zorntrunken, spielend, dort und da zum
        Schauenden Ufer und bei des Fremdlings

Besondrer Stimme stehen die Herden auf,
Es regen sich die Wälder, es hört tief Land
    Den Stromgeist fern, und schaudernd regt im
        Nabel der Erde der Geist sich wieder.

Der Frühling kömmt. Und jedes, in seiner Art,
Blüht. Der ist aber ferne; nicht mehr dabei.
    Irr ging er nun; denn allzugut sind
        Genien; himmlisch Gespräch ist sein nun.

(1802–3)

GANYMEDE

Why sleep, mountain son, lying askew, despondent,
  Shivering on the bare streambank, all patience?
    Not a thought for grace now, when once
      Was thirst at the tables, among gods?

The father's heralds, is there nothing of them you see
  Down there? Sharper winds in the gully at play?
    Or hear what he says, the much-traveled
      Man filled with old spirit?

Nevertheless the music sounds in his heart. As then,
  When high in the hills he slept, there is a gushing up,
    But now the prisoner washes himself
      Clean of his bonds, now he hurries,

Gauche, mocking the slag, seizes and breaks
  And hurls the splinters now, drunk with wrath,
    In play, hither and thither against
      The watchful streambank, and the flocks

Rise to their feet at the special voice of the stranger,
  Forests thrill, the plain below can hear
    The far spirit of streams and the shuddering
      Spirit thrills in earth's navel again.

Spring comes. And each thing in its fashion
  Breaks into flower. But he is gone, out of it,
    He went awry; they are too generous,
      The elementals; it is with gods now he speaks.

LEBENSALTER

Ihn Städte des Euphrats!
Ihr Gassen von Palmyra!
Ihr Säulenwälder in der Ebne der Wüste,
Was seid ihr?
Euch hat die Kronen,
Dieweil ihr über die Grenze
Der Othmenden seid gegangen,
Von Himmlischen der Rauchdampf und
Hinweg das Feuer genommen;
Jetzt aber sitz ich unter Wolken (deren
Ein jedes eine Ruh hat eigen) unter
Wohleingerichteten Eichen, auf
Der Heide des Rehs, und fremd
Erscheinen und gestorben mir
Der Seligen Geister.

(1802–3)

THE AGES OF LIFE

You cities of Euphrates!
Narrow streets of Palmyra!
Forests of columns in the desert plain,
What are you?
Fume of gods and
Fire stript off
Your crowns as you crossed
The boundary of breath;
But now I sit under clouds (each
With its own repose), under
Sumptuous oaks, on
The roebuck's heath, and alien
They seem to me, dead,
The blessèd souls.

DER WINKEL VON HARDT

Hinunter sinket der Wald,
Und Knospen ähnlich, hängen
Einwärts die Blätter, denen
Blüht unten auf ein Grund,
Nicht gar unmündig.
Da nämlich ist Ulrich
Gegangen; oft sinnt, über den Fußtritt,
Ein groß Schicksal
Bereit, an übrigem Orte.

(1802–3)

TILTED STONES AT HARDT

The forest subsides
And leaves hang inward
As buds do, a valley the flower
Thrusting up under them,
Really not inarticulate.
For it was there
Ulrich entered; over his footprint
Broods a great destiny
Often, poised
In the residue of the place.

HÄLFTE DES LEBENS

Mit gelben Birnen hänget
Und voll mit wilden Rosen
Das Land in den See,
Ihr holden Schwäne,
Und trunken von Küssen
Tunkt ihr das Haupt
Ins heilignüchterne Wasser.

Weh mir, wo nehm ich, wenn
Es Winter ist, die Blumen, und wo
Den Sonnenschein,
Und Schatten der Erde?
Die Mauern stehn
Sprachlos und kalt, im Winde
Klirren die Fahnen.

(1802–3)

THE HALF OF LIFE

With yellow pears the country,
Brimming with wild roses,
Hangs into the lake,
You gracious swans,
And drunk with kisses
Your heads you dip
Into the holy lucid water.

Where, ah where shall I find,
When winter comes, the flowers,
And where the sunshine
And shadows of the earth?
Walls stand
Speechless and cold, in the wind
The weathervanes clatter.

PATMOS

Dem Landgrafen von Homburg

Nah ist
Und schwer zu fassen der Gott.
Wo aber Gefahr ist, wächst
Das Rettende auch.
Im Finstern wohnen
Die Adler und furchtlos gehn
Die Söhne der Alpen über den Abgrund weg
Auf leichtgebaueten Brücken.
Drum, da gehäuft sind rings
Die Gipfel der Zeit, und die Liebsten
Nah wohnen, ermattend auf
Getrenntesten Bergen,
So gib unschuldig Wasser,
O Fittige gib uns, treuesten Sinns
Hinüberzugehn und wiederzukehren.

So sprach ich, da entführte
Mich schneller, denn ich vermutet,
Und weit, wohin ich nimmer
Zu kommen gedacht, ein Genius mich
Vom eigenen Haus. Es dämmerten
Im Zwielicht, da ich ging,
Der schattige Wald
Und die sehnsüchtigen Bäche
Der Heimat; nimmer kannt ich die Länder;
Doch bald, in frischem Glanze,
Geheimnisvoll
Im goldenen Rauche, blühte
Schnellaufgewachsen,
Mit Schritten der Sonne,
Mit tausend Gipfeln duftend,

PATMOS

For the Landgrave of Homburg

Near and
Hard to grasp is
            The God.
But where danger is,
      Deliverance also grows.
The eagles
      Dwell in obscurity
      And across chasms fearless go
            The sons of the Alps, on bridges
Lightly built. Wherefore,
            Since the peaks of time cluster
      High all around
And loved ones dwell
                  Near, languishing
            On mountains farthest apart,
Give us innocent
                  Water, O give us the wings
With truest mind to travel
            Across and to return.

Thus I spoke
And a spirit
            Rapid beyond my expectation
                  Carried me far
From my own house to where
            I never thought to go.
                  The shadowy forest
Darkened
      In twilight as I went,
And rivers of my native land,
            Yearning; countries there were
I never knew; but soon
            In the first sheen rose
Mysterious in golden haze,
            Rapidly full grown
With sunlight's paces, fragrant
      With a thousand peaks

Mir Asia auf, und geblendet sucht
Ich eines, das ich kennete, denn ungewohnt
War ich der breiten Gassen, wo herab
Vom Tmolus fährt
Der goldgeschmückte Paktol
Und Taurus stehet und Messogis,
Und voll von Blumen der Garten,
Ein stilles Feuer, aber im Lichte
Blüht hoch der silberne Schnee,
Und Zeug unsterblichen Lebens
An unzugangbaren Wänden
Uralt der Efeu wächst und getragen sind
Von lebenden Säulen, Zedern und Lorbeern,
Die feierlichen,
Die göttlichgebauten Paläste.

Es rauschen aber um Asias Tore
Hinziehend da und dort
In ungewisser Meeresebene
Der schattenlosen Straßen genug,
Doch kennt die Inseln der Schiffer.
Und da ich hörte,
Der nahegelegenen eine
Sei Patmos,
Verlangte mich sehr,
Dort einzukehren und dort
Der dunkeln Grotte zu nahn.
Denn nicht, wie Cypros,
Die quellenreiche, oder
Der anderen eine
Wohnt herrlich Patmos,

Asia, across my vision, all in bloom,
And dazzled
    I peered to find
        One thing I knew, being not
Familiar with the spacious lanes down which
      Paktolus travels, tricked
        With gold, from Tmolus,
And where Tauros stands,
           And Messogis, and
The garden, full of flowers,
          A calm fire, but in the light
High up the blush of silver snow
           And, stuff of life immortal
       On walls unapproachable,
    Primordial the ivy grows,
         And borne aloft
By living columns, cedar and laurel,
      The solemn godbuilt palaces.

But round the gates to Asia
Murmur
      Passing this way and that on the sea's
      Uncertain plain
        Shadowless roads enough, though any
Seafarer knows
      The islands. And since I heard
Patmos was among
      Those near at hand,
  Much I desired to put in there
         And be close
To the dark cave. For not
      In splendor, like Cyprus with
  Its abounding waters, nor
Like any other island
      Does Patmos dwell,

Gastfreundlich aber ist
Im ärmeren Hause
Sie dennoch
Und wenn von Schiffbruch oder klagend
Um die Heimat oder
Den abgeschiedenen Freund
Ihr nahet einer
Der Fremden, hört sie es gern, und ihre Kinder,
Die Stimmen des heißen Hains,
Und wo der Sand fällt, und sich spaltet
Des Feldes Fläche, die Laute,
Sie hören ihn und liebend tönt
Es wider von den Klagen des Manns. So pflegte
Sie einst des gottgeliebten,
Des Sehers, der in seliger Jugend war

Gegangen mit
Dem Sohne des Höchsten, unzertrennlich, denn
Es liebte der Gewittertragende die Einfalt
Des Jüngers und es sahe der achtsame Mann
Das Angesicht des Gottes genau,
Da, beim Geheimnisse des Weinstocks, sie
Zusammensaßen, zu der Stunde des Gastmahls,
Und in der großen Seele, ruhigahnend, den Tod
Aussprach der Herr und die letzte Liebe, denn nie genug
Hatt er von Güte zu sagen
Der Worte, damals, und zu erheitern, da
Ers sahe, das Zürnen der Welt.
Denn alles ist gut. Drauf starb er. Vieles wäre
Zu sagen davon. Und es sahn ihn, wie er siegend blickte,
Den Freudigsten die Freunde noch zuletzt,

But still hospitable
In her poorer house,
    And if a stranger comes
      From shipwreck or grieving
For his lost homeland or a far friend,
        She listens, and her children,
Voices of the hot thicket,
        A trickle of sand, earth
Splitting in a field, her sounds,
    They hear him and a loving echo
Flows from his lament.
          Thus did she care
Once for the Godbeloved
    Visionary who, in blessèd youth,

Had walked with the Son of the Highest
And inseparably,
      For the stormbearer loved the simpleness
    Of his disciple, and he, attentive, saw
Plainly the God's face
      When at supper they sat assembled
    And it was the mystery of the vine,
    And the Lord in his great
Soul with calm foreknowing spoke
    Of his death
       And of the ultimate love. For of goodness
He told, more than abundantly, and to bring
    Joy, seeing the fury of the world. For all
Is good. He died
      Thereafter. Much might be said
    Of that. And him they saw, and his
Victorious look, his friends
    Saw him gladdest at the last.

Doch trauerten sie, da nun
Es Abend worden, erstaunt,
Denn Großentschiedenes hatten in der Seele
Die Männer, aber sie liebten unter der Sonne
Das Leben und lassen wollten sie nicht
Vom Angesichte des Herrn
Und der Heimat. Eingetrieben war,
Wie Feuer im Eisen, das, und ihnen ging
Zur Seite der Schatte des Lieben:
Drum sandt er ihnen
Den Geist, und freilich bebte
Das Haus und die Wetter Gottes rollten
Ferndonnernd über
Die ahnenden Häupter, da, schwersinnend,
Versammelt waren die Todeshelden,

Itzt, da er scheidend
Noch einmal ihnen erschien.
Denn itzt erlosch der Sonne Tag,
Der Königliche, und zerbrach
Den geradestrahlenden,
Den Zepter, göttlichleidend, von selbst,
Denn wiederkommen sollt es,
Zu rechter Zeit. Nicht wär es gut
Gewesen, später, und schroffabbrechend, untreu,
Der Menschen Werk, und Freude war es
Von nun an,
Zu wohnen in liebender Nacht, und bewahren
In einfältigen Augen, unverwandt
Abgründe der Weisheit. Und es grünen
Tief an den Bergen auch lebendige Bilder,

Doch furchtbar ist, wie da und dort
Unendlich hin zerstreut das Lebende Gott.

Yet they were sorrowful, now
As night had begun, and were astonished,
    For great things destined
      They harbored in their souls,
        But life they loved
Under the sun, and wished not to leave
    The Lord's sight and their native land. It was
Driven deep in, this was,
      Like fire in iron, and the shadow
    Of him they loved walked at their side. So
He sent them the spirit,
    And the house, of course, shook
And God's far storms
      Rumbled over their heads, divining much,
  Now they were gathered, deep
In thought, the heroes of death,

  And in valediction
Again he appeared to them.
      For now the day-sun, royal, he quenched
      And broke the straight
Rayed scepter, nothing loath, in godly agony,
      For there should be
    Another coming, in good time. Not good
      Would it have been, later, and
Snapping off harshly
    Achievement of men, and joy it was
  To live the present and hereafter
In loving night and keep, steadfast, in simple eyes
      Chasms of wisdom. And deep among
    Foothills also living
      Images break into leafgreen,

But terrible it is, how infinitely
Far and wide God scatters what lives.
    For even to vanish from the sight

Denn schon das Angesicht
Der teuern Freunde zu lassen
Und fernhin über die Berge zu gehn
Allein, wo zweifach
Erkannt, einstimmig
War himmlischer Geist; und nicht geweissagt war es, sondern
Die Locken ergriff es, gegenwärtig,
Wenn ihnen plötzlich
Ferneilend zurück blickte
Der Gott und schwörend,
Damit er halte, wie an Seilen golden
Gebunden hinfort
Das Böse nennend, sie die Hände sich reichten—

   Wenn aber stirbt alsdenn,
An dem am meisten
Die Schönheit hing, daß an der Gestalt
Ein Wunder war und die Himmlischen gedeutet
Auf ihn, und wenn, ein Rätsel ewig füreinander,
Sie sich nicht fassen können
Einander, die zusammenlebten
Im Gedächtnis, und nicht den Sand nur oder
Die Weiden es hinwegnimmt und die Tempel
Ergreift, wenn die Ehre
Des Halbgotts und der Seinen
Verweht und selber sein Angesicht
Der Höchste wendet
Darob, daß nirgend ein
Unsterbliches mehr am Himmel zu sehn ist oder
Auf grüner Erde, was ist dies?

   Es ist der Wurf des Säemanns, wenn er faßt
Mit der Schaufel den Weizen,

Of his dear friends and go alone
            Far, over the mountains, when
        The spirit of heaven, doubly known,
Was one in mind; and not
            Foretold it was, but seized them, there
                That very moment
By the hair, when the God fast
                Far off suddenly looked
Back at them, and
        As they begged him
Stop, linked as by golden cords,
        Hereafter naming evil, they
Clasped each other's hands—

   But when he dies then
To whom beauty
            Most clung, making his form
Flesh of a miracle
            And the powers of heaven
Pointed to him, and when, eternally
        Riddles to one another, they
            Cannot grasp one another, who
Lived as one
   In memory, and when it takes away
Not the sand only, nor the willows,
                When it takes hold
    Of the temples, when the demigod
And his own are all
            Stript of honor, and even the Highest
Averts his gaze, whence not a shred
        Of immortality is seen in heaven or on
The green earth, what is this?

   It is the cast
Made by the sower when he scoops
        Wheat into the shovel and sweeps it

Und wirft, dem Klaren zu, ihn schwingend über die Tenne.
Ihm fällt die Schale vor den Füßen, aber
Ans Ende kommet das Korn,
Und nicht ein Übel ists, wenn einiges
Verloren gehet und von der Rede
Verhallet der lebendige Laut,
Denn göttliches Werk auch gleichet dem unsern,
Nicht alles will der Höchste zumal.
Zwar Eisen träget der Schacht,
Und glühende Harze der Aetna,
So hätt ich Reichtum,
Ein Bild zu bilden, und ähnlich
Zu schaun, wie er gewesen, den Christ,

   Wenn aber einer spornte sich selbst,
Und traurig redend, unterweges, da ich wehrlos wäre,
Mich überfiele, daß ich staunt und von dem Gotte
Das Bild nachahmen möcht ein Knecht—
Im Zorne sichtbar sah ich einmal
Des Himmels Herrn, nicht, daß ich sein sollt etwas, sondern
Zu lernen. Gütig sind sie, ihr Verhaßtestes aber ist,
Solange sie herrschen, das Falsche, und es gilt
Dann Menschliches unter Menschen nicht mehr.
Denn sie nicht walten, es waltet aber
Unsterblicher Schicksal und es wandelt ihr Werk
Von selbst, und eilend geht es zu Ende.
Wenn nämlich höher gehet himmlischer

In an arc
   Toward the clear
      Void over the threshingfloor,
The husk falls at his feet, but
      The grain does reach its goal,
And no bad thing it is, if
        Some disappears, the live sound
      Of speech
         Fades, for divine work too is akin
To ours, the Highest does not want
   All things at once. True,
     The shaft bears iron
       And Etna glowing resins,
So might I have the wherewithal
     To make an image, and see
Christ as he was,

   But suppose someone clapped the spurs
To himself, and on the road
      Morosely talking
    Set upon me, defenseless, much
To my surprise, and it was
      A mere minion trying his hand
      At the image of God—in wrath visible
Once I saw
    The Lord of heaven, not that I
Should be something, but to learn.
             They are benign
But hate most, as long
     As they are sovereign,
       Falseness which makes
Void the humanity between humans, for
    They do not rule, what rules
Is destiny, of immortals, and their work moves
     In its own motion
       Now speeding to an end.

Triumphgang, wird genennet, der Sonne gleich,
Von Starken der frohlockende Sohn des Höchsten,

Ein Losungszeichen, und hier ist der Stab
Des Gesanges, niederwinkend,
Denn nichts ist gemein. Die Toten wecket
Er auf, die noch gefangen nicht
Vom Rohen sind. Es warten aber
Der scheuen Augen viele,
Zu schauen das Licht. Nicht wollen
Am scharfen Strahle sie blühn,
Wiewohl den Mut der goldene Zaum hält.
Wenn aber, als
Von schwellenden Augenbraunen,
Der Welt vergessen
Stilleuchtende Kraft aus heiliger Schrift fällt, mögen,
Der Gnade sich freuend, sie
Am stillen Blicke sich üben.

Und wenn die Himmlischen jetzt
So, wie ich glaube, mich lieben,
Wie viel mehr Dich,
Denn Eines weiß ich,
Daß nämlich der Wille
Des ewigen Vaters viel
Dir gilt. Still ist sein Zeichen
Am donnernden Himmel. Und Einer stehet darunter
Sein Leben lang. Denn noch lebt Christus.
Es sind aber die Helden, seine Söhne,
Gekommen all und heilige Schriften
Von ihm und den Blitz erklären
Die Taten der Erde bis itzt,

For when heaven's triumph passes on
    Yet higher, then strong men call
The exultant Son of the Highest,
        Like the sun,

  A beacon, and here is the song's
Staff, pointing downward,
      For nothing is ordinary. It wakes
The dead not caught by crudeness
    Yet. But many
Timorous eyes are waiting still
        To see the light. They want
    Not to flower
        In the sharp ray, although
The golden halter curbs
        Their mettle. But when,
As from brown arched eyebrows,
    Oblivious to the world
      Energy ebbs in a glow assuaged
        From sacred scripture, they
May school themselves, glad of Grace to come,
      In that calm gaze.

  And if the gods of heaven now
Love me well as I believe,
      How much greater is
Their love for you, because
    One thing I know is that the will
    Of the eternal father means
Much to you. In the thundering sky
      His sign is silent. And one
Stands underneath it all
    His life long. For still
Christ is living. But the heroes came,
    His sons, all, and sacred scripture,

Ein Wettlauf unaufhaltsam. Er ist aber dabei. Denn seine
       Werke sind
Ihm alle bewußt von jeher.

  Zu lang, zu lang schon ist
Die Ehre der Himmlischen unsichtbar.
Denn fast die Finger müssen sie
Uns führen und schmählich
Entreißt das Herz uns eine Gewalt.
Denn Opfer will der Himmlischen jedes,
Wenn aber eines versäumt ward,
Nie hat es Gutes gebracht.
Wir haben gedienet der Mutter Erd
Und haben jüngst dem Sonnenlichte gedient,
Unwissend, der Vater aber liebt,
Der über allen waltet,
Am meisten, daß gepfleget werde
Der feste Buchstab, und Bestehendes gut
Gedeutet. Dem folgt deutscher Gesang.

(Late 1802)

From him, and actions
On earth elucidate, to this hour, the stroke
Of lightning, in a ceaseless race.
But he is there. For known to him
Are all his works from the beginning.

Too long invisible, too long
Honor that flows
From those heavenly ones. For almost
They have to guide our fingers, and
There is a force
Ripping the heart out, with insult. For
Each of the heavenly ones
Wants sacrifice, but if
One be omitted
Good never came of it. Earth,
Our mother, we have served, and
Latest of all have served
Unwittingly the sunlight, but
The Father loves most,
Who rules over all, care
For the firm written character
And sound interpretation of such things
As stand permanent. This end
German song pursues.

ANDENKEN

Der Nordost wehet,
Der liebste unter den Winden
Mir, weil er feurigen Geist
Und gute Fahrt verheißet den Schiffern.
Geh aber nun und grüße
Die schöne Garonne,
Und die Gärten von Bourdeaux
Dort, wo am scharfen Ufer
Hingehet der Steg und in den Strom
Tief fällt der Bach, darüber aber
Hinschauet ein edel Paar
Von Eichen und Silberpappeln;

Noch denket das mir wohl und wie
Die breiten Gipfel neiget
Der Ulmwald, über die Mühl,
Im Hofe aber wächset ein Feigenbaum.
An Feiertagen gehn
Die braunen Frauen daselbst
Auf seidnen Boden,
Zur Märzenzeit,
Wenn gleich ist Nacht und Tag,
Und über langsamen Stegen,
Von goldenen Träumen schwer,
Einwiegende Lüfte ziehen.

Es reiche aber,
Des dunkeln Lichtes voll,
Mir einer den duftenden Becher,
Damit ich ruhen möge; denn süß
Wär unter Schatten der Schlummer.
Nicht ist es gut,
Seellos von sterblichen
Gedanken zu sein. Doch gut
Ist ein Gespräch und zu sagen
Des Herzens Meinung, zu hören viel

REMEMBRANCE

The northeaster blows,
Best loved of all the winds
For me, as it promises
Fiery spirit and a good voyage
For seafarers. But now go and greet
The beautiful Garonne
And the gardens of Bordeaux,
Where on the steep
Riverbank the path slopes
Down and the stream
Falls into it, sheer, but
A noble pair of oaks upstands,
And silver poplars, gazing.

Thoughts of this are pleasant still, and how
The wide treetops of the elmwood
Bow across the mill,
But a figtree grows in the courtyard.
There on holidays
Brown women walk
On silken ground,
When March is come
And day and night are equal,
And over slow footpaths
Weighted with golden dreams
The lulling breezes move.

But hand me,
Someone, the fragrant cup
Brimming with dark light, that I
May rest; sleep
Would be sweet, in the shadows.
It is not good
To let mortal thoughts
Empty the soul. But conversation
Is good, and to say
What the heart means, to hear

Von Tagen der Lieb,
Und Taten, welche geschehen.

Wo aber sind die Freunde? Bellarmin
Mit dem Gefährten? Mancher
Trägt Scheue, an die Quelle zu gehn;
Es beginnet nämlich der Reichtum
Im Meere. Sie,
Wie Maler, bringen zusammen
Das Schöne der Erd und verschmähn
Den geflügelten Krieg nicht, und
Zu wohen einsam, jahrlang, unter
Dem entlaubten Mast, wo nicht die Nacht durchglänzen
Die Feiertage der Stadt,
Und Saitenspiel und eingeborener Tanz nicht.

Nun aber sind zu Indiern
Die Männer gegangen,
Dort an der luftigen Spitz
An Traubenbergen, wo herab
Die Dordogne kommt,
Und zusammen mit der prächtgen
Garonne meerbreit
Ausgehet der Strom. Es nehmet aber
Und gibt Gedächtnis die See,
Und die Lieb auch heftet fleißig die Augen,
Was bleibet aber, stiften die Dichter.

(Spring 1803)

Much about days of love
And deeds that have been done.

   But where are my friends, Bellarmin
With his companion? Some hesitate
To go to the source;
For in the sea
Plenitude does begin. They
Like painters compose
The beauty that is of earth, and do not shun
Winged war and to live
Years on end alone before the unleafed mast,
Where no town festivals
Make luminous the night,
Nor music, nor dancing of country folk.

   But now to the Indians
The men have gone,
There by the windy point,
By grape-clustering hills, down which
The Dordogne comes, and outward
With the glorious Garonne
Seawide the waters roll. But remembrance,
The sea takes it and gives it,
And love, too, intently steadies the gaze;
But poets alone ordain what abides.

WIE VÖGEL LANGSAM ZIEHN...

Wie Vögel langsam ziehn—
Es blicket voraus
Der Fürst und kühl wehn
An die Brust ihm die Begegnisse, wenn
Es um ihn schweiget, hoch
In der Luft, reich glänzend aber hinab
Das Gut ihm liegt der Länder, und mit ihm sind
Das erstemal siegforschend die Jungen.
Er aber mässiget mit
Der Fittige Schlag.

(Ca. 1804–6)

LIKE SLOW FLYING BIRDS...

Like slow flying birds—
                he looks ahead,
                        the prince,
      come whatever, it is
                    a current of air
cools his breast
        in a ring of silence
    up there, but
shining below and rich his
             dominion spreads
       and for the first time
his young are with him,
                strain
       to win—
      he with his wingbeat
  curbs
    and moderates them.

WIE MEERESKÜSTEN

Wie Meeresküsten, wenn zu baun
Anfangen die Himmlischen und herein
Schifft unaufhaltsam, eine Pracht, das Werk
Der Wogen, eins ums andere, und die Erde
Sich rüstet aus, darauf vom Freudigsten eines
Mit guter Stimmung, zurecht es legend, also schlägt es
Dem Gesang, mit dem Weingott, vielverheißend dem
               bedeutenden,
Und der Lieblingin
Des Griechenlandes,
Der meergeborenen, schicklich blickenden,
Das gewaltige Gut ans Ufer.

(Ca. 1804–6)

LIKE SEA COASTS...

Like sea coasts when the gods begin to build
  and
    rushing splendor the wave creations
  hove inshore
      and earth
        robes in her panoplies
soon
    with one
    joymost in good mood and hoarding it
    so
bearing the winegod
        for his importance much
      being promised
also of Greece the darling
          born of the sea
          her gaze modest
beats the tremendous
    billowing treasure
      up shores of song.

HEIMAT

Und niemand weiß

Indessen laß mich wandeln
Und wilde Beeren pflücken,
Zu löschen die Liebe zu dir
An deinen Pfaden, o Erd

Hier, wo — — —
          und Rosendornen
Und süße Linden duften neben
Den Buchen, des Mittags, wenn im falben Kornfeld
Das Wachstum rauscht, an geradem Halm,
Und den Nacken die Ähre seitwärts beugt
Dem Herbst gleich, jetzt aber unter hohem
Gewölbe der Eichen, da ich sinn
Und aufwärts frage, der Glockenschlag
Mir wohlbekannt
Fernher tönt, goldenklingend, um die Stunde, wenn
Der Vogel wieder wacht. So gehet es wohl.

(Ca. 1804–6)

HOMELAND

And no-one knows

Meanwhile let me walk
And pluck berries wild
To quench my love of you
Upon your paths, O earth

Here, where — — —
    and rose thorns
And fragrant limes beside
The beech trees, at noon, when in the yellowing
Wheatfield growth rustles, past the erect stalk
And the nodding wheat-ear sways
Like autumn, but now beneath the high
Vault of oaks as I think and
Question upward, the familiar
Bell note
Tolls from far, golden peal, the time
When the bird reawakens. Things are well so.

Wenn nämlich der Rebe Saft,
Das milde Gewächs, suchet Schatten
Und die Traube wächset unter dem kühlen
Gewölbe der Blätter,
Den Männern eine Stärke,
Wohl aber duftend den Jungfraun,
Und Bienen,
Wenn sie, vom Wohlgeruche
Des Frühlings trunken, der Geist
Der Sonne rühret, irren ihr nach
Die Getriebenen, wenn aber
Ein Strahl brennt, kehren sie
Mit Gesumm, vielahnend
            darob
        die Eiche rauschet,

(Ca. 1804–6)

WHEN THE JUICE OF THE VINE...

When the juice of the vine
            gentle growth
seeks the shade
and the grape cluster grows
            under the cool
vault of leaves
for men strength
            but fragrance
for girls
      and bees
            drunk with the scent
of springtime
      when the spirit of the sun
touches them
      possessed
they wander out seeking it
            but when
the ray burns
      they turn humming
divining much
            so
      the oak rustles

AUF FALBEM LAUBE...

Auf falbem Laube ruhet
Die Traube, des Weines Hoffnung, also ruhet auf der Wange
Der Schatten von dem goldenen Schmuck, der hängt
Am Ohre der Jungfrau.

Und ledig soll ich bleiben,
Leicht fanget aber sich
In der Kette, die
Es abgerissen, das Kälblein.

Fleißig

Es liebet aber der Sämann,
Zu sehen eine,
Des Tages schlafend über
Den Strickstrumpf.

Nicht will wohllauten
Der deutsche Mund,
Aber lieblich
Am stechenden Bart rauschen
Die Küsse.

(Ca. 1804–6)

On a pale yellow leaf the grape
Cluster reposes
       hope of wine
          thus on the cheek
The shadow of the gold
       pendant hung
         from a girl's ear.

And I must never marry,
But the little calf is
Easily caught
In the chain it has broken.

Busy

But the sower
      loves
  to see a lady fast asleep
In daytime
Over a sock she is knitting.

It will not speak
      with euphony,
The German mouth.
But in a prickly beard kisses make
A sweet murmur.

DIE TITANEN

Nicht ist es aber
Die Zeit. Noch sind sie
Unangebunden. Göttliches trifft Unteilnehmende nicht.
Dann mögen sie rechnen
Mit Delphi. Indessen, gib in Feierstunden
Und daß ich ruhen möge, der Toten
Zu denken. Viele sind gestorben,
Feldherrn in alter Zeit
Und schöne Frauen und Dichter
Und in neuer
Der Männer viel,
Ich aber bin allein.

              und in den Ozean schiffend
Die duftenden Inseln fragen,
Wohin sie sind.

Denn manches von ihnen ist
In treuen Schriften überblieben
Und manches in Sagen der Zeit.
Viel offenbaret der Gott.
Denn lang schon wirken
Die Wolken hinab
Und es wurzelt vielesbereitend heilige Wildnis.
Heiß ist der Reichtum. Denn es fehlet
An Gesang, der löset den Geist.
Verzehren würd er
Und wäre gegen sich selbst,
Denn nimmer duldet
Die Gefangenschaft das himmlische Feuer.

Es erfreuet aber
Das Gastmahl oder wenn am Feste
Das Auge glänzet und von Perlen
Der Jungfrau Hals.
Auch Kriegesspiel

THE TITANS

But it is not
The time. They are
Not fettered yet. Who stand aloof,
The divine does not touch them.
Then with Delphi
They may reckon. Grant me, meanwhile,
At my leisure and that I may rest,
Thoughts of the dead. Many
Have died, commanders in olden time,
Beautiful women, and poets,
And of late
Many men,
But I am alone.

                    and shipping
Across the sea to ask the fragrant isles
Where they have gone.

For something of them lives on
In faithful writ
And something in sagas of the time.
Much by God is revealed.
For clouds have long brought down
Their influence, and a holy wilderness
Has sunk roots, where much is being readied.
Hot, that plenitude. For we lack
Song, which frees the spirit.
It would be consuming,
It would be contrary to itself,
For never does the heavenly fire
Consent to be imprisoned.

But a banquet
We enjoy, or when at the feast
The eye shines, and with pearls
A girl's throat.
The games of war as well

und durch die Gänge
Der Gärten schmettert
Das Gedächtnis der Schlacht und besänftiget
An schlanker Brust
Die tönenden Wehre ruhn
Von Heldenvätern den Kindern.
Mich aber umsummet
Die Bien und wo der Ackersmann
Die Furchen machet, singen gegen
Dem Lichte die Vögel. Manche helfen
Dem Himmel. Diese siehet
Der Dichter. Gut ist es, an andern sich
Zu halten. Denn keiner trägt das Leben allein.

Wenn aber ist entzündet
Der geschäftige Tag
Und an der Kette, die
Den Blitz ableitet,
Von der Stunde des Aufgangs
Himmlischer Tau glänzt,
Muß unter Sterblichen auch
Das Hohe sich fühlen.
Drum bauen sie Häuser
Und die Werkstatt gehet
Und über Strömen das Schiff.
Und es bieten tauschend die Menschen
Die Händ einander, sinnig ist es
Auf Erden und es sind nicht umsonst
Die Augen an den Boden geheftet.

Ihr fühlet aber
Auch andere Art.
Denn unter dem Maße
Des Rohen brauchet es auch,
Damit das Reine sich kenne.
Wenn aber

and all among the garden
Walks trumpet
Battle memories, pacified
The loud weapons find repose
On slender breasts
Of children sired by heroes.
But around me hums
The bee, and where the plowman
Makes furrows, birds are singing
Up at the light. This
The poet sees. Some are helpers
To heaven. It is good
To lean on others. For none
Can bear life alone.

But when the busy
Day has been kindled,
And on the chain that guides
The lightning heavenly dew
Shines forth
From the moment of sunrise,
Among mortals too
The supernal must feel itself.
Therefore they build houses
And the workshop is running
And the ship across currents,
And men trading hold
Hands out to one another, it
Is pensive on the earth, and not
For nothing do the eyes gaze at the ground.

But also you feel
Another kind of being.
For crudeness within limits
Is needed, that purity
May come to know itself.
But when

107

Und in die Tiefe greifet,
Daß es lebendig werde,
Der Allerschütterer, meinen die,
Es komme der Himmlische
Zu Toten herab und gewaltig dämmerts
Im ungebundenen Abgrund,
Im allesmerkenden, auf.
Nicht möcht ich aber sagen,
Es werden die Himmlischen schwach,
Wenn schon es aufgärt.
Wenn aber

      und es gehet

An die Scheitel dem Vater, daß

      und der Vogel des Himmels ihm
Es anzeigt. Wunderbar
Im Zorne kommet er drauf.

(Ca. 1804–6)

And down into the depths,
Animating them,
He reaches, who is the shaker-up
Of all, they do suppose
The heavenly one descends,
Visiting the dead, and a great dawn
Breaks in the dissolute
All-observant abyss.
But I would not say
The heavenly ones are weakened,
Though now it seethes in ferment.
But when

      and it goes

To the crown of his head, the father's, that

     and to him the bird of the heavens
Shows it. Marvelous then
In his wrath he will be coming.

DER VATIKAN

                                    der Vatikan,
Hier sind wir   in der Einsamkeit
Und drunten gehet der Bruder, ein Esel auch dem braunen
        Schleier nach.
Wenn aber der Tag   , allbejahend von wegen des
        Spotts,
Schicksale macht, denn aus Zorn der Natur-
Göttin, wie ein Ritter gesagt von Rom, in derlei
Palästen, gehet itzt viel Irrsal, und alle Schlüssel des Geheimnisses
        wissend
Fragt bös Gewissen,
Und Julius Geist um derweil, welcher Kalender
Gemachet, und dort drüben, in Westfalen,
Mein ehrlich Meister.
Gott rein und mit Unterscheidung
Bewahren, das ist uns vertrauet,
Damit nicht, weil an diesem
Viel hängt, über der Büßung, über einem Fehler
Des Zeichens
Gottes Gericht entstehet.

THE VATICAN

the Vatican,
We are here   in the solitude
And down there
    a monk and a donkey
        follow the brown wimple.
But when the day   affirming all
          out of ridicule
Shapes destinies
   for (said a gentleman of Rome) there is
   a deal of wrongdoing in that sort of palace
        it comes of the goddess,
     nature, being angry
And bad conscience
    puts the questions (cognizant
      of all keys to the mystery)
    Caesar's ghost walks
      (he made the calendar) and
My honest master (up in Westphalia)

  to keep God
    pure   make the distinctions
That is our trust
    lest (since much
  hangs on this) contrition or some
Sign misinterpreted bring down
      judgment divine

Ach! kennet ihr den nicht mehr,
Den Meister des Forsts, und den Jüngling in der Wüste, der von
        Honig
Und Heuschrecken sich nährt. Still Geists ists. Fraun
             Oben wohl
Auf Monte   , wohl auch seitwärts,
Irr ich, herabgekommen
Über Tirol, Lombarda, Loretto, wo des Pilgrims Heimat
        auf dem Gotthard, gezäunt, nachlässig, unter
            Gletschern
Karg wohnt jener, wo der Vogel
Mit Eiderdünnen, eine Perle des Meers,
Und der Adler den Akzent rufet, vor Gott, wo das Feuer läuft
        der Menschen wegen,
Des Wächters Horn tönt aber über den Garden,
Der Kranich hält die Gestalt aufrecht,
Die majestätische, keusche, drüben
In Patmos, Morea, in der Pestluft.
Türkisch. Und die Eule, wohlbekannt, der Schriften
Spricht, heischern Fraun gleich in zerstörten Städten. Aber
Die erhalten den Sinn. Oft aber wie ein Brand
Entstehet Sprachverwirrung. Aber wie ein Schiff,

Ah have you forgotton him, the lord
     of the forest, the young man in the desert
Who feeds on honey and locusts
       It is the spirit
         at peace. Women
           perhaps up
On Monte Wherever, perhaps
      sideways too I wander
Down over Tyrol, Lombardy, Loretto, where the pilgrim
     houses, on the Gotthard,
        fenced casually in
    among glaciers

That one, he lives hard
      where the bird
    with eiderdowns, a sea pearl
And the eagle, in sight of God, gives
        the accent, where fires
Rush, because of men
     but the watchman's horn blares
    over the household guards.
The crane
   conserves his vertical form,
      majestic, chaste, yonder
  on Patmos, in Morea, in the fug of pestilence.
Turkish. And the owl,
     familiar, of scripture, speaks like
      yawping women in shattered
Towns. But they
    do get the sense. Often though
     like brushfire confusion of tongues
Breaks out

DER VATIKAN *(continued)*

Das lieget im Hafen, des Abends, wenn die Glocke lautet
Des Kirchturms, und es nachhallt unten
Im Eingeweid des Tempels und der Mönch
Und Schäfer Abschied nehmet, vom Spaziergang
Und Apollon, ebenfalls
Aus Roma, derlei Palästen, sagt
Ade! unreinlich bitter, darum!
Dann kommt das Brautlied des Himmels.
Vollendruhe. Goldrot. Und die Rippe tönet
Des sandigen Erdballs in Gottes Werk
Ausdrücklicher Bauart, grüner Nacht
Und Geist, der Säulenordnung, wirklich
Ganzem Verhältnis, samt der Mitt,
Und glänzenden

(Ca. 1804–6)

But like a ship, docked
   at nightfall
When the bell tolls from the church tower
      echoing in the temple bowels
And the monk
   and the shepherd part ways
      after a walk
And Apollo says goodbye to such palaces
    (filthily bitter, reason enough)
      then heaven's marriage song begins.
Peaceperfect. Gold-red. And the sandy globe's
   rib seasounds in God's artifice
     of explicit architecture
       green night
And ordered
   spirit of the peristyle, real
In complete proportion
     the center also
  and   splendid

GRIECHENLAND

Dritte Fassung

O ihr Stimmen des Geschicks, ihr Wege des Wanderers!
Denn an der Schule Blau,
Fernher, am Tosen des Himmels
Tönt wie der Amsel Gesang
Der Wolken heitere Stimmung, gut
Gestimmt vom Dasein Gottes, dem Gewitter.
Und Rufe, wie Hinausschauen, zur
Unsterblichkeit und Helden;
Viel sind Erinnerungen. Wo darauf
Tönend, wie des Kalbs Haut,
Die Erde, von Verwüstungen her, Versuchungen der Heiligen,
Denn anfangs bildet das Werk sich,
Großen Gesetzen nachgehet, die Wissenschaft
Und Zärtlichkeit und den Himmel breit lauter Hülle nachher
Erscheinend singen Gesangeswolken.

GREECE

Third version

O you voices of fate, you
           Pathways of man
                Traveling!
  For the unruffled mood
Of clouds, like blackbird song, sounds
      From afar in the blueness
    Of the school, in the rushing
              Of the sky, tuned
To harmony by storm that is
        God's being-there.

    And shouts, like
             Lookings-out toward
Immortality and heroes;
             Manifold
  Memories are, to which a vibrance
Clings, of earth, as to a drumskin, from
      Destructions,
          Temptations of saints,
  For the work shapes itself
In the beginning, obeys
        Great laws, and afterward
Choral
   Clouds appear, singing
          Knowledge, tenderness, the sweep
Of sky—all
    Integument.

Denn fest ist der Erde
Nabel. Gefangen nämlich in Ufern von Gras sind
Die Flammen und die allgemeinen
Elemente. Lauter Besinnung aber oben lebt der Aether. Aber
        silbern
An reinen Tagen
Ist das Licht. Als Zeichen der Liebe
Veilchenblau die Erde.
Zu Geringem auch kann kommen
Großer Anfang.
Alltag aber wunderbar zu lieb den Menschen
Gott an hat ein Gewand.
Und Erkenntnissen verberget sich sein Angesicht
Und decket die Lüfte mit Kunst.
Und Luft und Zeit deckt
Den Schröcklichen, daß zu sehr nicht eins
Ihn liebet mit Gebeten oder
Die Seele. Denn lange schon steht offen
Wie Blätter, zu lernen, oder Linien und Winkel
Die Natur
Und gelber die Sonnen und die Monde,

For fixed and firm is
The earth navel. Shores of grass
            Batten down
                The flames and universal
Elements. But pure
        And utter consciousness
                    Aither lives above. The light
Yet
    On clear days is
            Silver. Signifying love,
Earth is violet.

        Grand beginnings, too,
Can come to little. But day in, day out,
            God wears a garment
Wonderfully for the favor of man.
                    And his face hides
        From cognizance, and robes
                The air with art.
And air and time
        Robe God the Terrifier, lest
One thing love him
                Overmuch, or the soul do. For nature
        Was always news, an open book
To learn from, or lines
                And angles, yellower the suns,
                    Yellower the moons,

Zu Zeiten aber,
Wenn ausgehn will die alte Bildung
Der Erde, bei Geschichten nämlich,
Gewordnen, mutig fechtenden, wie auf Höhen führet
Die Erde Gott. Ungemessene Schritte
Begrenzt er aber, aber wie Blüten golden tun
Der Seele Kräfte dann, der Seele Verwandtschaften sich zusammen,
Daß lieber auf Erden
Die Schönheit wohnt und irgend ein Geist
Gemeinschaftlicher sich zu Menschen gesellet.
Süß ists, dann unter hohen Schatten von Bäumen
Und Hügeln zu wohnen, sonnig, wo der Weg ist
Gepflastert zur Kirche. Reisenden aber, wem,
Aus Lebensliebe, messend immerhin,
Die Füße gehorchen, blühn
Schöner die Wege, wo das Land

(Ca. 1804–6)

But times do come
When the old shaping imageries
                Of earth launch forth—
        In histories,
                Happenings past, brave
                Battlings, when God
Leads earth from height
        To height. But he sets
                A limit to the stride unchecked
By measure, then
        The soul's powers and
        Affinities draw in tight,
                As golden blossoms do, together,
    So that beauty may dwell on earth
More fondly, and a spirit of some kind
        Makes commoner cause with men.

    Sweet then it is to dwell
Sunnily in the tall
        Shade of tree and hill, where
                There is a paved path goes to the church.
But for travelers, with whom
        The feet comply, moving in measure, on and on
For love of life,
                The pathways flower, lovelier yet,
    Where the countryside

ZU SOKRATES' ZEITEN

Vormals richtete Gott.

        Könige.

     Weise.

          wer richtet denn itzt?

Richtet das einige
   Volk? die heilge Gemeinde?
   Nein! o nein! wer richtet denn itzt?
          ein Natterngeschlecht!   feig und falsch
             das edlere Wort nicht mehr
      Über die Lippe
O im Namen

                  ruf ich,

    Alter Dämon! dich herab

Oder   sende
   Einen Helden

Oder
    die Weisheit.

(Ca. 1804–6)

IN SOCRATES' TIMES

Time was when God judged.

                    Kings.

            Sages.

                    but who judges now?

Does the united
        People judge? The holy fellowship?
        No! O no! but who judges now?
                    a generation of vipers! Gutless and false
                        the noble word no more
                Passing the lips
O in the name
                        I call
        You, demon of old, down

Or   send
    a hero

Or
        wisdom

WENN AUS DER FERNE...

Wenn aus der Ferne, da wir geschieden sind,
  Ich dir noch kennbar bin, die Vergangenheit,
    O du Teilhaber meiner Leiden!
      Einiges Gute bezeichnen dir kann,

So sage, wie erwartet die Freundin dich?
  In jenen Gärten, da nach entsetzlicher
    Und dunkler Zeit wir uns gefunden?
      Hier an den Strömen der heilgen Urwelt.

Das muß ich sagen, einiges Gutes war
  In deinen Blicken, als in den Fernen du
    Dich einmal fröhlich umgesehen,
      Immer verschlossener Mensch, mit finstrem

Aussehn. Wie flossen Stunden dahin, wie still
  War meine Seele über der Wahrheit, daß
    Ich so getrennt gewesen wäre?
      Ja! ich gestand es, ich war die deine.

Wahrhaftig! wie du alles Bekannte mir
  In mein Gedächtnis bringen und schreiben willst,
    Mit Briefen, so ergeht es mir auch,
      Daß ich Vergangenes alles sage.

Wars Frühling? war es Sommer? die Nachtigall
  Mit süßem Liede lebte mit Vögeln, die
    Nicht ferne waren im Gebüsche
      Und mit Gerüchen umgaben Bäum uns.

Die klaren Gänge, niedres Gesträuch und Sand,
  Auf dem wir traten, machten erfreulicher
    Und lieblicher die Hyazinthe
      Oder die Tulpe, Viole, Nelke.

Um Wänd und Mauern grünte der Efeu, grünt'
  Ein selig Dunkel hoher Alleen. Oft
    Des Abends, Morgens waren dort wir,
      Redeten manches und sahn uns froh an.

IF FROM THE DISTANCE...

If from the distance, now we are far apart,
  You still can know me, if time past
    For you, the sharer of my sorrows,
      Has any feature at all of goodness,

Tell me, how does she wait for you, your love?
  In those gardens, when we found one another
    After a time of fright and darkness?
      Here by the streams of the holy underworld.

Some good there was, I must say, in your eyes
  Once you were gazing in far-off places
    Happily at things around you, always
      A taciturn person, and of somber

Appearance. Hours, how did they pass? My soul,
  How could it be so tranquil in the truth
    That I was separated? Yes,
      Yours I was and I confessed it.

That's how it is, just as you wish to write
  Into my mind everything you've known
    With letters, it is the same for me
      And all that has come to pass I tell you.

Was it spring? Was it summer? The nightingale
  Sweetly singing dwelt with birds that were
    Not far off in the bushes, trees
      Spread their fragrance all around us.

The sunny walks, the low shrubs, and the sand
  We trod on made yet more pleasant
    And sweeter still the hyacinth
      Or tulip, violet, carnation.

On wall and rampart ivyleaves were green, and green
  A blissful dark of lofty avenues. Often
    Morn and night we were there, talking,
      And looked with joy at one another.

In meinen Armen lebte der Jüngling auf,
  Der, noch verlassen, aus den Gefilden kam,
    Die er mir wies, mit einer Schwermut,
      Aber die Namen der seltnen Orte

Und alles Schöne hatt er behalten, das
  An seligen Gestaden, auch mir sehr wert,
    Im heimatlichen Lande blühet
      Oder verborgen, aus hoher Aussicht,

Allwo das Meer auch einer beschauen kann,
  Doch keiner sein will. Nehme vorlieb, und denk
    An die, die noch vergnügt ist, darum,
      Weil der entzückende Tag uns anschien,

Der mit Geständnis oder der Hände Druck
  Anhub, der uns vereinet. Ach! wehe mir!
    Es waren schöne Tage. Aber
      Traurige Dämmerung folgte nachher.

Du seiest so allein in der schönen Welt,
  Behauptest du mir immer, Geliebter! das
    Weißt aber du nicht,

(After 1806?)

126

In my embrace he was revived again,
   The young man, desolate still, who came
      From fields he showed me, with a sadness,
         But all the names of the abstruse places

He had remembered, and all the beauty which
   Blossoms in our native country
      On happy shores dear to me also,
         Or is hidden there, or a high lookout

Where one can even scan the ocean, but
   Where no one wants to be. Forgive and keep
      Her in your thoughts, who still is gratified
         Because on us the rapturous day did shine

Beginning with an avowal or pressure of hands,
   Uniting us. Ah, but alas now
      What lovely days they were, and what
         A sorry twilight came afterward.

So much alone you are in the beautiful world,
   You always tell me, my beloved, yet
      One thing you do not know

Eduard Mörike

AN EINEM WINTERMORGEN,
VOR SONNENAUFGANG

O flaumenleichte Zeit der dunkeln Frühe!
Welch neue Welt bewegest du in mir?
Was ist's, daß ich auf einmal nun in dir
Von sanfter Wollust meines Daseins glühe?

Einem Kristall gleicht meine Seele nun,
Den noch kein falscher Strahl des Lichts getroffen;
Zu fluten scheint mein Geist, er scheint zu ruhn,
Dem Eindruck naher Wunderkräfte offen,
Die aus dem klaren Gürtel blauer Luft
Zuletzt ein Zauberwort vor meine Sinne ruft.

Bei hellen Augen glaub' ich doch zu schwanken;
Ich schließe sie, daß nicht der Traum entweiche.
Seh ich hinab in lichte Feenreiche?
Wer hat den bunten Schwarm von Bildern und Gedanken
Zur Pforte meines Herzens hergeladen,
Die glänzend sich in diesem Busen baden,
Goldfarb'gen Fischlein gleich im Gartenteiche?

Ich höre bald der Hirtenflöten Klänge,
Wie um die Krippe jener Wundernacht,
Bald weinbekränzter Jugend Lustgesänge;
Wer hat das friedenselige Gedränge
In meine traurigen Wände hergebracht?

Und welch Gefühl entzückter Stärke,
Indem mein Sinn sich frisch zur Ferne lenkt!
Vom ersten Mark des heut'gen Tags getränkt,
Fühl' ich mir Mut zu jedem frommen Werke.
Die Seele fliegt, soweit der Himmel reicht,
Der Genius jauchzt in mir! Doch sage,
Warum wird jetzt der Blick von Wehmut feucht?
Ist's ein verloren Glück, was mich erweicht?
Ist es ein werdendes, was ich im Herzen trage?
—Hinweg, mein Geist! hier gilt kein Stillestehn:
Es ist ein Augenblick, und Alles wird verwehn!

ON A WINTER MORNING,
BEFORE SUNRISE

O feathery light time of the dark dawn,
What new world have you brought to life in me?
What can this mean, so suddenly to be
Aglow in you with joy to have been born?

My soul is like a crystal in this moment,
That no false ray of light as yet has stricken;
My spirit seems to flow, and to be pent,
Then to the touch of wondrous powers quicken
Thronging before my senses, summoned there
By magic out of the clear blue belt of air.

With open eyes I seem to lose all grip on earth;
I shut them lest the dream escape and go:
Now do I gaze on shining fairy realms below?
Who brings these motley thoughts and images to birth,
Crowding the portal of my heart and so
Luminous within me as they swim around
Like little goldfish in a garden pond?

The noise of shepherd pipings now I hear,
As by the crib that wondrous night they played;
Now young folk singing canticles of cheer;
Who brought with vineleaves crowned these people near,
In my sad room their peaceful cavalcade?

And what a sense of power thrills my mood
Now briskly as my thought moves far away,
And drenched with this first essence of the day
I feel the courage to be doing good.
My soul flies on, as far as heaven is,
My angel shouts for joy! And yet, how can this be,
What makes my gaze now moisten with a sadness?
Is it some lost joy that is softening me?
Or in my heart a burgeoning of bliss?
—On, on, my spirit! there's no stopping here,
A moment only, all will disappear.

AN EINEM WINTERMORGEN,
VOR SONNENAUFGANG *(continued)*

Dort, sieh, am Horizont lüpft sich der Vorhang schon!
Es träumt der Tag, nun sei die Nacht entflohn;
Die Purpurlippe, die geschlossen lag,
Haucht, halbgeöffnet, süße Atemzüge:
Auf einmal blitzt das Aug', und, wie ein Gott, der Tag
Beginnt im Sprung die königlichen Flüge!

(1825)

There, look, on the horizon see the curtain rise!
The dawn is dreaming night has reached an end.
The crimson lips are parting and they send
Sweet drafts of breath across the skies:
Then suddenly, the leaping eye a blaze of light,
Day like a god begins its royal flight!

GESANG ZU ZWEIEN IN DER NACHT

Sie: Wie süß der Nachtwind nun die Wiese streift,
Und klingend jetzt den jungen Hain durchläuft!
Da noch der freche Tag verstummt,
Hört man der Erdenkräfte flüsterndes Gedränge,
Das aufwärts in die zärtlichen Gesänge
Der reingestimmten Lüfte summt.

Er: Vernehm' ich doch die wunderbarsten Stimmen,
Vom lauen Wind wollüstig hingeschleift,
Indes, mit ungewissem Licht gestreift,
Der Himmel selber scheinet hinzuschwimmen.

Sie: Wie ein Gewebe zuckt die Luft manchmal,
Durchsichtiger and heller aufzuwehen;
Dazwischen hört man weiche Töne gehen
Von sel'gen Feen, die im blauen Saal
Zum Sphärenklang,
Und fleißig mit Gesang,
Silberne Spindel hin und wieder drehen.

Er: O holde Nacht, du gehst mit leisem Tritt
Auf schwarzem Samt, der nur am Tage grünet,
Und luftig schwirrender Musik bedienet
Sich nun dein Fuß zum leichten Schritt,
Womit du Stund um Stunde missest,
Dich lieblich in dir selbst vergissest—
Du schwärmst, es schwärmt der Schöpfung Seele mit!

(1825)

134

SONG FOR TWO IN THE NIG

She: How sweet the night wind glides across the
    And rippling through the coppice, how it runs!
    While brash day is silent still,
    You hear the thronged terrestrial powers' whisper
    Rise upward humming into delicate songs
    The tunèd airs and breezes sing and sing.

He: Yes, I hear most wondrous voices now
    By the warm wind drawn voluptuously along,
    While with its streaks of wavering light
    Heaven itself, it seems, might flow away.

She: Sometimes the air trembles like a skein,
    Then heaves aloft, brighter and more transparent;
    And in between one hears the soft tones move
    Of happy sprites who in the blue domain
    To music of the spheres
    And busy with their songs
    Are turning silver spindles now and then.

He: O beauteous night, with quiet tread you pass
    On black velvet only green by day,
    And now your feet for their light motions use
    A whirling airily celestial music
    With which you measure moment after moment,
    Rapt in yourself, yourself you do forget—
    You dream, and all creation dreams, adoring.

BESUCH IN URACH

Nur fast so wie im Traum ist mir's geschehen,
Daß ich in dies geliebte Tal verirrt.
Kein Wunder ist, was meine Augen sehen,
Doch schwankt der Boden, Luft und Staude schwirrt,
Aus tausend grünen Spiegeln scheint zu gehen
Vergangne Zeit, die lächelnd mich verwirrt;
Die Wahrheit selber wird hier zum Gedichte,
Mein eigen Bild ein fremd und hold Gesichte!

Da seid ihr alle wieder aufgerichtet,
Besonnte Felsen, alte Wolkenstühle!
Auf Wäldern schwer, wo kaum der Mittag lichtet
Und Schatten mischt mit balsamreicher Schwüle.
Kennt ihr mich noch, der sonst hieher geflüchtet,
Im Moose, bei süß-schläferndem Gefühle,
Der Mücke Sumsen hier ein Ohr geliehen,
Ach, kennt ihr mich, und wollt nicht vor mir fliehen?

Hier wird ein Strauch, ein jeder Halm zur Schlinge,
Die mich in liebliche Betrachtung fängt;
Kein Mäuerchen, kein Holz ist so geringe,
Daß nicht mein Blick voll Wehmut an ihm hängt:
Ein jedes spricht mir halbvergeßne Dinge;
Ich fühle, wie von Schmerz und Lust gedrängt
Die Träne stockt, indes ich ohne Weile,
Unschlüssig, satt und durstig, weiter eile.

Hinweg! und leite mich, du Schar von Quellen,
Die ihr durchspielt der Matten grünes Gold!
Zeigt mir die urbemoosten Wasserzellen,
Aus denen euer ewig's Leben rollt,
Im kühnsten Walde die verwachsnen Schwellen,
Wo eurer Mutter Kraft im Berge grollt,
Bis sie im breiten Schwung an Felsenwänden
Herabstürzt, euch im Tale zu versenden.

URACH REVISITED

Almost as in a dream I found myself
Wandering back in this beloved valley.
What I can see is not a miracle,
But the ground shifts, air and bushes whirl,
From green and countless mirrors bygone time
Now seems to move and smiles bewildering me;
Here truth itself becomes a very poem,
A strange and lovely vision my own image.

There towered up again you all appear,
Sunlit cliffs, the ancient thrones of cloud
Topping the woods which sun at noon scarce pierces,
To mix the shadows with a warmth perfumed—
Do you still know me, once a fugitive here,
Upon the moss with a sweet and drowsy feeling,
Who listened to the buzzing of the flies,
Ah, do you wish to stand and know me still?

Here any bush or blade of grass becomes
A noose to snare me in sweet meditation;
No tiny bank of earth, no piece of wood
Too small for me to look upon with sadness:
Each speaks to me of half-forgotten things;
Feeling how pain and joy press back the tears
Which hesitate, I do not stop but hasten
Onward and undecided, full and thirsting.

Onward! and be my guides, you host of waters,
Which play among the green and golden fields!
Show me the cells with primal moss encrusted,
From which your everlasting life is poured,
The thresholds overgrown in wildest woodland,
Where among hills your mother's plunging force
Sweeps down, until cascading over walls
Of rock, she sends you out across the valley.

O hier ist's, wo Natur den Schleier reißt!
Sie bricht einmal ihr übermenschlich Schweigen;
Laut mit sich selber redend will ihr Geist,
Sich selbst vernehmend, sich ihm selber zeigen.
—Doch ach, sie bleibt, mehr als der Mensch, verwaist,
Darf nicht aus ihrem eignen Rätsel steigen!
Dir biet ich denn, begier'ge Wassersäule,
Die nackte Brust, ach, ob sie dir sich teile!

Vergebens! und dein kühles Element
Tropft an mir ab, im Grase zu versinken.
Was ist's, das deine Seele von mir trennt?
Sie flieht, und möcht' ich auch in dir ertrinken!
Dich kränkt's nicht, wie mein Herz um dich entbrennt,
Küssest im Sturz nur diese schroffen Zinken;
Du bleibest, was du warst seit Tag und Jahren,
Ohn ein'gen Schmerz der Zeiten zu erfahren.

Hinweg aus diesem üpp'gen Schattengrund
Voll großer Pracht, die drückend mich erschüttert!
Bald grüßt beruhigt mein verstummter Mund
Den schlichten Winkel, wo sonst halb verwittert
Die kleine Bank und wo das Hüttchen stund;
Erinnrung reicht mit Lächeln die verbittert
Bis zur Betäubung süßen Zauberschalen;
So trink' ich gierig die entzückten Qualen.

Hier schlang sich tausendmal ein junger Arm
Um meinen Hals mit inn'gem Wohlgefallen.
O säh ich mich, als Knaben sonder Harm,
Wie einst, mit Necken durch die Haine wallen!
Ihr Hügel, von der *alten* Sonne warm,
Erscheint mir denn auf keinem von euch allen
Mein Ebenbild, in jugendlicher Frische
Hervorgesprungen aus dem Waldgebüsche?

O here it is that nature rends her veil.
For once she breaks her superhuman silence;
Her spirit, speaking to itself aloud,
And listening, desires self-revelation.
But nature, ah, more so than man, is orphaned
And cannot step outside her own enigma.
My naked breast I offer you, O greedy stream,
Hoping to you some share of her might fall.

But all in vain, and your cool element
Has trickled off, to vanish in the grass.
What makes your soul elude me? It escapes,
Even if I might wish to drown in you.
You do not take offence, if my heart burns for you,
But kiss, as down you pour, only these rocky spurs,
You are just what you were, time out of mind,
And never do you feel the pangs of time.

Away from this luxuriant shady dell
Which with its splendid grandeur makes me tremble.
My mouth, more calm, though striken dumb, now greets
The simple nook where stood the little bench,
Much weather-worn, and then the little house.
Bitter they have become, her toxic cups
Of sweetness memory hands me with a smile;
Thus greedily I drink the ecstatic torments.

A thousand times with intimate delight
A young arm here was twined around my neck.
Could I but see myself, an innocent lad,
Walking as once and bantering through the trees.
You hills, which still are warm with the old sun,
Does not my image appear on one of you,
On any single one, in all the sparkle of youth
Leaping out from among the undergrowth?

O komm, enthülle dich! dann sollst du mir
Mit Freundlichkeit ins dunkle Auge schauen!
Noch immer, guter Knabe, gleich ich dir,
Uns beiden wird nicht voreinander grauen!
So komm und laß mich unaufhaltsam hier
Mich deinem reinen Busen anvertrauen!—
Umsonst, daß ich die Arme nach dir strecke,
Den Boden, wo du gingst, mit Küssen decke!

Hier will ich denn laut schluchzend liegen bleiben,
Fühllos, und alles habe seinen Lauf!—
Mein Finger, matt, ins Gras beginnt zu schreiben:
Hin ist die Lust! hab' alles seinen Lauf!
Da, plötzlich, hör ich's durch die Lüfte treiben,
Und ein entfernter Donner schreckt mich auf;
Elastisch angespannt mein ganzes Wesen
Ist von Gewitterluft wie neu genesen.

Sieh! wie die Wolken finstre Ballen schließen
Um den ehrwürd'gen Trotz der Burgruine!
Von weitem schon hört man den alten Riesen,
Stumm harrt das Tal mit ungewisser Miene,
Der Kuckuck nur ruft sein einförmig Grüßen
Versteckt aus unerforschter Wildnis Grüne,—
Jetzt kracht die Wölbung, und verhallet lange,
Das wundervolle Schauspiel ist im Gange!

Ja nun, indes mit hoher Feuerhelle
Der Blitz die Stirn und Wange mir verklärt,
Ruf ich den lauten Segen in die grelle
Musik des Donners, die mein Wort bewährt:
O Tal! du meines Lebens andre Schwelle!
Du meiner tiefsten Kräfte stiller Herd!
Du meiner Liebe Wundernest! ich scheide,
Leb wohl!—und sei dein Engel mein Geleite!

(May 1827)

O come, now show yourself! And then for sure
You'll gaze with friendship into my somber eyes!
Good lad, I still resemble you today,
We shall not be afraid of one another.
So come, and I shall tell you everything,
Confiding everything to your pure heart.
In vain I stretch my arms to capture you,
And kiss the earth that once you walked upon.

Here then I'll lie and sob aloud, unfeeling,
Let all things take their course, what do I care!
My finger, weak, begins to write in the grass:
"All joy is gone. Let all things take their course."
Then suddenly I hear the breezes quicken,
And distant thunder brings me to my feet,
Ethereally tensed through all my being
I seem to have been healed by the stormy air.

Look how around the venerable ruined fort's
Defiance gloomy thunderheads are shaping;
One hears the ancient ogre from afar,
The valley seems to waver, holds its breath,
Only the cuckoo's constant greeting sounds
From the unfathomed wilderness of verdure,—
And now the vault roars and is echoing,
The pageantry of marvels has begun.

So then, as with its rays of fire aloft
The lightning clarifies my brow and cheek,
Into the strident music of the thunder
I shout my blessing, and it keeps my word:
O valley, second threshold of my life,
Unruffled focus of my deepest powers,
Wondrous nest of my love, farewell, I go,
And may your guardian spirit be my company!

SEPTEMBERMORGEN

Im Nebel ruhet noch die Welt,
Noch träumen Wald und Wiesen:
Bald siehst du, wenn der Schleier fällt,
Den blauen Himmel unverstellt,
Herbstkräftig die gedämpfte Welt
In warmem Golde fließen.

(18 October 1827)

SEPTEMBER MORNING

Sleeps the world still
In folds of mist.
  Meadow and woodland
Still are dreaming.
  Soon when the veil
Down has slid,
  You shall see
Blue sky manifest
  And autumn-vivid
The calm world amid
  A warm gold streaming.

ERSTES LIEBESLIED EINES
MÄDCHENS

Was im Netze? Schau einmal!
Aber ich bin bange;
Greif' ich einen süßen Aal?
Greif' ich eine Schlange?

Lieb' ist blinde
Fischerin;
Sagt dem Kinde,
Wo greift's hin?

Schon schnellt mir's in Händen!
Ach Jammer! o Lust!
Mit Schmiegen und Wenden
Mir schlüpft's an die Brust.

Es beißt sich, o Wunder!
Mir keck durch die Haut,
Schießt's Herze hinunter!
O Liebe, mir graut!

Was tun, was beginnen?
Das schaurige Ding,
Es schnalzet da drinnen,
Es legt sich im Ring.

Gift muß ich haben!
Hier schleicht es herum,
Tut wonniglich graben
Und bringt mich noch um!

(June 1828)

GIRL'S FIRST LOVE SONG

Look, in the net
What's this? I feel
Afraid, am I touching
A snake or an eel?

Love's a fishergirl,
Blind, blind,
Say where it's going,
Comfort her mind.

It whips through my hands,
What pleasures, they hurt!
Coiling and snuggling
Inside my shirt!

Bites clean through my skin,
Now what's this, and O
It shoots my heart down
And frightens me so.

Help! What can I do?
The horrible thing,
Smacking its lips,
It coils in a ring.

Its poison has got me,
The cunning, the sly,
The sweet burrowing creature,
I'm certain to die.

SCHERZ

Einen Morgengruß ihr früh zu bringen,
Und mein Morgenbrot bei ihr zu holen,
Geh ich sachte an des Mädchens Türe,
Öffne rasch, da steht mein schlankes Bäumchen
Vor dem Spiegel schon und wascht sich emsig.
O wie lieblich träuft die weiße Stirne,
Träuft die Rosenwange Silbernässe!
Hangen aufgelöst die süßen Haare!
Locker spielen Tücher und Gewänder.
Aber wie sie zagt und scheucht und abwehrt!
Gleich, sogleich soll ich den Rückzug nehmen!
Närrchen, rief ich, sei mir so kein Närrchen:
Das ist Brautrecht, ist Verlobtensitte.
Laß mich nur, ich will ja blind und lahm sein,
Will den Kopf und alle beiden Augen
In die Fülle deiner Locken stecken,
Will die Hände mit den Flechten binden—
,,Nein, du gehst!" Im Winkel laß mich stehen,
Dir bescheidentlich den Rücken kehren!
,,Ei, so mag's, damit ich Ruhe habe!"

Und ich stand gehorsam in der Ecke,
Lächerlich, wie ein gestrafter Junge,
Der die Lektion nicht wohl bestanden,
Muckste nicht und kühlte mir die Lippen
An der weißen Wand mit leisem Kusse,
Eine volle, eine lange Stunde;
Ja, so wahr ich lebe. Doch, wer etwa
Einen kleinen Zweifel möchte haben
(Was ich ihm just nicht verargen dürfte),
Nun, der frage nur das Mädchen selber:
Die wird ihn—noch zierlicher belügen.

(1829)

JOKE

To wish her early in the day good-morning,
And to have my breakfast down at her place,
I steal up to her door, open it quickly,
And there my little tree is standing, busy
Washing herself and looking in the mirror.
Oh what a lovely sparkling of moistures
On her white forehead and her cheeks so rosy!
How sweetly disarrayed her chevelure is!
And hanging loose the play of robes and towels.
Yet how she quails, quite overcome with shyness;
She tells me I must get me gone, be off,
I shout: "You little fool, don't be so silly,
Since we're engaged I have the right, it's legal!
I shall pretend I'm paralyzed, a blind man,
I'll hide my head and eyes, the both of them,
By burying them in your abundant hairdo,
What's more, I'll tie my hands up with your braids—"
"No, out you go!—" "Just let me stay in the corner,
I'll turn my back, surely that's not immodest?"
"Oh, all right then, just so I shan't be bothered."

And so I stood, obedient, in the corner,
Ridiculous, like a schoolboy being punished,
Who hasn't passed a test or done his homework.
I didn't move an inch and cooled my lips
Against the white wall with a kiss, a quiet one,
For all of an hour, and that hour was a long one.
Yes, it's the truth. But anyone who doubts it,
Perhaps, who doubts it even just a little
(For which, of course, he really needn't blame me)
Well, he should put the girl herself his question:
She'll tell him, with a lie that's even neater.

PEREGRINA

I

Der Spiegel dieser treuen, braunen Augen
Ist wie von innerem Gold ein Widerschein;
Tief aus dem Busen scheint er's anzusaugen,
Dort mag solch Gold in heil'gem Gram gedeihn.
In diese Nacht des Blickes mich zu tauchen,
Unwissend Kind, du selber lädst mich ein—
Willst, ich soll kecklich mich und dich entzünden,
Reichst lächelnd mir den Tod im Kelch der Sünden!

II

Aufgeschmückt ist der Freudensaal.
Lichterhell, bunt, in laulicher Sommernacht
Stehet das offene Gartengezelte.
Säulengleich steigen, gepaart,
Grün-umranket, eherne Schlangen,
Zwölf, mit verschlungenen Hälsen,
Tragend und stützend das
Leicht gegitterte Dach.

Aber die Braut noch wartet verborgen
In dem Kämmerlein ihres Hauses.
Endlich bewegt sich der Zug der Hochzeit,
Fackeln tragend,
Feierlich stumm.
Und in der Mitte,
Mich an der rechten Hand,
Schwarz gekleidet, geht einfach die Braut;
Schön gefaltet ein Scharlachtuch
Liegt um den zierlichen Kopf geschlagen.
Lächelnd geht sie dahin; das Mahl schon duftet.

Später im Lärmen des Fests
Stahlen wir seitwärts uns beide
Weg, nach den Schatten des Gartens wandelnd,
Wo im Gebüsche die Rosen brannten,

PEREGRINA

I

The mirror of these brown and loyal eyes
Is as of inner gold the afterglow;
Sucked from the heart the splendor seems to rise;
Such gold might flourish there in holy sorrow.
To plunge into this dark night of your gaze
You ask me, child, but this you cannot know;
To set us both on fire with wild beguiling:
Death in the cup of sin you hand me, smiling.

II

The place of joy is adorned for festival.
Glittering with lamps and colors the pavilion
Stands open in the summery night.
Like columns, in pairs,
Green vines over them, serpents of brass,
Twelve, with necks entwined,
Hold and support the
Lightly latticed roof.

But the bride waits, hidden still
At home in her chamber.
At last the wedding procession has begun,
Torches aloft,
In solemn silence.
And in the midst of it walks,
With me on her right hand,
The bride in simple black;
Around her delicate head in lovely folds
Is looped a cloth of scarlet.
Smiling she walks along; a fragrance
Floats from the banquet.

Later we left the clamor of feasting
And went aside together,
Walking away toward the garden shadows,
Where the roses glowed in the bushes,

Wo der Mondstrahl um Lilien zuckte,
Wo die Weymouthsfichte mit schwarzem Haar
Den Spiegel des Teiches halb verhängt.

Auf seidnem Rasen dort, ach, Herz am Herzen,
Wie verschlangen, erstickten meine Küsse den scheueren Kuß!
Indes der Springquell, unteilnehmend
An überschwänglicher Liebe Geflüster,
Sich ewig des eigenen Plätscherns freute;
Uns aber neckten von fern und lockten
Freundliche Stimmen,
Flöten und Saiten umsonst.

Ermüdet lag, zu bald für mein Verlangen,
Das leichte, liebe Haupt auf meinem Schoß.
Spielender Weise mein Aug' auf ihres drückend
Fühlt' ich ein Weilchen die langen Wimpern,
Bis der Schlaf sie stellte,
Wie Schmetterlingsgefieder auf und nieder gehn.

Eh' has Frührot schien,
Eh' das Lämpchen erlosch im Brautgemache,
Weckt' ich die Schläferin,
Führte das seltsame Kind in mein Haus ein.

III

Ein Irrsal kam in die Mondscheingärten
Einer einst heiligen Liebe.
Schaudernd entdeckt' ich verjährten Betrug.
Und mit weinendem Blick, doch grausam,
Hieß ich das schlanke,
Zauberhafte Mädchen
Ferne gehen von mir.
Ach, ihre hohe Stirn
War gesenkt, denn sie liebte mich;
Aber sie zog mit Schweigen
Fort in die graue
Welt hinaus.

Where the moonray flickered around lilies,
Where the weeping pine, with black hair,
Half hid the mirror of the pool.

There on silken turf, ah, heart to heart,
We embraced, my kisses stifling her more timid kiss,
While the fountain took no share
In the whispers of frenzied love
But pleasure only in its own splashing,
And we could hear the far
Friendly voices,
Flutes and strings,
Taunting and enticing us in vain.

Her dear light head
Lay weary in my arms, too soon
For my desiring. Playfully I pressed
My eyes on hers and felt for a while
Her long eyelashes, until sleep
Stilled them,
Rise and fall like plumes of a butterfly.

Before the sun rose,
Before the lamp in our bridal chamber was quenched,
I woke the sleeper,
Led the strange child into my house.

III

Into the moonlit gardens of a love once holy,
Wrongness came.
I found with a shudder
She had deceived me long ago.
And with tears, but cruelly,
I told the slender
Magical girl
To go from me.
Ah, her high forehead

Krank seitdem,
Wund ist und wehe mein Herz.
Nimmer wird es genesen!

Als ginge, luftgesponnen, ein Zauberfaden
Von ihr zu mir, ein ängstig Band,
So zieht es, zieht mich schmachtend ihr nach!
—Wie? wenn ich eines Tags auf meiner Schwelle
Sie sitzen fände, wie einst, im Morgen-Zwielicht,
Das Wanderbündel neben ihr,
Und ihr Auge, treuherzig zu mir aufschauend,
Sagte, da bin ich wieder
Hergekommen aus weiter Welt!

IV

Warum, Geliebte, denk ich dein
Auf einmal nun mit tausend Tränen,
Und kann gar nicht zufrieden sein,
Und will die Brust in alle Weite dehnen?

Ach, gestern in den hellen Kindersaal,
Beim Flimmer zierlich aufgesteckter Kerzen,
Wo ich mein selbst vergaß in Lärm und Scherzen,
Tratst du, o Bildnis mitleid-schöner Qual;
Es war dein Geist, er setzte sich ans Mahl,
Fremd saßen wir mit stumm verhaltnen Schmerzen;
Zuletzt brach ich in lautes Schluchzen aus,
Und Hand in Hand verließen wir das Haus.

V

Die Liebe, sagt man, steht am Pfahl gebunden,
Geht endlich arm, zerrüttet, unbeschuht;
Dies edle Haupt hat nicht mehr, wo es ruht,
Mit Tränen netzet sie der Füße Wunden.

Ach, Peregrinen habe ich so gefunden!
Schön war ihr Wahsinn, ihrer Wange Glut,
Noch scherzend in der Frühlingsstürme Wut,
Und wilde Kränze in das Haar gewunden.

Was bowed, for she loved me;
But she went away,
In silence,
Into the gray world.
Since then my heart
Is sick and sore and wounded,
It never will be well again.

As if between herself and me, braided of air,
A magic thread were tied, a timorous bond,
And it draws me, draws me languishing toward her.
—How would it be if one day at my door
I found her sitting, as once, in the dusk of sunrise,
Her traveling bundle beside her,
And if her eyes, looking up at me with candor,
Said: Well, here I am,
Back again from the wide wide world!

IV

Suddenly weeping as the thoughts return,
Why do I think of you, my love, like this?
And why with discontent forever burn
And want my heart to fill the world's wide distances?

Ah, into the room of children yesterday,
With candles flickering gracefully and tall,
As I forgot myself in the noise and play,
You came, with pain and pity beautiful;
It was your ghost that came to share our meal,
We sat like strangers, grieving the words away,
Until at last I broke out sobbing, and
We left the house together, hand in hand.

V

Love, so they say, is martyred at the stake,
And walks unshod, poor, broken in mind.
No resting place this noble head can find;
Love laves the wounded feet for loving's sake.

War's möglich, solche Schönheit zu verlassen?
—So kehrt nur reizender das alte Glück!
O komm, in diese Arme dich zu fassen!

Doch weh! o weh! was soll mir dieser Blick?
Sie küßt mich zwischen Lieben noch und Hassen,
Sie kehrt sich ab, und kehrt mir nie zurück.

(I: before spring 1828; II: possibly summer 1824; III: early version
7 June 1824, revised by 1867; IV: before spring 1828; V: ca.
June 1828. Variant versions of I, II, III, and V in *Maler Nolten*,
1832).

Ah, thus I found Peregrina, found her fair
In all her madness, and her way of blushing;
She'd laugh amid the furious storms of spring,
And put wild flower garlands in her hair.

How could I ever forsake such loveliness?
—The joys gone by, more joyous yet, in vain—
Come to my arms, come back to my embrace!

But O, her telling look, and O, the pain!
Loving and hating me she gives her kiss.
She turns away, she'll not come back again.

IN DER FRÜHE

Kein Schlaf noch kühlt das Auge mir,
Dort gehet schon der Tag herfür
An meinem Kammerfenster.
Es wühlet mein verstörter Sinn
Noch zwischen Zweifeln her und hin
Und schaffet Nachtgespenster.
—Ängste, quäle
Dich nicht länger, meine Seele!
Freu' dich! schon sind da und dorten
Morgenglocken wach geworden.

(1828)

DAYBREAK

No sleep has come to cool my eyes;
The daystar now begins to rise
At my window.
My troubled mind, tossed about,
To and fro, between this doubt
And that, is making
Specters of the night. Now let self-torment go,
Have no more fear,
Soul, be glad for here
And there the bells are waking.

DIE TRAURIGE KRÖNUNG

Es war ein König Milesint,
Von dem will ich euch sagen:
Der meuchelte sein Bruderskind,
Wollte selbst die Krone tragen.
Die Krönung ward mit Prangen
Auf Liffey-Schloß begangen.
O Irland! Irland! warst du so blind?

Der König sitzt um Mitternacht
Im leeren Marmorsaale,
Sieht irr in all die neue Pracht,
Wie trunken von dem Mahle;
Er spricht zu seinem Sohne:
,,Noch einmal bring die Krone!
Doch schau, wer hat die Pforten aufgemacht?"

Da kommt ein seltsam Totenspiel,
Ein Zug mit leisen Tritten,
Vermummte Gäste groß und viel,
Eine Krone schwankt in Mitten;
Es drängt sich durch die Pforte
Mit Flüstern ohne Worte;
Dem Könige, dem wird so geisterschwül.

Und aus der schwarzen Menge blickt
Ein Kind mit frischer Wunde;
Es lächelt sterbensweh und nickt,
Es macht im Saal die Runde,
Es trippelt zu dem Throne,
Es reichet eine Krone
Dem Könige, des Herze tief erschrickt.

Darauf der Zug von dannen strich,
Von Morgenluft berauschet,
Die Kerzen flackern wunderlich,
Der Mond am Fenster lauschet;
Der Sohn mit Angst und Schweigen
Zum Vater tät sich neigen,—
Er neiget über eine Leiche sich.

(1828)

MOURNFUL CORONATION

A king there was called Milesint,
His story now I sing.
He killed his brother when a child,
He wanted to be king.
He was crowned at Liffey Castle
With pomp of every kind:
Ireland, O Ireland, could you be so blind?

The king he sits at midnight
In his empty marble hall,
Swivels his eyes like a drunkard
At the new glory and all.
And to his son he speaks:
"Fetch me the crown again—
But look, the door, who's this acoming in?"

Many and tall death-dancers
Crowd through with quiet tread,
In masks the faces muffled,
The crown held overhead.
All whisper without words
Now they're inside the door,
The king quakes and sweats in every pore.

Out of the black throng stares
A boy with a fresh wound,
He grins and nods like hurt to death
And he walks the hall around.
He totters to the throne,
That crown to render up,
And the king's heart squirms in terror's grip.

The dancers swirl and vanish
In the cooler morning air,
Weirdly the candles flicker,
The moon is listening there:
Aghast in dread and silence
What does the son discover—
It is a corpse that he is leaning over.

DAS VERLASSENE MÄGDLEIN

Früh, wann die Hähne krähn,
Eh' die Sternlein verschwinden,
Muß ich am Herde stehn,
Muß Feuer zünden.

Schön ist der Flamme Schein,
Es springen die Funken;
Ich schaue so drein,
In Leid versunken.

Plötzlich, da kommt es mir,
Treuloser Knabe,
Daß ich die Nacht von dir
Geträumet habe.

Träne auf Träne dann
Stürzet hernieder;
So kommt der Tag heran—
O ging er wieder!

(May 1829)

THE FORSAKEN GIRL

Early, in starlight still,
And the cocks crowing,
I must stand at the hob,
Must get the fire going.

Sparks leap, and lovely
The flames ablaze;
Sunk in sorrow,
At them I gaze.

Suddenly then recall,
Faithless lover,
Last night I dreamed of you,
Over and over.

Tear upon tear now
Tumbling down;
So the day comes and comes—
Would it were gone.

RAT EINER ALTEN

Bin jung gewesen,
Kann auch mitreden,
Und alt geworden,
Drum gilt mein Wort.

Schön reife Beeren
Am Bäumchen hangen:
Nachbar, da hilft kein
Zaun um den Garten;
Lustige Vögel
Wissen den Weg.

Aber, mein Dirnchen,
Du laß dir raten:
Halte dein Schätzchen
Wohl in der Liebe,
Wohl im Respekt!

Mit den zwei Fädlein
In eins gedrehet,
Ziehst du am kleinen
Finger ihn nach.

Aufrichtig Herze,
Doch schweigen können,
Früh mit der Sonne
Mutig zur Arbeit,
Gesunde Glieder,
Saubere Linnen,
Das machet Mädchen
Und Weibchen wert.

Bin jung gewesen,
Kann auch mitreden,
Und alt geworden,
Drum gilt mein Wort.

(23 March 1832)

OLD WOMAN'S ADVICE

Was young once too,
So I can talk,
And now am old,
So I talk sense.

Lovely ripe berries
Hang on the tree;
Neighbor, it's no use
Putting a fence up;
The merry birdies,
They know the way.

But you, young lady,
Here's my advice:
Once you've a sweetheart
Love him and give him
All your respect.

With those two threads
Twined in one,
You'll lead him around
With your little finger.

Straight from the heart,
But watch your tongue,
Up with the sun
And on with your work,
A healthy body
And linen clean,
That makes a girl
Or wife a credit.

Was young once too,
So I can talk,
And now am old,
So I talk sense.

GEBET

Herr! schicke, was du willt,
Ein Liebes oder Leides;
Ich bin vergnügt, daß beides
Aus deinen Händen quillt.

Wollest mit Freuden
Und wollest mit Leiden
Mich nicht überschütten!
Doch in der Mitten
Liegt holdes Bescheiden.

(Lines 5–9: 1832; lines 1–4:
ca. 31 January 1846)

PRAYER

Send me what you will, Lord,
Be it pain or pleasure;
Each in welcome measure
From your hands is poured.

Do not overwhelm me, pray,
With sorrow or delight;
The fairest share, it seems,
Of either ever lay
Between extremes.

DER STRÄFLING

Elegische Balladière
Im Kerker zu Stuttgart gedichtet
den 5 April 1837

In des Zwingers Mißgerüchen
    Fröstelnd sitz ich da;
Weil man mich der königlichen
    Zwiebel dräuen sah.

Denn ich wähnt', es wär nicht übel,
    Wenn wir unserem Aquavit,*
Statt gemeiner Zähren-Zwiebel
    Zärtern Schmälzling teilten mit.**

Und ich schlich zum Herrscher-Garten
    Wo der Silberstöszling† schwimmt,
Wo die Afrikanen†† schnarrten
    Und die Tulpe flimmt.

„Ihre Knolle auszuwarken,
    Hilf, o Küpris,††† mir!
Niemand wird mir dies verargen,
    Niemand lauschet hier!"

Und schon bohrt' ich auf die Neige,
    Und schon gab sie nach,
Als aus nahem Lustgezweige
    Still ein Bosmann brach.

Und ich trat mit meinem Zweke
    Floskelnhaft hervor,
Doch der goldbordierte Reke****
    Wismet' mir kein Ohr.—

—Wie notwendig Junge brechen
    Aus dem Hühner-Ei,
So folgt jeglichem Verbrechen
    Stets die Polizei.

From The Wispeliads

THE PRISONER

Elegiac balladière,
Written in the Stuttgart
Prison, 5 April 1837

Down among the smelly dungeons
 Shivering I sit,
Caught for jabbadizing onions,
 Royal ones, to wit.

My intent in onion-stealing
 Was to splice our soup
With onions of far finer feeling
 Than the common weepful group. *

And I crept to the king's garden,
 Where the silverthruster† swims,
Where the afrikaaners†† quaaken
 And the tulip glims.

"Help me now your bulb to hoe
 Up, O Cypris, ††† please!
No one possibly can know,
 Not a person sees!"

Soon a sloping hole I grub,
 Soon my plea she hears,
When suddenly from out the shrub
 A pesky man appears.

Flowerily I said, uprisen,
 What had brought me here.
But would the braided donzel*** listen?
 He did not lend me ear.

Sure as little chickens poke
 From eggs to find release,
Crimes of any kind provoke
 Action by police.

In des Zwingers Mißgerüchen
Fröstelnd sitz ich da,
Weil man mich der königlichen
Zwiebel dräuen sah.

* Euphemism, pour Wasser-Soupe.
** Auch mein Kochwerk anzubessern ***
    Pröblings wollt' ich's tun;
    Diesen Wissenszweig zu größern
    Kann mein Geist nicht ruhn.

*** Der Verfasser beabsichtigte die Herausgabe eines Kochbuches
    nach baichenen Ideen, welches sein Bruder drucken wollte.

† Der Schwan.

†† Eine Art ausländischer Enten; sehr schön, aber von häßlichem
    Geschrei.

††† Göttin der Botanique.

**** Altteutsch pour: Portier.

(1837)

Down among the smelly dungeons
Shivering I sit,
Caught for jabbadizing onions,
Royal ones, to wit.

* My cooking to improve somewhat
Was also what I meant,
This field of knowledge to unclot
My mind is restless bent. **

** The author aimed to publish a cookbook using his boriginal ideas, which his brother was going to print.

† The swan.

†† A sort of foreign duck, very beautiful, but with an ugly screech.

††† Goddess of Botanique

*** Ancient term for "porter."

DER TAMBOUR

Wenn meine Mutter hexen könnt',
Da müßt' sie mit dem Regiment,
Nach Frankreich, überall mit hin,
Und wär' die Marketenderin.
Im Lager, wohl um Mitternacht,
Wenn niemand auf ist als die Wacht,
Und alles schnarchet, Roß und Mann,
Vor meiner Trommel säß' ich dann:
Die Trommel müßt' eine Schüssel sein,
Ein warmes Sauerkraut darein,
Die Schlegel Messer und Gabel,
Eine lange Wurst mein Sabel,
Mein Tschako wär ein Humpen gut,
Den füll ich mit Burgunderblut.
Und weil es mir an Lichte fehlt,
Da scheint der Mond in mein Gezelt;
Scheint er auch auf franzö'sch herein,
Mir fällt doch meine Liebste ein:
Ach weh! Jetzt hat der Spaß ein End!
—Wenn nur meine Mutter hexen könnt!

(1837)

THE DRUMMER BOY

I wish my mother were a witch,
Then with the regiment she'd march
To France, or everywhere with me,
And canteen lady's what she'd be.
At midnight in the camp I'd take,
When no one but the guard's awake,
And all are snoring, horse and man,
My drum, but it would be a saucepan
Filled with nice warm sauerkraut.
Next I'd take my drumsticks out,
But they would be a knife and fork,
My saber's now a sausage, look,
My military cap a cup
Of Burgundy for drinking up.
And since I am bereft of light,
Moonbeams fill my tent at night;
If in French they chance to shine,
Promptly I think of that girl of mine.
Ah, end of joke, for there's the hitch.
—I wish my mother were a witch.

JOHANN KEPLER

Gestern, als ich vom nächtlichen Lager den Stern mir im Osten
    Lang betrachtete, den dort mit dem rötlichen Licht,
Und des Mannes gedachte, der seine Bahnen zu messen,
    Von dem Gotte gereizt, himmlischer Pflicht sich ergab,
Durch beharrlichen Fleiß der Armut grimmigen Stachel
    Zu versöhnen, umsonst, und zu verachten bemüht:
Mir entbrannte mein Herz von Wehmut bitter; ach! dacht ich,
    Wußten die Himmlischen dir, Meister, kein besseres Los?
Wie ein Dichter den Helden sich wählt, wie Homer von Achilles'
    Göttlichem Adel gerührt, schön im Gesang ihn erhob,
Also wandtest du ganz nach jenem Gestirne die Kräfte,
    Sein gewaltiger Gang war dir ein ewiges Lied.
Doch so bewegt sich kein Gott von seinem goldenen Sitze,
    Holdem Gesang geneigt, den zu erretten, herab,
Dem die höhere Macht die dunkeln Tage bestimmt hat,
    Und euch Sterne berührt nimmer ein Menschengeschick;
Ihr geht über dem Haupte des Weisen oder des Toren
    Euren seligen Weg ewig gelassen dahin!

(1837)

JOHANN KEPLER

Last night lying in bed as I looked at the eastern star,
  Taking a good long look, that star with the reddish light,
And thought of the man who, being impelled by the god,
  Bowed to the heavenly task of calculating its course,
And who endeavored with steadfast work to dull and despise
  Poverty's terrible sting, though the endeavor was vain:
My heart blazed with bitter grief and, ah, master, I thought,
  Was this fate of yours all that the gods could give?
Homer exalted Achilles, stirred by his noble and godlike
  Grandeur, and poets do choose them a hero in song,
Likewise upon that star you turned all the force of your mind
  And its tremendous course was your eternal theme.
Yet a song's not the thing that occasions a god to flutter
  Down from his golden throne, bringing deliverance
For a man to whom dark days the loftier power has ordained,
  And you stars up there, never touched by a human fate,
Over the heads of the wise and foolish blithely you move
  Eternally calm as you pass unperturbed on your ways.

AN EINE ÄOLSHARFE

Tu semper urges flebilibus modis
Mysten ademptum: nec tibi Vespero
Surgente decedunt amores,
Nec rapidum fugiente Solem.

Horaz

Angelehnt an die Efeuwand
Dieser alten Terrasse,
Du, einer luftgebornen Muse
Geheimnisvolles Saitenspiel,
Fang an,
Fange wieder an
Deine melodische Klage!

Ihr kommet, Winde, fern herüber,
Ach! von des Knaben,
Der mir so lieb war,
Frisch grünendem Hügel.
Und Frühlingsblüten unterweges streifend,
Übersättigt mit Wohlgerüchen,
Wie süß bedrängt ihr dies Herz!
Und säuselt her in die Saiten,
Angezogen von wohllautender Wehmut,
Wachsend im Zug meiner Sehnsucht,
Und hinsterbend wieder.

Aber auf einmal,
Wie der Wind heftiger herstößt,
Ein holder Schrei der Harfe
Wiederholt, mir zu süßem Erschrecken,
Meiner Seele plötzliche Regung;
Und hier—die volle Rose streut, geschüttelt,
All ihre Blätter vor meine Füße!

(1857, before June 14)

174

TO AN AEOLIAN HARP

Tu semper urges flebilibus modis
Mysten ademptum: nec tibi Vespero
Surgente decedunt amores,
Nec rapidum fugiente Solem.

Horace

Leaning against the ivy wall
Of this old terrace,
You, instrument mysterious
Of a muse born of the air,
Begin,
And again begin
Your melodious lament.

Winds, you are coming from far,
Ah, from the fresh green
Hill he is under,
The boy I loved so well.
And combing springtime blossoms as you pass,
Drenched with perfumes,
How sweetly you press at my heart,
And whisper among the strings,
Ondrawn by sonorous sorrow's moan,
Rising in the motion of my grief,
And dying away again.

But all at once,
As the wind heaves a heavier sigh,
A tender cry from the harp
Repeats, sweetly startling me,
The sudden tremor through my soul;
And here—the full rose loosens, shaken,
At my feet all its petals.

AN FRIEDR. VISCHER,
PROFESSOR DER ÄSTHETIK ETC.

mit meinen Gedichten

Oft hat mich der Freund verteidigt,
Oft sogar gelobt; doch nun?
Der Professor ist beeidigt,
Und da hilft kein Traulich-tun.

Also geht, ihr braven Lieder,
Daß man euch die Köpfe wascht!
Seht auch, daß ihr hin und wieder
Einen guten Blick erhascht.

Er ist Vater: um so minder
Denk' ich ihn euch abgeneigt;
Sind doch seine eignen Kinder
Auf der Schulbank nicht gezeugt!

(1838)

TO FRIEDRICH VISCHER,
PROFESSOR OF ESTHETICS, ETC.

with my book of poems

Though my friend has spoken many a
Word of praise in my defence,
Since professors have their tenure
One can't presume on confidence.

So off you scamper, songs of mine,
Let the fellow wipe your noses.
You'll take care from time to time
To earn his favor, one supposes.

Such non-displeasure, I've believed,
Befits a father who's no fool:
His own children weren't conceived
Sitting on a bench in school.

AN PHILOMELE

Tonleiterähnlich steiget dein Klaggesang
Vollschwellend auf, wie wenn man Bouteillen füllt:
   Es steigt und steigt im Hals der Flasche—
      Sieh, und das liebliche Naß schäumt über.

O Sängerin, dir möcht' ich ein Liedchen weihn,
Voll Lieb und Sehnsucht! aber ich stocke schon;
   Ach, mein unselig Gleichnis regt mir
      Plötzlich den Durst und mein Gaumen lechzet.

Verzeih! im Jägerschlößchen ist frisches Bier
Und Kegelabend heut: ich versprach es halb
   Dem Oberamtsgerichtsverweser,
      Auch dem Notar und dem Oberförster.

(22 May 1841)

178

TO PHILOMEL

Like a musical scale your lamentation ascends in
   Swelling crescendo like flasks filling with liquid:
      Up the neck of the flask it mounts—
         Look, the delectable foam runs over.

Songstress! Much as I'd like to devote to you
   A ditty, loving and soulful, here I'm stuck;
      Ah, my infelicitous image
         Has made me thirsty all of a sudden.

Sorry, there's cool beer at the Huntsman's Rest
   And a game of skittles tonight: I've a date, sort of,
      With the county judiciary superintendent,
         The notary too, and the chief forester.

WALDPLAGE

Im Walde deucht mir alles miteinander schön,
Und nichts Mißliebiges darin, so vielerlei
Er hegen mag; es krieche zwischen Gras und Moos
Am Boden, oder jage reißend durchs Gebüsch,
Es singe oder kreische von den Gipfeln hoch,
Und hacke mit dem Schnabel in der Fichte Stamm,
Daß lieblich sie ertönet durch den ganzen Saal.
Ja, machte je sich irgend etwas unbequem,
Verdrießt es nicht, zu suchen einen andern Sitz,
Der schöner bald, der allerschönste, dich bedünkt.
Ein einzig Übel aber hat der Wald für mich,
Ein grausames und unausweichliches beinah.
Sogleich beschreib' ich dieses Scheusal, daß ihr's kennt;
Noch kennt ihr's kaum, und merkt es nicht, bis unversehns
Die Hand euch und, noch schrecklicher, die Wange schmerzt.
Geflügelt kommt es, säuselnd, fast unhörbarlich;
Auf Füßen, zweimal dreien, ist es hoch gestellt
(Deswegen ich in Versen es zu schmähen auch
Den klassischen Senarium mit Fug erwählt);
Und wie es anfliegt, augenblicklich lässet es
Den langen Rüssel senkrecht in die zarte Haut;
Erschrocken schlagt ihr schnell darnach, jedoch umsonst,
Denn, graziöser Wendung, schon entschwebet es.
Und alsobald, entzündet von dem raschen Gift,
Schwillt euch die Hand zum ungestalten Kissen auf,
Und juckt und spannt und brennet zum Verzweifeln euch
Viel Stunden, ja zuweilen noch den dritten Tag.
So unter meiner Lieblingsfichte saß ich jüngst—
Zur Lehne wie gedrechselt für den Rücken, steigt
Zwiestämmig, nah dem Boden, sie als Gabel auf—
Den Dichter lesend, den ich jahrelang vergaß:
An Fanny singt er, Cidly und den Zürcher See,
Die frühen Gräber und des Rheines goldnen Wein
(O sein Gestade brütet jenes Greuels auch
Ein größeres Geschlechte noch und schlimmres aus,
Ich kenn es wohl, doch höflicher dem Gaste wars.)—

PLAGUE OF THE FOREST

Everything in the forest, I find, is beautiful,
And nothing nasty, despite the multitude of things
Which flourish there: whether they creep in grass or moss
Along the ground, or hurtle through the shrubs full tilt;
Whether they sing in the tops of trees, or squawk in them,
Or hammer on the trunks of fir trees with their beaks,
Making the sweet sound echo all around the place.
Indeed, if anything might be a nuisance, why,
It's no trouble at all to sit down somewhere else,
In an even nicer place, the best imaginable.
Yet for me the forest harbors one iniquity,
A cruel one and almost inescapable.
I shall describe this monster, then you'll know of it;
You hardly know or notice it until, unwarned, your hand
Or else, more frightful still, your cheek begins to hurt.
It comes on wings, and humming, hardly audible;
And then it perches, at a tilt, on twice three feet
(That's why, for this invective, I have settled on
The classical senarius—most appropriate).
As soon as it arrives immediately it sinks
Its vertical proboscis into your tender skin;
Scared out of your wits you swipe at it, in vain,
For, with a graceful turnabout, the thing has gone.
Inflamed by the venom it has left, your hand at once
Is swollen like a cushion that has lost its shape,
Itching, stretching, burning, you'll be desperate
For hours on end, and sometimes it may last three days.
Thus I was sitting, lately, under my favorite fir—
It forks, near to the ground, with twin dividing boles
Molded like an upright chair to fit your back—
Reading the poet I'd forgotten about for years:
He sings his ladyfriend, called Fanny, and the Lake
Of Zürich, Cidli, early graves, and gold Rhine wine
(O but these monsters hatch on the banks of the Rhine, I know,
A larger breed, what's more, and worse, though more polite
They were to me the time when I was visiting there).

Nun aber hatte geigend schon ein kleiner Trupp
Mich ausgewittert, den geruhig Sitzenden;
Mir um die Schläfe tanzet er in Lüsternheit.
Ein Stich! der erste! er empört die Galle schon.
Zerstreuten Sinnes immer schiel' ich übers Blatt.
Ein zweiter macht, ein dritter, mich zum Rasenden.
Das holde Zwillings-Nymphenpaar des Fichtenbaums
Vernahm da Worte, die es nicht bei mir gesucht;
Zuletzt geboten sie mir flüsternd Mäßigung:
Wo nicht, so sollt' ich meiden ihren Ruhbezirk.
Beschämt gehorcht' ich, sinnend still auf Grausamtat.
Ich hielt geöffnet auf der flachen Hand das Buch,
Das schwebende Geziefer, wie sich eines naht',
Mit raschem Klapp zu töten. Ha! da kommt schon eins!
,,Du fliehst! o bleibe, eile nicht, Gedankenfreund!''
(Dem hohen Mond rief jener Dichter zu dies Wort.)
Patsch! Hab ich dich, Canaille, oder hab ich nicht?
Und hastig—denn schon hatte meine Mordbegier
Zum stillen Wahnsinn sich verirrt, zum kleinlichen—
Begierig blättr' ich: ja, da liegst du plattgedrückt,
Bevor du stachst, nun aber stichst du nimmermehr,
Du zierlich Langgebeinetes, Jungfräuliches!
—Also, nicht achtend eines schönen Buchs Verderb,
Trieb ich erheitert lange noch die schnöde Jagd,
Unglücklich oft, doch öfter glücklichen Erfolgs.

So mag es kommen, daß ein künftiger Leser wohl
Einmal in Klopstocks Oden, nicht ohn einiges
Verwundern, auch etwelcher Schnaken sich erfreut.

(Shortly before 8 September 1841)

Well now, a little fiddling troup had nosed me out
Beneath my fir, as there I sat and took my ease.
They're dancing all around my head in high delight.
I'm stung—the first, enough to make me furious.
I keep on squinting at the page, with errant mind.
A second sting, a third! and now I'm hopping mad.
The fair twin firtree nymphs were hearing words
They never had expected, so they asked me, murmuring,
To moderate myself or leave their place of peace.
And I complied, in shame, but plotting secretly the worst:
I held the book wide in the flat of my hand,
Meaning to kill the hovering varmints when they came
By clapping it shut. Ha! I see one coming now:
"Thou fleest, depart not, tarry, pray, thou friend of thought!"
(Thus did this poet once apostrophize the moon.)
Whack! Did I get you, rascal, did I? Yes? Or not?
And quickly as I could, for the desire to kill
Had turned into a quiet madness, paltry enough—
Greedily I turned the pages, yes: you're squashed,
Before you stung me, nevermore to sting again,
You delicate longlegged virginal creature, you!
—Thereafter, unconcerned by damage done to the book,
Long and merrily I maintained this vile pursuit,
Without success quite often, but more often with.

So may it come to pass that, at some future date,
A reader will be glad, perusing Klopstock's Odes,
And quite amazed to find some natty jokes in them.

AN LONGUS

Von Widerwarten eine Sorte kennen wir
Genau und haben ärgerlich sie oft belacht,
Ja, einen eignen Namen ihr erschufest du,
Und heute noch beneid' ich dir den kühnen Fund.

Zur Kurzweil gestern in der alten Handelsstadt,
Dich mich herbergend einen Tag langweilete,
Ging ich vor Tisch, der Schiffe Ankunft mit zu sehn,
Nach dem Kanal, wo im Getümmel und Geschrei
Von tausendhändig aufgeregter Packmannschaft,
Faßwalzender, um Kist' und Ballen fluchender,
Der tätige Faktor sich zeigt und, Gaffens halb,
Der Straßenjunge, beide Händ' im Latze, steht.
Doch auf dem reinen Quaderdamme ab und zu
Spaziert' ein Pärchen; dieses faßt' ich mir ins Aug'.
Im grünen, goldbeknöpften Frack ein junger Herr
Mit einer hübschen Dame, modisch aufgepfauscht.
Schnurrbartsbewußtsein trug und hob den ganzen Mann
Und glattgespannter Hosen Sicherheitsgefühl,
Kurz, von dem Hütchen bis hinab zum kleinen Sporn
Belebet' ihn vollendete Persönlichkeit.
Sie aber lachte pünktlich jedem dürft'gen Scherz.
Der treue Pudel, an des Herren Knie gelockt,
Wird, ihr zum Spaße, schmerzlich in das Ohr gekneipt,
Bis er im hohen Fistelton gehorsam heult,
Zu Nachahmung ich weiß nicht welcher Sängerin.

Nun, dieser Liebenswerte, dächt' ich, ist doch schon
Beinahe was mein Longus einen *Sehrmann* nennt;
Und auch die Dame war in hohem Grade *sehr*.
Doch nicht die affektierte Fratze, nicht allein
Den Gecken zeichnet dieses einz'ge Wort, vielmehr,
Was sich mit Selbstgefälligkeit Bedeutung gibt,
Amtliches Air, vornehm ablehnende Manier,
Dies und noch manches andere begreifet es.

TO LONGUS

We know full well a certain sort of loathsomeness,
And often angrily we both have laughed at it,
Indeed you even coined for it a proper name,
Bold find for which to this very day day I envy you.

Yesterday to pass the time in the old trade town
Where I was putting up, just for a day, and which
I found was getting me down with all its tedium,
Before my lunch, wishing to see the ships come in,
I walked to the canal where amid shouts and rumpus
Of a thousand-handed bustling crew of porters,
Cursing around their bales and crates, rolling their casks,
The work factor is evident and the urchin stands
To watch agape, his hands thrust in his jacket flaps.
But on the spotless crossway, up and down, there walked
A couple, and I took a good long look at them.
A gentleman in a green goldbuttoned cutaway, young,
With a pretty dame dolled up in the latest fashion kit.
Mustache-mindedness bore the whole fellow along,
And the feel of being safe in trousers tight as drums,
Briefly he was, from hatlet down to his tiny spurs,
Electrified accomplished personality.
But punctually she laughed at every feeble joke,
The lady did. The faithful poodle, lured to his master's
Knee, is tweaked by the ear to amuse her, painfully,
Until he emits, obedient, a high-pitched howl—
Which opera star he's imitating I don't know.

Well, this amiable person, so I thought, is just
About what my friend Longus called a Very Man;
And very, too, his lady friend, in high degree.
Yet the term denotes not merely the affected look,
Nor yet alone the swank, much more it is whatever
Has given itself importance with complacency,
The official air, a grand disdainful manner, these
And certain other features too the term implies.

Der Principal vom Comptoir und der Canzellei
Empfängt den Assistenten oder Commis—denkt,
Er kam nach elfe gestern nacht zu Hause erst—
Den andern Tag mit einem langen Sehrgesicht.
Die Kammerzofe, die kokette Kellnerin,
Nachdem sie erst den Schäker kühn gemacht, tut bös,
Da er nun vom geraubten Kusse weitergeht:
„Ich muß recht, recht sehr bitten!" sagt sie wiederholt
Mit seriösem Nachdruck zum Verlegenen.

Die Tugend selber zeiget sich in Sehrheit gern.
O hättest du den jungen Geistlichen gesehn,
Dem ich nur neulich an der Kirchtür hospitiert!
Wie Milch und Blut ein Männchen, durchaus musterhaft;
Er wußt' es auch: im wohlgezognen Backenbart,
Im blonden, war kein Härchen, wett' ich, ungezählt.
Die Predigt roch mir seltsamlich nach Leier und Schwert,
Er kam nicht weg vom schönen Tod fürs Vaterland;
Ein paarmal gar riskiert' er liberal zu sein,
Höchst liberal,—nun, halsgefährlich macht' er's nicht,
Doch wurden ihm die Ohren sichtlich warm dabei.
Zuletzt, herabgestiegen von der Kanzel, rauscht
Er strahlend, Kopf und Schultern wiegend, rasch vorbei
Dem duft'gen Reihen tiefbewegter Jungfräulein,
Und richtig macht er ihnen ein Sehrkompliment.

Besonders ist die Großmut ungemein sehrhaft.
Denn der Student, von edlem Burschentum erglüht,
Der hochgesinnte Leutnant, schreibet seinem Feind
(Ach *eine* Träne Juliens vermochte das!)
Nach schon erklärtem Ehrenkampfe, schnell versöhnt,
Lakonisch schön ein Sehr-Billett—es rührt ihn selbst.
So ein Herr X, so ein Herr Z, als Rezensent,
Ist großer Sehrmann, Sehr-Sehrmann, just wenn er dir
Den Lorbeer reicht, beinahe mehr noch, als wenn er
Sein höhnisch Sic! und Sapienti sat! hintrumpft.

TO LONGUS (continued)

The senior bank executive and office chief
Receives his clerk or his assistant—think,
He was not home last night before eleven o'clock—
The next day with a long censorious Very Face.
The chambermaid, the barmaid who is built to tease,
After she makes some rascal daring, acts annoyed
As soon as, from a stolen kiss, he ventures on
For something more: "The very idea!" she says, again
And again, with varying stress, to the embarrassed lad.

Virtue itself is pleased to parade in Veryness.
I wish you could have seen the youthful clergyman
Whose lecture I attended not so long ago
(Standing by the church door). Pink and white he was,
Like blood and milk, the little fellow, quite
Exemplary. He knew it, too: his mutton chops
Well-trained and blond did not contain a single hair,
I bet, he had not counted. From his sermon rose
A curious reek of *Leier und Schwert*, I thought; the theme
Pro patria mori—he would not let it drop,
And once or twice he even risked a liberal tone,
Most liberal—well, he played it safe, but you
Could see his ears glow at the mere thought of it.
At length, dismounted from the pulpit, radiant
He rushes, bobbing head and shoulders, past the rows
Of fragrant maidens who are deeply moved, and makes
Unerringly to all around his Very Bow.

Especially big-heartedness is very—most.
The student hot with high fraternity ideals,
The lofty-minded subaltern, will write his foe
(Ah, but a single tear from Julia does the trick),
Although the duel of honour is arranged, a note,
A Very Note, he's reconciled, it's beautiful,
Laconic, to the point, he's even stirred himself.
A Mr. X or Y, reviewer, likewise, is
A big Very Man, Very Very Man, when he gives
The laurel to you, almost more than when, with scorn,
He ends by trumping: *Sic*! and *Sapienti sat*!

187

Hiernächst versteht sich allerdings, daß viele auch
Nur teilweis und gelegentlich Sehrleute sind.
So haben wir an manchem herzlich lieben Freund
Ein unzweideutig Äderchen der Art bemerkt,
Und freilich immer eine Faust im Sack gemacht.
Doch wenn es nun vollendet erst erscheint, es sei
Mann oder Weib, der Menschheit Afterbild—o wer,
Dem sich im Busen ein gesundes Herz bewegt,
Erträgt es wohl? wem krümmte sich im Innern nicht
Das Eingeweide? Gift und Operment ist mirs!
Denn wären sie nur lächerlich! sie sind zumeist
Verrucht, abscheulich, wenn du sie beim Licht besiehst.
Kein Mensch beleidigt wie der Sehrmann und verletzt
Empfindlicher; wär's auch nur durch die Art wie er
Dich im Gespräch am Rockknopf faßt. Du schnöde Brut!
Wo einer auftritt, jedes Edle ist sogleich
Gelähmt, vernichtet neben ihnen, nichts behält
Den eignen, unbedingten Wert. Geht dir einmal
Der Mund in seiner Gegenwart begeistert auf,
Und was es sei—der Mann besitzt ein bleiernes,
Grausames Schweigen; völlig bringt dich's auf den Hund.
—Was hieße gottlos, wenn es dies Geschlecht nicht ist?
Und nicht im Schlaf auch fiel es ihnen ein, daß sie
Mit Haut und Haar des Teufels sind. Ich scherze nicht.
Durch Buße kommt ein Arger wohl zum Himmelreich:
Doch kann der Sehrmann Buße tun? O nimmermehr!
Drum fürcht' ich, wenn sein abgeschiedner Geist dereinst
Sich, frech genug, des Paradieses Pforte naht,
Der rosigen, wo, Wache haltend, hellgelockt
Ein Engel lehnet, hingesenkt ein träumend Ohr
Den ew'gen Melodien, die im Innern sind:
Aufschaut der Wächter, misset ruhig die Gestalt
Von Kopf zu Fuß, die fragende, und schüttelt jetzt
Mit sanftem Ernst, mitleidig fast, das schöne Haupt,
Links deutend, ungern, mit der Hand, abwärts den Pfad.
Befremdet, ja beleidigt stellt mein Mann sich an,

TO LONGUS (*continued*)

Next it is obvious, of course, that many
Are only Very People sometimes or in part.
We have observed the trait in several friends we love,
An unambiguous minor vein, and noticing it
Have clenched a fist inside a trouser pocket, true.
But when the thing is manifest in full attire,
Fake image of humanity, male or female, who
Can tolerate it if he has a healthy heart?
Who does not feel a twisting in his guts? It is
For me a poison, orpiment. If only they
Were laughable, but they are not. Mostly they are
Repugnant, horrid, when you see them in the light.
No one offends as strictly as the Very Man,
Or wounds as sensitively, even if it's just
The way he buttonholes you when he's talking. Mean!
Forthwith if one of them appears all finer things
Are numbed, abolished, nothing retains the least
Intrinsic absolute value. Should you once
Open your mouth to speak at all in a spirited way
When he is present, say what you will he meets it with
A leaden cruel silence; sure, it gets you down.
—Godless, what does it signify if not this breed?
And never even in their sleep to them occurs
The thought that they're the devil's creatures. Joking apart.
By penitence a sinner enters paradise:
But can a Very Man repent? Not on your life!
When his departed spirit in due course arrives,
Presumptuously enough, before the Gate of Heaven,
The rosy gate, where, keeping watch, with lustrous curls
An angel leans, his dreaming ear intent upon
Eternal molodies that sound from deep within,
Then, I'm afraid, the guardian looks up, so cool,
Measures this questioning form from top to toe and shakes
With gentle gravity, with pity almost, loath,
His lovely head and points to the left, the downward path.
Surprised, the man I'm talking of, offended even, still

Und zaudert noch; doch da er sieht, hier sei es Ernst,
Schwenkt er in höchster Sehrheit trotziglich, getrost
Sich ab und schwänzelt ungesäumt der Hölle zu.

(1841, before 24 November)

He hesitates; but when he sees that hereabouts
Matters are serious, he turns defiant on his heel
With a display of utmost Veryness, and struts
Promptly, cheerily, down the road that leads to Hell.

AN WILHELM HARTLAUB

Durchs Fenster schien der helle Mond herein;
Du saßest am Klavier im Dämmerschein,
Versankst im Traumgewühl der Melodien,
Ich folgte dir an schwarzen Gründen hin,
Wo der Gesang versteckter Quellen klang,
Gleich Kinderstimmen, die der Wind verschlang.

Doch plötzlich war dein Spiel wie umgewandt,
Nur blauer Himmel schien noch ausgespannt,
Ein jeder Ton ein lang gehaltnes Schweigen.
Da fing das Firmament sich an zu neigen,
Und jäh daran herab der Sterne selig Heer
Glitt rieselnd in ein goldig Nebelmeer,
Bis Tropf' um Tropfen hell darin zerging,
Die alte Nacht den öden Raum umfing.

Und als du neu ein fröhlich Leben wecktest,
Die Finsternis mit jungem Lichte schrecktest,
War ich schon weit hinweg mit Sinn und Ohr,
Zuletzt warst du es selbst, in den ich mich verlor;
Mein Herz durchzückt' mit eins ein Freudenstrahl:
Dein ganzer Wert erschien mir auf einmal.
So wunderbar empfand ich es, so neu,
Daß noch bestehe Freundeslieb und Treu!
Daß uns so sicherer Gegenwart Genuß
Zusammenhält in Lebensüberfluß!

Ich sah dein hingesenktes Angesicht
Im Schatten halb und halb im klaren Licht;
Du ahntest nicht, wie mir der Busen schwoll,
Wie mir das Auge brennend überquoll.
Du endigtest; ich schwieg—Ach warum ist doch eben
Dem höchsten Glück kein Laut des Danks gegeben?

Da tritt dein Töchterchen mit Licht herein,
Ein ländlich Mahl versammelt Groß und Klein,
Vom nahen Kirchturm schallt das Nachtgeläut,
Verklingend so des Tages Lieblichkeit.

(Ca. April 1842)

TO WILHELM HARTLAUB

Moonlight through the windowpane shone in;
You sat at the piano in the twilight,
Sunk in the dream surge of melodies;
I followed you, along beside dark valleys
Where the song of hidden rivulets was sounding,
Like children's voices swallowed by the wind.

But suddenly your playing turned around:
A blue expanse of sky seemed all there was,
And each tone like a silence long sustained.
Then all the firmament began to tilt,
The blithe remote host of stars was sliding
Down into a sea of golden mist,
Drop by drop flashing and fading in it,
Till ancient night enfolded empty space.

Then wakening a joyous life once more,
With fresh young light you terrified the darkness.
But I was far away, in thought and hearing,
And it was in yourself that I was lost.
Suddenly a ray of joy transfixed my heart,
I saw your virtues whole and all at once.
I sensed, and it was wonderful, so new,
That loyalty and friendship do persist;
And that delight in such a certain presence
Should keep our friendship firm in life's rampage.

I saw your face, poised at a certain angle
Half in the shadow, half in the clear light;
You did not know what feelings swelled my heart,
Nor how the burning tears came to my eyes.
You stopped. I did not say a word. Why is there
Never a murmur of thanks for purest joy?

Your little daughter came in then, with lights;
The people, big and small, sat round a country meal,
The evening bell tolled from the nearby steeple,
And faded with the sweetness of the day.

DIE SCHÖNE BUCHE

Ganz verborgen in Wald kenn' ich ein Plätzchen, da stehet
    Eine Buche, man sieht schöner im Bilde sie nicht.
Rein und glatt, in gediegenem Wuchs erhebt sie sich einzeln,
    Keiner der Nachbarn rührt ihr an den seidenen Schmuck.
Rings, soweit sein Gezweig' der stattliche Baum ausbreitet,
    Grünet der Rasen, das Aug' still zu erquicken, umher;
Gleich nach allen Seiten umzirkt er den Stamm in der Mitte;
    Kunstlos schuf die Natur selber dies liebliche Rund.
Zartes Gebüsch umkränzet es erst; hochstämmige Bäume,
    Folgend in dichtem Gedräng', wehren dem himmlischen Blau.
Neben der dunkleren Fülle des Eichbaums wieget die Birke
    Ihr jungfräuliches Haupt schüchtern im goldenen Licht.
Nur wo, verdeckt vom Felsen, der Fußsteig jäh sich hinabschlingt,
    Lässet die Hellung mich ahnen das offene Feld.
—Als ich unlängst einsam, von neuen Gestalten des Sommers
    Ab dem Pfade gelockt, dort im Gebüsch mich verlor,
Führt' ein freundlicher Geist, des Hains auflauschende Gottheit,
    Hier mich zum erstenmal, plötzlich, den Staunenden, ein.
Welch Entzücken! Es war um die hohe Stunde des Mittags,
    Lautlos alles, es schwieg selber der Vogel im Laub.
Und ich zauderte noch, auf den zierlichen Teppich zu treten;
    Festlich empfing er den Fuß, leise beschritt ich ihn nur.
Jetzo gelehnt an den Stamm (er trägt sein breites Gewölbe
    Nicht zu hoch), ließ ich rundum die Augen ergehn,
Wo den beschatteten Kreis die feurig strahlende Sonne,
    Fast gleich messend umher, säumte mit blendendem Rand.
Aber ich stand und rührte mich nicht; dämonischer Stille,
    Unergründlicher Ruh lauschte mein innerer Sinn.
Eingeschlossen mit dir in diesem sonnigen Zauber-
    Gürtel, o Einsamkeit, fühlt' ich und dachte nur dich!

(Summer 1842)

194

THE BEAUTIFUL BEECH TREE

Hidden deep in the wood I know of a place where a beech tree
   Stands, in beauty beyond any a picture can show.
Clean and smooth it rises up, strong-bodied, aloof,
   Swathed in silken allure none of its neighbors can touch.
Round it, far as the noble tree puts branches forth,
   Grows, delighting the eye, turf in a ring of green;
With radius always constant it circles the trunk in the center,
   Artlessly nature herself shaped this charming surround.
First it is fringed by wispy bushes; further back
   Trees with towering boles fend the heavenly blue.
Fulsome the dark oak grows and beside it the virginal
   Crest of the birch that, shy, sways in the golden light.
Only the spot where the path disappears, half-hidden by rocks,
   Out of the glade gives a hint of open country beyond.
—Not long since, walking alone, as the summery shapes,
   New, had lured me away from the path and I lost myself
In the bushes, a friendly spirit, the listening god of the grove,
   Led me here for the first time and in wonder I stood.
What delight! It was the moment of high noon,
   Everything was hushed, even the birds in the leaves.
And I was hesitant still to tread on the exquisite carpet;
   A ceremony it seemed, at length as I stole across.
Then, as I leaned against the trunk (its canopy billows
   Out not much overhead), freely my widening gaze
Followed the burning ray of the sun as it ran in a circle,
   Edging the shadowy round, almost measuring it.
There I stood, without moving, listening deep in myself
   To the demonic stillness, calm unfathomable.
With you enclosed in this magic circle of sun my only
   Thought, O solitude, my only feeling was you.

BEI DER MARIEN-BERGKIRCHE

O liebste Kirche sondergleichen,
Auf deinem Berge ganz allein,
Im Wald, wo Linden zwischen Eichen
Ums Chor den Maienschatten streun!

Aus deinem grünen Rasen steigen
Die alten Pfeiler prächtig auf,
An Drachen, Greifen, Laubgezweigen
Reich bis zum letzten Blumenknauf.

Und Nachtigall und Kukuk freuen
Sich dein- und ihrer Einsamkeit,
Sie kommen jährlich und erneuen
Dir deine erste Frühlingszeit.

Der Wohllaut deiner Orgeltöne
Schläft, ach, manch lieben langen Tag,
Bis einmal sich dein Tal der Schöne
Deines Geläutes freuen mag.

Dort, wo aus gelbem Stein gewunden
Die Treppe hängt, *ein* Blumenkranz,
Vertieft sich heut in Abendstunden
Mein Sinn in ihre Zierde ganz.

Sieh! ihre leicht geschlungenen Glieder
Verklären sich in rotes Gold!
Und horch, die Spindel auf und nieder
Gehn Melodien wunderhold!

Musik der hundertfachen Flöte,
Die mit dem letzten Strahl verschwebt,
Und schweigt,—bis sie die Morgenröte
Des gleichen Tages neu belebt.

(29 May 1845)

196

THE CHURCH OF
MARY AMONG THE HILLS

O loveliest church, without compare,
Alone upon the hill, in woods
Where lindens cast, among the oaks,
Shadows of Maytime round your nave.

Stately from your green turf the ancient
Columns rise, all richly wrought
With dragons, griffins, leafy sprays
Up to the flowered capitals.

And nightingale and cuckoo take
Joy in your solitude and theirs,
Yearly arriving they redeem
The time of your original spring.

The harmony of your organ notes,
Ah, many a good long day has slept,
Until your vale anon delight,
Charmed by the beauty of your bells.

There, woven of yellow stone,
The staircase hangs, a single wreath;
My mind on it this evening dwells,
Rapt in its delicate ornament.

Look how its loosely braided limbs
Become illumined, gold and red!
And up and down the spirals, listen,
Wondrous lovely melodies move!

Music of the hundredfold
Flute that fades as fades the light,
To silence—till it rouse anew
The rose dawn of the selfsame day.

GÖTTLICHE REMINISZENZ

Πάντα δι' αὐτοῦ ἐγένετο
Ev. Joh. 1,3

Vorlängst sah ich ein wundersames Bild gemalt,
Im Kloster der Kartäuser, das ich oft besucht.
Heut, da ich im Gebirge einsam ging,
Umstarrt von wild zerstreuter Felsentrümmersaat,
Trat es mit frischen Farben vor die Seele mir.

An jäher Steinkluft, deren dünn begraster Saum,
Von zweien Palmen überschattet, magre Kost
Den Ziegen beut, den steilauf weidenden am Hang,
Sieht man den Knaben Jesus sitzend auf Gestein;
Ein weißes Vlies als Polster ist ihm unterlegt.
Nicht allzu kindlich deuchte mir das schöne Kind;
Der heiße Sommer, sicherlich sein fünfter schon,
Hat seine Glieder, welche bis zum Knie herab
Das gelbe Röckchen decket mit dem Purpursaum,
Hat die gesunden, zarten Wangen sanft gebräunt;
Aus schwarzen Augen leuchtet stille Feuerkraft,
Den Mund jedoch umfremdet unnennbarer Reiz.
Ein alter Hirte, freundlich zu dem Kind gebeugt,
Gab ihm soeben ein versteinert Meergewächs,
Seltsam gestaltet, in die Hand zum Zeitvertreib.
Der Knabe hat das Wunderding beschaut, und jetzt,
Gleichsam betroffen, spannet sich der weite Blick,
Entgegen dir, doch wirklich ohne Gegenstand,
Durchdringend ew'ge Zeiten-Fernen, grenzenlos:
Als wittre durch die überwölkte Stirn ein Blitz
Der Gottheit, ein Erinnern, das im gleichen Nu
Erloschen sein wird; und das welterschaffende,
Das Wort von Anfang, als ein spielend Erdenkind
Mit Lächeln zeigt unwissend dir sein eigen Werk.

(1845, before 22 August)

198

DIVINE REMINISCENCE

Πάντα δι'αὐτοῦ ἐγένετο
St. John 1,3

I saw a strange painting, quite some time ago,
In the Carthusian abbey where I've often been.
Today in the mountains over there, walking alone,
Round me the bone-hard wilderness of shattered rocks,
It came back to my mind with colors live and fresh.

Beside a steep ravine, its edge of meager grass
Shaded by a pair of palms the tenuous fare
Of goats feeding aslant on the precipitous slope,
One sees the young boy Jesus sitting on some stones;
Beneath him for his cushion a white fleece is spread.
I thought the child less childish than he might have been;
The heat of summer (this must be his fifth at least)
Has given his skin, clad as he is down to the knees
In the yellow robe with crimson hem, a delicate tan,
Likewise his face, the cheeks gentle and full of health.
In his dark eyes a quiet fiery energy glows,
Yet a strange charm, ineffable, surrounds the mouth.
An old shepherd amiably stoops before the child
And has this moment handed him a fossil shell,
Curiously formed, to help him pass the time away.
The boy has looked upon this wondrous thing and now,
As if taken aback, his wide gaze opens out
And looks straight at you, but, since nothing is there,
Pierces eternal vistas of unbounded time:
As if there flashed out of his cloudy brow the light
Divine, a memory, which in the selfsame instant will
Vanish without a trace; it is the maker of all,
The original Word, as an earthly child at play, who smiles
And shows you, not that he knows of it, this work, his own.

KEINE RETTUNG

Kunst! o in deine Arme wie gern entflöh ich dem Eros!
　　Doch, du Himmlische, hegst selbst den Verräter im Schoß.

(Before 30 August 1845, possibly some years earlier)

NO ESCAPE

Art, how gladly I'd seek your embrace and escape from love—
But the betrayer is there, held in your heavenly arms!

VOM KIRCHHOF

Gräschen, wenn auch noch so schlicht,
Eine Hand verschmäht dich nicht.
Bring ihr eine leise Kunde
Von dem mütterlichen Grunde,
Dem bescheiden du entsprossen,
Wo der Tau auf dich geflossen,
Den, die Mitternacht zu weihen,
Jenes Gartens Wächter streuen.

(1845)

FROM THE CHURCHYARD

Blade of grass, plain though you be,
One hand hath no scorn of thee.
Go to her, a word to breathe
Of the mother-ground beneath,
Whence in modesty you grew,
Moistened by the falling dew
That garden's watchers scatter far,
To consecrate the midnight hour.

AUF EINE LAMPE

Noch unverrückt, o schöne Lampe, schmückest du,
An leichten Ketten zierlich aufgehangen hier,
Die Decke des nun fast vergeßnen Lustgemachs.
Auf deiner weißen Marmorschale, deren Rand
Der Efeukranz von goldengrünem Erz umflicht,
Schlingt fröhlich eine Kinderschar den Ringelreihn.
Wie reizend alles! lachend, und ein sanfter Geist
Des Ernstes doch ergossen um die ganze Form—
Ein Kunstgebild der echten Art. Wer achtet sein?
Was aber schön ist, selig scheint es in ihm selbst.

(1846)

ON A LAMP

Not yet disturbed, O lovely lamp, you still adorn,
Gracefully suspended here on slender chains,
The ceiling of this pleasance, near-forgotten now.
On your white marble bowl, around whose rim is twined
A wreath of ivy leaves in greenish golden bronze,
Children happily join to dance a roundelay.
What charm throughout! laughing, yet the whole form
Ringed by a gentle flowing spirit of seriousness.
A work of art, the genuine thing. Who notices it?
Yet blithely beauty seems to shine in self-content.

WEIHGESCHENK

Von kunstfertigen Händen geschält, drei Äpfelchen, zierlich,
    Hängend an *einem* Zweig, den noch ein Blättchen umgrünt;
Weiß wie das Wachs ihr Fleisch, von lieblicher Röte durch-
        schimmert;
    Dicht aneinander geschmiegt, bärgen die nackten sich gern.
Schämet euch nicht, ihr Schwestern! euch hat ein Mädchen
        entkleidet,
    Und den Chariten fromm bringet ein Sänger euch dar.

(Early June 1846)

OFFERING

Peeled by dexterous hands, three little apples, so delicate,
    Hung on a single twig still with a circlet of leaf;
White as wax their flesh suffused with a shimmer of rose,
    Close together they cling, naked and eager to hide.
Do not be bashful, sisters, it was a girl who undressed you;
    And to the Graces Three he brings you, a poet demure.

NEUE LIEBE

Kann auch ein Mensch des andern auf der Erde
Ganz, wie er möchte, sein?
—In langer Nacht bedacht' ich mir's, und mußte sagen, nein!

So kann ich niemands heißen auf der Erde,
Und niemand wäre mein?
—Aus Finsternissen hell in mir aufzückt ein Freudenschein:

Sollt ich mit Gott nicht können sein,
So wie ich möchte, Mein und Dein?
Was hielte mich, daß ich's nicht heute werde?

Ein süßes Schrecken geht durch mein Gebein!
Mich wundert, daß es mir ein Wunder wollte sein,
Gott selbst zu eigen haben auf der Erde!

(1846)

NEW LOVE

Is there no way, on earth, for anyone,
Wanting it so, to belong to another being?
—Far into the night I thought, and had to answer: none.

So cannot I belong, on earth, to anyone
Or call another being mine?
—Out of the dark in me a ray of joy begins to shine:

Now should I not so share with God my being,
Wanting it, that he shares his with mine?
Why I should not today be his, there is no reason.

A sweet amazement thrills me to the bone:
I marvel to have thought it such a marvel
That God himself, on earth, should be my own.

ERBAULICHE BETRACHTUNG

Als wie im Forst ein Jäger, der, am heißen Tag
Im Eichenschatten ruhend, mit zufriednem Blick
Auf seine Hunde niederschaut, das treue Paar,
Das, Hals um Hals geschlungen, brüderlich den Schlaf,
Und schlafend noch des Jagens Lust und Mühe teilt:
So schau ich hier an des Gehölzes Schattenrand
Bei kurzer Rast auf meiner eignen Füße Paar
Hinab, nicht ohne Rührung; in gewissem Sinn
Zum ersten Mal, so alt ich bin, betracht ich sie,
Und bin fürwahr von ihrem Dasein überrascht,
Wie sie, in Schuhn bis überm Knöchel eingeschnürt,
Bestäubt da vor mir liegen im verlechzten Gras.

Wie manches Lustrum, ehrliche Gesellen, schleppt
Ihr mich auf dieser buckeligen Welt umher,
Gehorsam eurem Herren jeden Augenblick,
Tag oder Nacht, wohin er nur mit euch begehrt.
Sein Wandel mochte töricht oder weislich sein,
Den besten Herrn, wenn man euch hörte, trugt ihr stets.
Ihr seid bereit, den Unglimpf, der ihm widerfuhr,
—Und wäre sein Beleidiger ein Reichsbaron—
Alsbald zu strafen mit ergrimmtem Hundetritt
(Doch hiefür hat er selber zu viel Lebensart).
Wo war ein Berg zu steil für euch, zu jäh ein Fels?
Und glücklich immer habt ihr mich nach Haus gebracht;
Gleichwohl noch nie mit einem Wörtchen dankt' ich euch,
Vom Schönsten was mein Herz genoß erfuhrt ihr nichts!

Wenn, von der blausten Frühlingsmitternacht entzückt,
Oft aus der Gartenlaube weg vom Zechgelag
Mein hochgestimmter Freund mich noch hinausgelockt,
Die offne Straße hinzuschwärmen raschen Gangs,
Wir Jünglinge, des Jugendglückes Übermaß
Als baren Schmerz empfindend, ins Unendliche
Die Geister hetzten, und die Rede wie Feuer troff,
Bis wir zuletzt an Kühnheit mit dem sichern Mann
Wetteiferten, da dieser Urwelts-Göttersohn

EDIFYING OBSERVATION

Like as an hunter in the woods, on a hot day
Reposing in the shade of an oak, with gaze content
Might look upon his hounds, the loyal twain
Which, neck entwined with neck, fraternally share
Their sleep and even in sleep the chase's toil and joy—
So do I here, at the shady edge of a thicket
Resting awhile, gaze down upon my pair
Of feet, with some emotion; in a certain sense
I see them for the first time, old as I am,
And am surprised indeed that they exist,
Lying before me as they do, laced to the ankles
In shoes all over dust in the parched grass.

For many a lustrum, loyal mates, you've been
Carrying me around upon this humpy world,
Obedient to your master every moment,
Night or day, wherever he might go.
Whether his conduct was advised or foolish
You bore him as the best of possible masters,
At least in your opinion. You are prepared
To punish any insult offered him
(Even if the offender were a baron)
With an angry kick in the ass (though, to be sure,
For such a dealing he's far too polite).
Was ever a hill or crag too steep for you?
And always you have brought me safely home:
Albeit I never thanked you with a single word—
Perfection of desire, and you knew nothing!

When in the bluest midnight hour of springtime
My fond ecstatic friend would lure me on
To leave the arbor where we sat imbibing,
And along the open road we rushed in a stampede
Of dreams and longings, for we felt, being young,
The exuberance of youth as a mere tenuous pain,
And chasing after spirits into the infinite,
Our speech a stream of fire, until at length

211

In Flößerstiefeln vom Gebirg' zum Himmel sich
Verstieg und mit der breiten Hand der Sterne Heer
Zusammenstrich in einen Habersack und den
Mit großem Schnaufen bis zum Rand der Schöpfung trug,
Den Plunder auszuschütteln vor das Weltentor—
Ach, gute Bursche, damals war't ihr auch dabei,
Und wo nicht sonst, davon ich jetzo schweigen will!

Bleibt mir getreu, und altert schneller nicht als ich!
Wir haben, hoff' ich, noch ein schön Stück Wegs vor uns;
Zwar weiß ich's nicht, den Göttern sei es heimgestellt.
Doch wie es falle, laßt euch nichts mit mir gereun.
Auf meinem Grabstein soll man ein Paar Schuhe sehn,
Den Stab darüber und den Reisehut gelegt,
Das beste Sinnbild eines reisenden Wandersmanns.
Wer dann mich segnet, der vergißt auch eurer nicht.
Genug für jetzt! denn dort seh' ich's gewitterschwer
Von Mittag kommen, und mich deucht, es donnert schon.
Eh' uns der Regen übereilt, ihr Knaben, auf!
Die Steig' hinab! zum Städtchen langt sich's eben noch.

(Between 22 May and 29 June 1846)

We emulated that huge creature of our legends,
The Certain Man, son of gods and the primeval world
Who climbed up from the mountaintops to heaven
In boots as big as rafts and swept the stars
Into his haversack, which then he lugged
Panting and snorting to the edge of creation
And dumped the lot at the gate of the universe—
Ah, my good fellows, you were there as well;
In other places too, which I'll not mention.

Stay loyal to me and age no faster than I shall.
We have, I hope, a good long way to go;
Of course, I cannot tell, the gods decide,
But come what may, do not repent of me.
My tombstone shall display a pair of shoes
And, over them, a hat and walking stick:
The traveler at rest, his perfect emblem.
If someone blesses me, he'll bless you too.
Enough for now. The southern sky looks dark,
There'll be a storm, I think it's thundering.
Let's go, my boys, before the rain can catch us up—
Down here, we'll reach the little town in time.

IM PARK

Sieh, der Kastanie kindliches Laub hängt noch wie der feuchte
  Flügel des Papillons, wenn er die Hülle verließ;
Aber in laulicher Nacht der kürzeste Regen entfaltet
  Leise die Fächer und deckt schnelle den luftigen Gang.
—Du magst eilen, o himmlischer Frühling, oder verweilen
  Immer dem trunkenen Sinn fliehst du, ein Wunder, vorbei.

(Probably spring 1847)

IN A PARK

Look how they hang, the childish leaves of the chestnut, still
  Moist like butterfly wings fresh from the broken cocoon;
But nights are warm and the briefest sprinkle of rain descending
  Quietly spreads their fans, roofing the alley of air.
Whether you hurry or stay, heavenly spring, always you sweep
  Over the drunken mind, soon like a miracle gone.

DENK' ES, O SEELE

Ein Tännlein grünet wo,
Wer weiß, im Walde,
Ein Rosenstrauch, wer sagt,
In welchem Garten?
Sie sind erlesen schon,
Denk' es, o Seele,
Auf deinem Grab zu wurzeln
Und zu wachsen.

Zwei schwarze Rößlein weiden
Auf der Wiese,
Sie kehren heim zur Stadt
In muntern Sprüngen.
Sie werden schrittweis gehn
Mit deiner Leiche;
Vielleicht, vielleicht noch eh'
An ihren Hufen
Das Eisen los wird,
Das ich blitzen sehe!

(Ca. September 1851)

THINK NOW, O SOUL

A little pine is sprouting
Somewhere in a forest,
A rose bush, who can tell
The garden that it grows in?
Already they are destined,
Think now, O soul,
To take root in your grave
And to grow there.

Two black ponies crop
Grass in the pasture,
Back to town they go,
Happily cantering.
They'll walk step by step
Pulling your corpse;
Perhaps, perhaps before
Their hoofs let fall
The iron shoes
That I see shining.

CORINNA

Wir sahn dich im geschwisterlichen Reigen
Voll Anmut, Blume unter Blumen, schweben,
Im Lächeln blühete die Seele dir
Ganz *eines* mit der sichtbaren Gestalt
—Sie wußt' es nicht—, heraus aufs Angesicht
Unschuld'ge Freude, dem Beschauer fast
So innig fühlbar wie der Tänzerin!

O wessen ganzes Sein und Leben doch
Sich so bewegte durch des Jahres Kreis
In holdem Gleichmaß jeglichen Moment,
Sich selber so zu seliger Genüge
Und alle Welt zu letzen, zu erbaun!

(June 1854)

CORINNA

We saw with your sisters in the ring dance,
A flower mid flowers, swaying, full of grace,
Your soul was blossoming in your smile, it was
Entirely one with the body that was visible
—Not knowing it—and risen to your face
Innocent joy, by the beholder almost
As inly to be felt as by the girl who danced.

O, whose entire life and being yet
Might move throughout the circle of the year,
Each moment in a sweetly balanced measure,
So blessèd and so blithe in self-contentment,
Meaning delight and uplift for us all.

ERINNA AN SAPPHO

Erinna, eine hochgepriesene junge Dichterin des griechischen
Altertums, um 600 v.Chr., Freundin und Schülerin Sapphos zu
Mitylene auf Lesbos. Sie starb als Mädchen mit neunzehn
Jahren. Ihr berühmtestes Werk war ein episches Gedicht, „Die
Spindel," von dem man jedoch nichts Näheres weiß. Überhaupt
haben sich von ihren Poesien nur einige Bruchstücke von
wenigen Zeilen und drei Epigramme erhalten. Es wurden ihr
zwei Statuen errichtet, und die Anthologie hat mehrere Epigramme
zu ihrem Ruhme von verschiedenen Verfassern.

„Vielfach sind zum Hades die Pfade," heißt ein
Altes Liedchen—„und einen gehst du selber,
Zweifle nicht!" Wer, süßeste Sappho, zweifelt?
Sagt es nicht jeglicher Tag?
Doch den Lebenden haftet nur leicht im Busen
Solch ein Wort, und dem Meer anwohnend ein Fischer von Kind auf
Hört im stumpferen Ohr der Wogen Geräusch nicht mehr.
—Wundersam aber erschrak mir heute das Herz. Vernimm!

Sonniger Morgenglanz im Garten,
Ergossen um der Bäume Wipfel,
Lockte die Langschläferin (denn so schaltest du jüngst Erinna!)
Früh vom schwüligen Lager hinweg.
Stille war mein Gemüt; in den Adern aber
Unstet klopfte das Blut bei der Wangen Blässe.

Als ich am Putztisch jetzo die Flechten löste,
Dann mit nardeduftendem Kamm vor der Stirn den Haar-
Schleier teilte,—seltsam betraf mich im Spiegel Blick in Blick.
Augen, sagt' ich, ihr Augen, was wollt ihr?
Du, mein Geist, heute noch sicher behaust da drinne,
Lebendigen Sinnen traulich vermählt,
Wie mit fremdendem Ernst, lächelnd halb, ein Dämon,
Nickst du mich an, Tod weissagend!
—Ha, da mit eins durchzuckt' es mich
Wie Wetterschein! wie wenn schwarzgefiedert ein tödlicher Pfeil
Streifte die Schläfe hart vorbei,

ERINNA TO SAPPHO

(Erinna, a highly esteemed young poetess of Greek antiquity,
was a friend and pupil of Sappho's around 600 B.C. She
died when she was nineteen. Her most famous work was an
epic, *The Spindle*, of which only the title is known. Of
her work, indeed, only some fragments of a few lines and
three epigrams have survived. Two statues were erected
to her, and the Greek anthology contains several epigrams
by various authors in praise of her.)

"Manifold are the paths to Hades," says an
Old song—"and one of them will be yours to walk,
Have no doubt of it!" Who, Sappho sweetest, doubts it?
Doesn't each day say the same?
But the living aren't likely to take such a saying
Heavily to heart, and the fisherman down by the sea
From childhood on, he hardly hears the wavebeat falling.
—Yet strangely my heart took fright today. Listen!

Early sunlight in the garden
Circling the tops of trees
Enticed this lazybones (not long ago that's what you called me)
Out of my sultry bed betimes.
I felt at peace; but through my veins
The blood pulsed fitfully, and my cheeks were pale.

Then as I unloosed my braids at the dressing table,
And with my scented comb parted in front the hanging
Veil of hair—a strange meeting of eyes occurred in the mirror.
Eyes, I said, what can it be you want of me?
Spirit of mine, you're safe at home in there today,
Faithfully wed to living senses,
As with a serious look, to put me off, half smiling, a demon now,
You nod at me and prophesy death!
—Ha! then the shiver pierced me
Like lightning! as if a deadly blackflighted arrow
Shot past hardly missing my head,

Daß ich, die Hände gedeckt aufs Antlitz, lange
Staunend blieb, in die nachtschaurige Kluft schwindelnd hinab.

Und das eigene Todesgeschick erwog ich;
Trockenen Aug's noch erst,
Bis da ich dein, o Sappho, dachte,
Und der Freundinnen all,
Und anmutiger Musenkunst,
Gleich da quollen die Tränen mir.

Und dort blinkte vom Tisch das schöne Kopfnetz, dein Geschenk,
Köstliches Byssosgeweb', von goldnen Bienlein schwärmend.
Dieses, wenn wir zunächst das blumige Fest
Feiern der herrlichen Tochter Demeters,
Möcht' ich *ihr* weihn, für meinen Teil und deinen;
Daß sie hold uns bleibe (denn viel vermag sie),
Daß du zu früh dir nicht die braune Locke mögest
Für Erinna vom lieben Haupte trennen.

(1863, before 27 June)

And covering my face with my hands I sat there a long time,
Staring down amazed into the dizzying dark abyss.

And I pondered my own death;
Dry-eyed at first,
Until my thoughts turned, Sappho, to you
And to all my friends
And the graceful art of the Muses,
It was then the flood of tears came.

There, gleaming on the table, I saw your gift, the beautiful
                hairnet,
Fine fabric of Byssos, swarming with little golden bees.
This, when next we celebrate the flowery feast
Of Demeter's sovereign daughter,
I wish to consecrate to her, on my behalf and yours;
That she may favor us (for she is powerful),
That you may not need to sheer too soon from your beloved head
The brown curl, in mourning for Erinna.

Aus: BILDER AUS BEBENHAUSEN

I
Kunst und Natur

Heute dein einsames Tal durchstreifend, o trautestes Kloster,
Fand ich im Walde zunächst jenen verödeten Grund,
Dem du die mächtigen Quader verdankst und was dir zum
Schmucke
Deines gegliederten Turms alles der Meister verliehn.
Ganz ein Gebild des fühlenden Geistes verleugnest du dennoch
Nimmer den Mutterschoß drüben am felsigen Hang.
Spielend ahmst du den schlanken Kristall und die rankende
Pflanze
Nach und so manches Getier, das in den Klüften sich birgt.

V
Sommer-Refektorium

Sommerlich hell empfängt dich ein Saal; man glaubt sich in
einem
Dom; doch ein heiterer Geist spricht im Erhabnen dich an.
Ha, wie entzückt aufsteiget das Aug' im Flug mit den schlanken
Pfeilern! Der Palme vergleicht fast sich ihr luftiger Bau.
Denn vielstrahlig umher aus dem Büschel verlaufen die Rippen
Oben und knüpfen, geschweift, jenes unendliche Netz,
Dessen Felder phantastisch mit grünenden Ranken der Maler
Leicht ausfüllte; da lebt was nur im Walde sich nährt:
Frei in der Luft ein springender Eber, der Hirsch und das
Eichhorn;
Habicht und Kauz und Fasan schaukeln sich auf dem Gezweig.
—Wenn, von der Jagd herkommend als Gast hier speiste der
Pfalzgraf,
Sah er beim Becher mit Lust über sich sein Paradies.

VIII
Am Kirnberg

Hinter dem Bandhaus lang hin dehnt sich die Wiese nach Mittag,
Längs dem hügligen Saum dieser bewaldeten Höhn,

From PICTURES FROM BEBENHAUSEN

I
Nature and Art

Walking today in your lonely vale, O abbey of mine,
  Soon in the forest I found that empty abandoned dell
To which you owe your massive stones and all the adornments
  The master builder himself gave to your jointed tower.
Image you are of the sensing spirit but never deny
  The womb that gave you birth, on the rocky slope over there.
Playful you mime the slender crystal and rambling plant,
  Various animals too, lurking there in the clefts.

V
The Summer Refectory

A room receives you, bright as summer, you think you have
                entered
    A cathedral, and yet sublimity's language is light.
Ha, the joy of the eye as it mounts in flight with the slender
    Columns! Airy their form, and a palmtree springs to mind,
For all around at the top the ribbings in radiant lines
    Arch out from the tufts, weaving that infinite net
Into whose fields the painter touched, fantastic, these tendrils
    Of green, filling them up; you see what feeds in the woods:
Floating in air a boar in mid-leap, squirrel and roebuck;
    Hawk and pheasant and owl balance among the boughs.
—The Count Palatinate, come from the hunt to dine as a guest
                here,
    Quaffing his wine would have seen his own paradise overhead.

VIII
The Kirnberg

Behind the granary, far to the south the meadow extends,
    Undulating along the edge of these woody heights,

Bis querüber ein mächtiger Damm sich wirft wie mit grünem
    Sammet gedeckt: ehdem faßte das Becken den See,
Welcher die Schwelle noch netzte des Pförtleins dort in der Mauer,
    Wo am eisernen Ring spielte der wartende Kahn.
Sah ich doch jüngst in der Kirche das Heiligenbild mit dem
        Kloster
    Hinten im Grund: tiefblau spiegelt der Weiher es ab.
Und auf dem Schifflein fahren in Ruh zwei Zisterzienser,
    Weiß die Gewänder und schwarz, Angel und Reuse zur Hand.
Als wie ein Schattenspiel, so hell von Farben, so kindlich,
    Lachte die Landschaft mich gleich und die Gruppe mich an.

X
Nachmittags

Drei Uhr schlägt es im Kloster. Wie klar durch die schwülige
        Stille
    Gleitet herüber zum Waldrande mit Beben der Schall,
Wo er lieblich zerfließt, in der Biene Gesumm sich mischend,
    Das mich Ruhenden hier unter den Tannen umgibt.

(September–October 1863)

To the point where a thick dam traverses it, mantled it looks
  In green velvet; but once this basin was framing the lake
Which lapped against the step to the little gate in the wall there.
  Here a boat would be bobbing, moored to an iron ring,
As I know from a picture I saw in the chapel, the background
            showing
  First the abbey itself, mirrored dark blue in the pool,
Then two Cistercians peacefully drifting along in the boat,
  Robed in black and in white, with basket and fishing rod.
Like a magic lantern display, so clear and childish the colors,
  The landscape sparkled for me with laughter, and so did the
            monks.

X
Afternoon

Three o'clock strikes in the abbey. How clear the trembling sound
  Slides through the breathless hush down to the edge of the
            wood,
Where it trickles away and sweetly melts into the hum of bees
  Surrounding me here as I sit quietly under the pines.

IN GEDANKEN AN
UNSERE DEUTSCHEN KRIEGER

Bei euren Taten, euren Siegen
Wortlos, beschämt hat mein Gesang geschwiegen,
Und manche, die mich darum schalten,
Hätten auch besser den Mund gehalten.

(Ca. March 1871)

THOUGHTS CONCERNING
OUR GERMAN WARRIORS

Through all your victories and achievements
Wordless, in shame, my song kept silence.
Better for some who found me wrong
Also to have held their tongue.

NOTES

POEMS BY FRIEDRICH HÖLDERLIN

ALS ICH EIN KNABE WAR / WHEN I WAS A BOY: This mythological
epitome of H.'s boyhood could have been arrived at via a Rouss-
eauistic model, possibly *Emile* (see note to "The Rhine"). H.'s
actual early education, at the Denkendorf theological seminary,
was strictly monastic.

HYPERIONS SCHICKSALSLIED / HYPERION'S SONG OF FATE: Published
in the second volume of H.'s novel *Hyperion*, 1799; probably
written toward the end of 1797.

DIE KÜRZE / BREVITY: Among H.'s earlier poems (1786–87) there
are several in quasi-classical stanza form (alcaics), which show
Klopstock's influence; likewise during his first year as a student at
Tübingen (1788–89). But from about 1790 until 1796 H. culti-
vated the trochaic four-beat or five-beat line in eight-line stanzas
with Schiller as his model (hymns to Freedom, Love, Beauty,
Truth, Humanity, Immortality). During 1796 he returned to the
classical forms and developed his own modifications of them,
limiting himself to the asclepiadic and the alcaic stanza forms.
'Die Kürze' is asclepiadic:

$$/ \; \cup \quad / \quad \cup \; \cup \; / \qquad\qquad / \quad\quad \cup \; \cup \quad / \quad \cup \qquad /$$
Warum bist du so kurz? | liebst du, wie vormals, denn

$$/ \quad \cup \qquad / \quad \cup \quad \cup\, / \qquad / \qquad\quad \cup \; \cup \quad / \quad \cup \qquad\quad /$$
  Nun nicht mehr den Gesang? | fandst du, als Jüngling, doch,

$$/ \quad \cup \quad / \quad \cup \quad \cup \; / \quad \cup \; /$$
    In den Tagen der Hoffnung,

$$/ \qquad \cup \quad / \quad \cup \quad \cup \; / \quad \cup \; /$$
      Wenn du sangest, das Ende nie!

Cesura (vertical line) occurs in the first two lines after the third
beat.

    "Dem Sonnengott," which follows, is alcaic:

$$\cup \quad / \quad \cup \qquad / \quad \cup \quad / \qquad \cup \quad \cup \qquad / \, \cup \quad /$$
    Wo bist du? trunken dämmert die Seele mir

$$\cup \quad / \quad \cup \quad / \quad \cup \quad \cup \quad / \quad / \, \cup \quad /$$
    Von aller deiner Wonne; denn eben ist's

$$\cup \quad / \qquad \cup \, / \qquad \cup \qquad / \; \cup \; / \quad \cup$$
      Daß ich gesehn, wie, müde seiner

$$/ \qquad \cup \; \cup \; \cup \quad / \; \cup \; \cup \quad / \qquad \cup$$
        Fahrt, der entzückende Götterjüngling [. . .]

Here the cesura normally occurs in the first two lines after the second beat; H. syncopates by introducing a grammatical pause (with the question: "Wo bist du?) before the cesura following "trunken." The cesura in line 2 would normally come after "deiner"; but in the line given the grammar ("sense") liquefies the cesura (no pause in the phrase "Von aller deiner Wonne"), and introduces a grammatical pause in the middle of the third measure (dactylic): "Wonne; denn . . ."

The rugous verbal textures so achieved, with their varying tensions and eccentric word ordering, meant a refiguring of the German lyric idiom on levels reaching to the roots of the language. Orthodox nineteenth- and early twentieth-century metricians (such as Andreas Heusler) censured H.'s metric for being at points out of accord with his Greek (quantitative) models, as when he places a dactylic foot at the end of an asclepiadic stanza, instead of a cretic. Actually H.'s new and singularly German symphonic structures are comparable to those which Horace had brought into Latin poetry, also by modifying Greek measures.

The mood tonalities of the two types of stanza are different. Friedrich Beissner characterizes the asclepiadic as "darkly pensive, hesitant," and the alcaic as "bright and rapid, rushing." In musical terms: the asclepiadic rhythm ranges between andante and adagio, the alcaic between allegro and presto.

The translations only approximate to the original measures.

AN DIE PARZEN / TO THE FATES: Capital *E* in lines 1 and 11 of the German conventionally indicates emphasis on the whole word.

DER MENSCH / MAN: Alcaic. The first three stanzas and line 1 of stanza 4 consist, despite the period at the end of stanza 2, of a single sentence: an opening dependent clause ("Kaum sproßten . . .") completed by a main clause ("da . . . wo . . . lag . . . dein schönstes Kind"). The ensuing *Und* (stanza 4, line 2) continues this sentence, which advances like a great wave to the end of stanza 6, announcing man's desire to resemble nature, by being, like her, all-embracing. The imagery of man's origin and desire is then succeeded by six stanzas (of which the last four are self-contained) presenting in sections, with a kind of ebbing motion, ritardando, the actuality of man's fate.

MEIN EIGENTUM / MY POSSESSION: Alcaic. Some translators (Hamburger, Henderson) translate the title into the plural, "My Possessions." But the possession in question is the gift of poetry (*Gesang*): H. evidently means *Eigentum* in the sense of that which is intrinsic (*eigen*) to oneself. After the first three descriptive and contemplative stanzas, H. addresses here a series of presences in turn: light, the breeze, heavenly altitudes, song, and heavenly powers. As in some other poems, this makes for a kind of *canto clusus*: one overhears the voice enclosed in a monologue, though that monologue is addressed to presences whose response is desired, or who provoke the monologue by occupying the poet's imagination (cf. "Man").

DER NECKAR / THE NECKAR: Alcaic. The Neckar is the preeminent river in Swabia. An earlier draft of the poem has the title "Der Main," another river but, like the Danube (Donau), less exclusively Swabian. Rivers figure strongly in H.'s poems; he was versed in the topography of Europe, at least below the 49th parallel, from the Middle East, including Turkey, across the Alps, to the Atlantic coast (see also "Brot und Wein"). It is said that, in one room where he was living, the walls were covered with maps.

Pactolus: river in Lydia (now western Turkey) once renowned for its gold deposits.

Smyrna: port on west coast of Turkey, now Izmir.

Ilium's woodland: forests around ancient Troy.

Sounium: the southernmost promontory of Attica, where there is a ruined temple of Poseidon.

Olympion: sanctuary of the temple of the Olympian Zeus in Athens.

Mastic tree: evergreen resinous tree or shrub (*Pistacia lenticus*).

DER ABSCHIED / THE FAREWELL: Asclepiadic ("Lebenslauf," above, also). Beissner provides two versions of this poem; Mieth, in his Hanser Verlag edition (1970), follows Hellingrath's earlier provision of three versions, with the present text as the third, not second, version. The poem concerns H.'s separation from Susette Gontard (Diotima). After he left the Gontard household on about 25 September 1798, H. lived at Homburg, not far from Frankfurt-am-Main, and he was able occasionally to meet Susette in secret. They last saw each other on 8 May 1800.

In stanzas 7–9 I read the present tense verbs *ist*, *gehn*, and *führet* in such a way as to bring out the future tense which they can grammatically imply, and which they do imply with a certain force if *die Vergessenen* is read (as Beissner suggests) as a deponent (Latin *obliti*: "we who are to be forgotten"). The result is a more complex time pattern than that given in Hamburger's Bollingen translation. The implied future occurs in an eternal place which can only be imagined in the present actual place of farewell ("die Stelle des Abschieds"). The last stanza refers to the actual present again.

DICHTERBERUF / THE POET'S VOCATION: This paraphrase may help:

Stanzas 1–2: Dionysus (Bacchus), the god, roused up the peoples of the East; we too live in a time of deep disturbance—shall we be awakened by such a god?

Stanzas 3–12: the poet's concern is not so much practical affairs as the most lofty and divine modes of being; the poet sings the divine ever anew, so that people may feel it more clearly. Yet, whereas nature was the context of the poet's first inspirational meeting with the divine, should he not sing of nature (stanzas 5–6)? Should he not sing of the great actions of history in his time (stanza 7)? And, if he were to relate the divine to nature and to history, should he not guard against any profaning of the divine (stanza 10), which might result in his own loss of soul (stanza 12)?

Stanzas 13–16: Divine things are now in danger of such profaning (secularization). Knowledge, including scientific or statistical enquiry, can tend to sacrilege, disastrous for man. Yet man's power is limited by God himself. Our gratitude for being, as a divine mystery, is knowledge: and the poet likes to have communion with other human beings, since they may help him to understand the mystery (cf. "Bread and Wine" IV). In society, the poet has a mediating function. Yet, if necessary, the poet as man still stands alone before God. If God is not there, a man has his simplicity to protect him; and even the lack of God may eventually help him to realize his inner resources of strength and vision.

Penultimate stanza: difficulties in the German here are the indeterminate *es* of line 2, indeterminate predicate of *helfen*, and the word order of "damit verstehn sie helfen." "Ihn kennt der Dank": the *Ihn* probably refers back to *Himmel*. The translation leans heavily on explanatory notes in Beissner's edition.

BROT UND WEIN / BREAD AND WINE: Meter: elegiac distichs (coupled hexameters, the second with a masculine cesura after the third beat). One of the six monumental elegies written 1799–1801. Translations of others can be read in Michael Hamburger's Bollingen *Poems and Fragments*: "The Archipelago," "Menons Lament for Diotima," and "Homecoming."

Heinze: Wilhelm Heinse (1749–1803), to whom the poem is dedicated, was the author of the extraordinary hellenophile-utopian-bohemian novel *Ardinghello* (1787), which influenced H.'s novel *Hyperion* and his conception of pre-Socratic Greek philosophy. Heinse also wrote a novel about music and a long treatise on chess games. He was a friend of the Gontard family and was host to H. and Susette Gontard, accompanied by her four children and the Swiss governess Marie Rätzer, when they arrived in Kassel in July 1796 as refugees from the Frankfurt area, which had been overrun by Napoleon's Sambre-Maass army. He was the one older living writer who was consistently friendly toward Hölderlin.

There are three MS texts of the poem, of which the earliest was entitled "Der Weingott." Lines 1–18 were published by Leo von Seckendorf in his *Musenalmanach für das Jahr 1807*; their first recorded admirers appear to have been the poet Clemens Brentano and his wife Sophie Mereau.

The poem unfolds the fabulous vista of H.'s Hellenic imagery, clouded with anguish (however tempered) at the godlessness of his own times. The presiding "god" of the poem is Dionysus;

Christ appears at the end of VI and in lines 5–6 of VIII much less forcefully. The Christian symbols of bread and wine are detached from their doctrinal context (historically a rather late context, in any case), and are attached to Dionysus as a joyous god who mediates in transactions between heaven and earth (as in the growing of grapes). However, the poem is consistently a *social* text. It bears on the mythic and on the historical contexts of the urban scene of the first section. In IX, the phrase "fruit of the Hesperides" connotes, as in some earlier poems, Western youth of the changed culture that is coming to be, guided by spiritual values, outcome of the age of revolution and of the "night" during which the gods are withdrawn. A more Christian-mystical vision of sacred night, as cosmic source of divine and human being, appears in the *Hymns to the Night* by Novalis (Friedrich von Hardenberg, 1772–1801), published in the periodical *Athenäum* in 1800 and in the 1802 edition of Novalis' works.

Thebe: a river nymph (pronounced *theebee*).

Ismenos: river in Boeotia, near the city of Thebes.

Kadmos: legendary founder of Thebes, Dionysus' birthplace, from which the Dionysian or Bacchic rites spread to other parts of Greece.

Fackelschwingend, in IX ("bearing the torch"), is linked in the texture of light-symbolism with the phrase "mit Fackeln geschmückt" ("twinkling") of line 2 in I. Dionysus (the "Syrian") is traditionally pictured as bearing a torch through the subterranean darkness (as in the Eleusinian initiation rites). Hence *Cerberus*: the monstrous dog which guards the entrance to the Greek underworld.

DER RHEIN / THE RHINE: In 1801 H. was beginning to write the poems which have been called *Vaterländische Gesänge*, and which were inspired to some extent by Pindar (ca. 522–435 B.C.). These are anything but "patriotic" poems, but the burden of them is H.'s quest for the meaning of his Germany in the history of the human spirit. There are eleven of these poems (which are often called "hymns"); three are reprinted here, "The Rhine," "Patmos," and "Remembrance." "The Rhine" was probably begun while H. was a transient house-tutor at Hauptwil in Switzerland, from mid-January to mid-April 1801, and it was completed during the same year. There are three Ms texts and some variant readings. The poem was first published in Leo von Seckendorf's *Musenalmanach für das Jahr 1808*. Originally the dedication was to Wilhelm Heinse, but this was changed after Heinse's death in 1803. Isaak von Sinclair (1775–1815) was a revolutionary democrat, a jurist by profession, and a supporter of the French revolutionary cause even after Napoleon came to power. H. and he had been friends since 1795, when they met in Jena; Sinclair was expelled from the university there for his part in student disturbances. He was later a civil servant in Homburg, employed by Landgrave Friedrich V of Hessen-Homburg, and he made it possible for H. to live there from about 26 June 1804 until September 1806. On 26 February 1805, Sinclair was arrested and subsequently tried for high treason against the Grand Duke of Württemberg. During the proceedings, questions were asked about H., but the poet's eccentricities appear to have frustrated the commission of enquiry. By 1805, H., though losing his sanity, was preoccupied with his last Pindar translations and commentary, and he used to improvise, night and day, at the piano, often with wild hammerings on the keyboard (see *Hölderlin: Eine Chronik in Text und Bild*, ed. A. Beck and P. Raabe, Frankfurt am Main, 1970, 72–74; also M. B. Benn, *Hölderlin and Pindar*, The Hague, 1962). It was Sinclair who brought the mad H. to Tübingen in 1806.

As for the dialectical structure of "The Rhine," H. wrote the following marginal note: "The law of this poem [*dieses Gesanges*] is that the first two parts are formally opposed as progression and regression, but are alike in subject matter; the two succeeding parts are formally alike but are opposed as regards subject matter; the last part, however, balances everything out with a continuous metaphor." The fifteen strophes are divisible into five sets of three strophes each (triads). H.'s "first two parts" would be strophes 1–3 and 4–6; his "two succeeding parts" strophes 7–9 and 10–12; and his "last part" strophes 13–15. For further information, see F. Beissner's notes in the Grosse Stuttgarter Ausgabe, *Sämtliche Werke* 2: 438–40; also B. Boeschenstein, *Hölderlins Rheinhymne* (Zürich-Freiburg i.Br. 1959).

Morea: the Peloponnesus (southern part of Greece).

Tessin, Rhodanus (*Ticino, Rhodanus*): rivers which rise near the source of the Rhine.

Nach Asia (*toward Asia*): the Rhine flows east from its source, turning northward only when it reaches Chur in the Graubünden mountains.

Zerreißt er die Schlangen (*he rends those snakes*): allusion to Hercules, who is said to have been assailed in his cradle by two snakes sent by the goddess Hera.

Rousseau: There is an unfinished ode to R. by H. (ca. 1799–1800). H. had admired him as a "sage" since student days in Tübingen, both on account of his inspiring the libertarian forces of the French Revolution and for his analysis of the tensions arising between nature and culture.

Bielersee (*Lake Bienne*): Rousseau stayed during 1765 on the Peterinsel in this lake. The translation gives the (usual) French name.

Ein Weiser (*one wise man*): Socrates is meant, at the symposium which later provided the name for Plato's dialogue on love.

Im Stahl (In the steel blade): might allude to Sinclair's revolutionary activism. Pierre Bertaux, in a 1968 address to the Hölderlin Society, considerably surprised his audience with his hypothesis that Sinclair and H. were members of a revolutionary (Jacobin) conspiracy in 1799, aimed at the establishing of a Swabian Republic. Extracts of this (seemingly far-fetched) lecture appeared in *Alternative* (Berlin), April-June 1968, no. 4, and the whole appeared in *Hölderlin-Jahrbuch* 1969.

VULKAN / VULCAN: Alcaic. This poem, and the five which follow, were among the nine poems which H. called *Nachtgesänge* ("Night Songs"). It is believed that some of the poems were begun during the summer of 1802, soon after H.'s return from France. The "Night Songs" were published by Friedrich Wilmans (1764–1830), the Frankfurt publisher, in his *Taschenbuch für das Jahr 1805*.

An earlier version of "Vulkan" has the title "Winter." Vulcan, Roman god of artificers, especially of smiths, is a presiding deity of fire. The poem is one of few by H. in which an immediate context of conception or of composition can be detected: here a fireside indoors, while the north wind (Boreas) blows outside (cf. "Greece" for another such context).

BLÖDIGKEIT / BEING DIFFIDENT: Asclepiadic. Two earlier drafts are entitled "Dichtermut" ("The Poet's Courage").

Line 9: the elliptical grammar here can be spelled out as "Denn seit die Menschen gleich den Himmlischen ein einsam Wild waren" ("For, since men and gods alike were lonely animals"). *Schicklich* (last line) connotes *pure*; as it follows the previous "Geschickt einem zu etwas," one is tempted to read into *schicklich* a muted sense of the noun *Geschick*, which for H. denotes *skill* (Greek *techne*). The image of the gods holding humans like children on "leading strings" (in American English "harnesses") can be traced back to Homer, *Iliad* VIII, 18 ff., and to Plato, *Theaetetus* 155, and *Laws* 644. The phrase "zur Wende der Zeit" has strong Christian apocalyptic associations: in the ripeness of time, when the cycle of the spiritual life shall have brought again the moment of harmony between divine and human spheres of being.

GANYMED / GANYMEDE: Alcaic. An earlier version was entitled "Der gefesselte Strom" ("The Enchained Stream").

Ganymede, in Greek myth, was the son of the Trojan king Tros and the nymph Kallirrhoe, thus grandson of the river Skamander (which rises in the Ida Mountains), and great-grandson of the aquatic Titans Okeanos and Tethys. Zeus was captivated by Ganymede's beauty and, taking the form of an eagle, carried him off to become his cupbearer. The poem telescopes human and elemental features in a riverine personification of the coming of spring. On another level, the poem concerns the eruptive force of poetic inspiration.

LEBENSALTER / THE AGES OF LIFE: One of the most original features in Hölderlin's view of ancient Greece was his sense for Asiatic components in Greek mythology—long before Creuzer and half a century before Gérard de Nerval's *Voyage en Orient* (1851). This poem gives a flash of the Asia which Hölderlin imagined, including Syria, source of the Adonis myth.

Städte des Euphrats (*cities of Euphrates*): Babylon, Nineveh, cities on the river Euphrates.

Palmyra: ancient city in Syria, destroyed by the Romans in A.D. 273.

Der Seligen Geister (*the blessed souls*): literally "spirits of the blest." *Geister* is the subject of *erscheinen*.

DER WINKEL VON HARDT / TILTED STONES AT HARDT: Refers to a structure of two massive inclined slabs of stone near Hardt, between Nürtingen and Denkendorf. From under the trees here one sees the Aich valley (*Grund*). The popular Duke Ulrich of Württemberg took refuge inside the structure when he was being hunted down by other Swabian nobles in 1519. It is said that a spider's web across the opening dissuaded the pursuers from looking inside. Condensed space-time imagery in lines 2–4: the leaves of the trees are like buds insofar as you can detect below and beyond them the valley, as you can detect in a bud the flower to be.

HÄLFTE DES LEBENS / THE HALF OF LIFE:

Heilignüchtern: translated as "holy lucid" rather than "holy sober." The adjective epitomizes a complex of ideas with which H. was concerned at the time (1801–3). "Holy" connotes the ecstatic otherness of divine elemental being—the "fire from heaven," and "holy pathos," which H. regarded as the source of Greek poetic art. "Lucid:" H. regarded lucidity or sobriety of imagination and of reason as the *antithetic* source of Western ("Hesperian") poetic art. The two sources are dialectically related: the Greek poet is in quest of sobriety, the Hesperian in quest of "holy pathos." This formulation simplifies a much-discussed area in H.'s later thought and poetics. There is a consensus that his statements concerning these matters in his letter to Casimir Ulrich Böhlendorff, dated 4 December 1801, meant that he no longer saw classical Greek poetic art as an all-time model for poetry. "Modern" poetry must be constructed on its own fundamental cultural premises, and the modern poet should learn from the Greeks how to make "free use" of what is peculiarly "his own." Peter Szondi argues that this did not mean (as has often been thought) a "return" to autochthonous poetic impulses (the so-called *vaterländische Umkehr*), but an *integration* of "alien" and autochthonous values, an alliance of precision and passion (*Präzision, Wärme*) such as is found in the new tonalities of H.'s poems after 1801. See P. Szondi, *Hölderlin-Studien* (Frankfurt am Main, 1967), 95–100.

The poem itself, with its ellipses, plasticity, or "phanopoeia," and magical evocativeness, prefigures post-Symbolist poetry of more than a century later. Note also the abrupt change of key between lines 7 and 8. There is a comment on the poem in Michael Hamburger's *Contraries* (New York, 1970), 268–69.

PATMOS: The text reprinted is that of the dedication copy, which Sinclair handed to Landgrave Friedrich on 6 February 1803. H. may have been working on the poem and on his poem 'Der Einzige' ('The Only One,' about Christ) during the period autumn 1801–autumn 1802. But the last months of 1802 seem a more likely date. Variant readings occur in Ms texts of a somewhat later date (summer and autumn 1803). Michael Hamburger's Bollingen selection contains a translation of a later version. Landgrave Friedrich V (1748–1820) was a religious man and in politics a liberal authoritarian. In 1794 he published a book inveighing against "dangerous" irreligious books which might lead to "false freedom and Jacobinism," and he wrote in 1797–98 a sharp critique of the French Revolution. But he also protested against oppression by authority and insisted on rights under the law. H. met him in October 1802 in Regensburg. The dedication text was first published by Leo von Seckendorf in his *Musenalmanach für das Jahr 1808*. Like "The Rhine," the poem consists of five triads. In the original, each strophe has fifteen lines. In translating the text, I opted for a freer layout, while keeping the strophic divisions intact. My aim in this was to sharpen the profiles of particular words and phrases, and to invest the English with some of the glowing and vigorous rugosity which H. achieves by rhythmical turns, elliptical syntax, eccentric word order, and changes of key.

Patmos: an island in the Sporades (Aegean Ocean), where St. John the Divine is said to have written his Book of Revelations. H. shared the common belief that this John was identical with the apostle John. By an act of astonishing creative audacity, the poem is made to travel in space and time to that region, and on to the Holy Land during the period of Christ's death and transfiguration, thence to the descent of the spirit at Pentecost. Eventually it returns to the present and future of German spirituality and "German song."

Strophe 3. Pactolus: gold-bearing river which rises in Mt. Tmolus (old Asia Minor, now Turkey). *Tauros, Messogis*: mountains in the same region.

Strophe 7: da nun es Abend geworden (as night had begun): the "night" is brought on by Christ's absence. The "shadow" here refers to Christ's appearance to the disciples on the way to Emmaus (Luke 24, 13 ff.).

Strophe 9. Alludes to Christ's transfiguration.

Strophe 11. Bild (image): usually understood as a graven image.
Strophe 12 entails a warning against any image making which is
not grounded in illumination; the sense here—across ellipsis and
the silence marked by the dash after *Knecht*—is that punishment
is visited upon those who commit such hubristic sacrilege (cf.
"The Poet's Vocation"; for parallels in H.'s *Empedocles*, see the
translations of that drama in Hamburger's Bollingen selection).
The second part of strophe 12 is complicated by H.'s insistence
that "they" (the divine powers), be their context Greek or
Christian, are subject to omnipotent fate, *Schicksal*.

Strophe 13: der Stab / des Gesanges (the song's / Staff): the
image has a prototype in Moses' shamanic rod in Exodus 17,6 or
in the angel's staff of Judges 6,21. *Augenbraunen*: older form of
Augenbrauen.

Strophe 14: Dich (you): Landgrave Friedrich. *Seine Werke
(his works)*: "Known unto God are all his works from the begin-
ning of the world, "Acts 15,18 (cf. Mörike's "Göttliche Reminis-
zenz").

ANDENKEN / REMEMBRANCE: The scenes remembered are French;
the poem was probably written in spring 1803, about nine months
after H.'s return from Bordeaux. The poem appeared in Leo von
Seckendorf's *Musenalmanach für das Jahr 1808*.

Geh nun (but now go): addressing the northeast wind ("best
loved" because it would be blowing from Germany and finding
H. in southwest France). The "remembrance" throughout
presents events as happening now, not merely as a recollected
past.

Garonne: river which flows from the southeast into the sea
near Bordeaux, after joining with the Dordogne, which flows
from east to west (cf. strophe 5).

Bellarmin: a friend of Hyperion's in H.'s novel *Hyperion*; it is
probable that H. had Sinclair in mind.

An der luftigen Spitz (by the windy point): a point of land where
the two rivers meet.

Die See (The sea): here both a physical presence (the Atlantic)
and a symbolic one. Tentative paraphrase: the men of action go
out to sea where raw unreflected life is experienced in all its
fullness (strophe 4). This going-to-the-source is exacting and
dangerous, whether the quest is physical or spiritual. From the
ulterior fullness (both matter and spirit?) come the elements
that can be composed into the work which has beauty; from there,
too, memory comes, and to it memory returns. Love, which makes
us look upon persons and things with steady and intent gaze, can
stabilize the flux and variety of the fullness. But the poet, who
remembers and loves, actually inaugurates (the deeper sense of
stiften) what is perennial in the flux (whatever has authentic
constancy). The sea appears to have features of the human psyche.

WIE VÖGEL LANGSAM ZIEHN / LIKE SLOW FLYING BIRDS: This and the next four poems are fragmentary texts from the so-called *Hymnische Entwürfe*—drafts for hymnic poems sketched during the two or three years before H. became insane in 1806. I have translated, again, with a freer layout, prompted by the gaps and silences in some of the originals of this period.

DIE TITANEN / THE TITANS: In H.'s later mythological world view the revolt and overthrow of the Titans, as hubristic usurpers of divine roles, precedes the return of the "gods." Here, as the Titans have not yet been "fettered" (line 3), mankind is still in a transitional period of "night," of waiting, during which divine being cannot be perceived immediately (cf. the last 3 strophes of "Patmos").

DER VATIKAN / THE VATICAN: The original text has no strophic divisions at all. The liberty I have taken in dividing the translation into five sections rests on the following considerations: (1) a massive, but fragmentary, text may be more readable in this format; (2) the divisions are made at points where motifs do change; (3) such divisions, consistent with the breakup of the straight lefthand margin, serve to suggest an imaginable unity of which one can lose track while reading a cryptic text which *appears* as a typographic continuum; (4) the contemporary English reader's typographic sense will have followed, through the works of Pound, Williams, and Olsen, a course of development on which, I believe, H. would not have frowned.

Beissner considers that "The Vatican" contains echoes of Heinse's novel *Ardinghello* (see note to "Bread and Wine"). Heinse is meant by "my honest master (up in Westphalia)", for he lived at Bad Driburg, near Paderborn.

Julius Geist (*Caesar's ghost*): Julius Caesar reformed the Roman calendar in 46 B.C.

Türkisch (*Turkish*): Greece at this time was under Turkish rule.

die Rippe tönet (*the rib seasounds*): the "rib" analogy is based on the French *côte* = either "rib" or "coast."

GRIECHENLAND / GREECE: The original has no strophic divisions; for English layout, see note on 'The Vatican.' The pretext of composition (or conception) might have been the sight of a school building and sounds of children shouting (English strophes 1–2). *Griechenland* would then be the name H. gave to the images and to the thoughts on history which assailed him as he looked and listened. The poem is a fleeting conspectus of the Hellenic sense of *measure*, as a coordinate between human and divine being. The end of (English) strophe 2 and parts of 3 are reminiscent of Heraclitus. But the conspectus makes "Greece" a real presence, in the mind, in the air, in the landscape, sharply in focus, but so volatile that it enters, with a key change as chromatic as some of those in Bach's Cantata BWV.169, into the vision of what perennially occurs at turning points in history (English strophe 5).

English strophe 5: I translate *ausgehn* as "launch forth," not "extinguished" as Hamburger does. I construe the passage to mean that earth contains an occult vein of *Urbilder*, primordial images, which emerge spontaneously in times of historical crisis and shape events (metaphysical patterns of history). The poem peters out on the edge of a vision of civilization made safe, while the traveler, the "spirit unappeasable and peregrine," continues his walk, with *measured* stride, out into a world further on that is made more ravishingly beautiful by his "love of life."

ZU SOKRATES' ZEITEN / IN SOCRATES' TIMES: Though the original is fragmentary, it might appear that it was not a draft for a contemplative hymn (like "The Vatican"), but the whole outline of a shorter poem, possibly a ferocious invective against the times. Or it could be a sketch for a monologue from the mouth of Timon of Athens.

WENN AUS DER FERNE / IF FROM THE DISTANCE: Alcaic. The (unfinished) poem was probably written during the very early period of H.'s madness. It has the fullness, starkness, and tension which are missing from his subsequent verse. The speaker is selfevidently Diotima: Susette Gontard had died in June 1802, while H. was on the way back from France. *You* refers to H., who is likewise the "young man" of stanza 9.

NOTES

POEMS BY EDUARD MÖRIKE

AN EINEM WINTERMORGEN, VOR SONNENAUFGANG / ON A WINTER
MORNING, BEFORE SUNRISE: The translation is somewhat of a make-
shift fake antique. Not that much of the sense of the original is
lost, but the sinuous taut feel of the original is absent. Some lines
slacken the pull of the original rhythms. Other difficulties posed
by the German are the internal sound patterns, the subtle cross-
weave of masculine and feminine rhymes, and the elements of
Romantic vocabulary. The original refreshed such words as *Herz,
Busen, Genius, Wunderkräfte,* even *schwanken*; but these
seraphic terms cannot be re-enlivened now. Further: every line
in the German is a sense unit. It is anachronistic to insert, as I
have done, the enjambment between lines 5 and 6 of stanza 3.
True, the run-on line was familiar in German after Goethe's
early lyrics; but in historical terms, however desirable it may be
to "make it new," an enjambment like "and so / Luminous" is
a jarring anachronism. The sense unit line is a formal validation
of the "sense of a universe" (Paul Valéry) in the poem; other
validation occurs through the sensory and perceptual detail and
by verbal minutiae, such as rhythmic shifts, key changes, and
shifts in perspective (from sight to sound, from touch to sight).
As a text about "inspiration," the poem might be compared with
Hölderlin's "Ganymed," or with stanzas 5–10 of Hölderlin's
"Dichterberuf."

GESANG ZU ZWEIEN IN DER NACHT / SONG FOR TWO IN THE NIGHT:
The poem appears also in M.'s "fantasmagoric interlude," "The
Last King of Orplid" (in his novel *Malter Nolten*, 1832), where
it is spoken by the wicked enchantress Thereile and the aged
but undying king Ulmon. It also appears in a fragment called
"Spillner," written while M. was a student at Tübingen. There
it is preceded by comments from Spillner, a student in the
university jail, which may record an actual moment of "in-
spiration:" "I had stayed up by the light of my lamp until
midnight: suddenly I get a ringing in my ears, and, as if some

kind of enchantment is pressing on my brain, I am that moment
transported into a most strange orbit of thoughts; as if bewitched,
I gaze at the milling motions which start to occur in my head,
amid sounds of ringing and buzzing; I feel my condition clearly,
but I could not shake off the mild madness of it, as it settled quietly,
numbingly, more and more, around my head. I wondered if I
was awake or asleep, for a few moments I thought I had become
clairvoyant, it was as if my thoughts all culminated in the sharpest
points. And I was afraid, as one is afraid of ghosts, indeed I was in
a frightful state. Then suddenly nearby a thrush begins to sing; it
was in the window of my friend I——. Never in my life have I felt
such a deep inner comfort, my heart leaped in my body, and all
the uncanny thoughts were dissipated by the simple natural notes
of this bird; I walked to the bars and let the night air blow in
upon me. Everything quiet in the narrow streets. I felt a piety
I'd never known before, fervor, healthy bright-eyed life; I pressed
my face against the bars to see if the morning star was rising over
a rooftop, but there was nothing to be seen. The thrush kept
singing in long bursts, and in among them I could hear, so I felt,
quite different sounds, the trembling of the air, which is so strange,
when the night feels the first touches of morning. My imagination
set me free, and some verses formed themselves involuntarily on
my lips . . ." (tense changes as in original).

BESUCH IN URACH / URACH REVISITED: M. had been at the Urach
Klosterschule from his fourteenth to his eighteenth year (1818–22).
The trees, torrent, valley, hills, and fortress are still much as he
saw them. See Introduction for other remarks. I have not
attempted a rhymed translation.

  Stanza 10, line 7. Elastisch angespannt (ethereally tensed): in
M.'s Tübingen the word *elastisch* would have applied to bodies
capable of expansion without change of substance, rather than
to textiles (as for us). He may, too, have been familiar with the
young Hegel's use of the word as an attribute of air—the Greek
aithēr. The "primary form" of light's "reality" is, for the young
Hegel, "infinite elasticity" (see Rosenkrantz, *Hegels Leben*,
Berlin, 1844, 116, quoted by Emil Staiger, *Meisterwerke deutscher
Sprache*, Zürich-Berlin, 1943, 15). Hölderlin uses the noun
Elastizität ["Deines Geistes" ("elasticity of your spirit")] in his
letter to Böhlendorff, dated 4 December 1801. The Greek original
is ἐλαυνεῖν (*elaunein*): to drive.

ERSTES LIEBESLIED EINES MÄDCHENS / GIRL'S FIRST LOVE SONG: In
several early poems, as in the late poem 'Erinna to Sappho,' M.
"lends his voice" to a girl. One may or may not choose to construe
this stratagem as (a) a way of making the *anima* speak, and (b)
an indirect form of self-expression.

SCHERZ / JOKE: 1829 (14 August) is the year of M.'s engagement to
Luise Rau (1806–91). The engagement was broken off in 1833.

The poem 'Scherz' imitates Catullan hendecasyllabics: *passer mortuus est meae puellae, | passer, deliciae meae puellae* . . . M.'s Catullus translations appeared in his *Classische Blumenlese*, 1840. In his little preface to the Catullus section, he wrote: "Of course he is lascivious in high degree, but his purer erotic poems have an enchanting coloration. If he lets himself go sometimes, this is perhaps very closely connected with what makes him so attractive as a human being."

PEREGRINA: The biographical context of this cycle is still fairly dark. The girl whom M. called Peregrina was found in a species of somnambulistic trance on the roadside outside Ludwigsburg, around Easter 1823. Nobody knew who she was, and she was very beautiful. An innkeeper employed her at his bar for a few months, during which time M., on vacation from Tübingen, made her acquaintance briefly. She soon disappeared again (going to Heidelberg, where she was also found in a trance). Hearing that her magic was dubious, M. broke with her during the winter 1823–24 (no letters survive). It is likely that he did not see her again after the brief Ludwigsburg encounter. Twice she tried to see him in Tübingen (June 1824 and April 1826), but he apparently was obdurate. The girl's actual name was Maria Meyer, and she came from Schaffhausen (East Switzerland). She was born in 1802, the illegitimate daughter of a Helena Meyer (born 1777), and spent much of her early youth in the poorhouse. In late July 1817 she ran away, with the itinerant group of malcontents and religious eccentrics who formed the entourage of Mme. von Krüdener, wandering wife of the Russian liberal General von Krüdener. Maria stayed with the group for three or four months, reaching Kassel. Thence she returned to Schaffhausen. After a period of some months in Rheinfelden (East Switzerland) as housemaid (where she is recorded to have been a religious self-flagellant), she disappeared again. She emerged in Berne toward the end of 1820 (here she is said to have had an epileptic fit in a church). Then she was sent back to Schaffhausen. Little is known of her then until she came to Ludwigsburg. Eventually she married a cabinetmaker, lived indigently for several years in Winterthur, and lastly in the tiny Swiss village of Wilen, Canton Thurgau, where she died in 1865. Source: P. Korrodi, *Das Urbild von M.'s Peregrina. Jahrbuch der literarischen Vereinigung Winterthur*, 1923.

At the time of her acquaintance with M., she used to profess admiration for Karl Ludwig Sand, the student who had assassinated the playwright Kotzebue, on the grounds that the latter was a Czarist spy, in 1817. Sand was executed in 1820.

A variant version of the cycle appears in *Maler Nolten*: there the half-gipsy cousin of Nolten, Elisabeth, who brings doom to all and sundry, was modeled on Maria. Section III did not appear in the present form until the fourth edition of M.'s poems in 1867.

Weymouthsfichte (*weeping pine*): botanically this tree does not exist. It is probable that M. felt an association between *Weymouth* and *Wehmut* (sadness).

DIE TRAURIGE KRÖNUNG / MOURNFUL CORONATION: M.'s popular fame rests largely on his ballads (and narrative idylls). This is the only one I risked translating. I cannot advise the reader to fill the gap by reading the translations in Cruikshank-Cunningham (see bibliography).

DER STRÄFLING / THE PRISONER: The English removes one of Wispel's footnotes (after *Aquavit*, stanza 2). *Jabbadizing*: English Wispelese for "jeopardizing" (dräuen = drohen).

As early as 1826 M. is recorded (by Ludwig Bauer) as inventing eccentric characters during fantastic spates of vocal improvisation. Liebmund Maria Wispel—"barber's apprentice and *bel esprit*"— was one of these. He eventually found his way into *Maler Nolten*, where he appears usually in disguise (as an artist, as an art dealer) and speaking with liberal doses of curious French. In fact the Wispel of *Maler Nolten* is a malicious and pretentious nonentity. These diabolic traits had been softened by 1837, when M. wrote out his eleven poems for Ludwig Bauer, in an extravagantly flowery script (varying from poem to poem). There was also a special high fluting voice which M. invented for the recital of his works. The poems were called *Sommersprossen* ("Freckles"), and they are unique among other nonsense poems of the nineteenth century (Edward Lear, Lewis Carroll, Wilhelm Busch, Paul Scheerbart), not least for their being largely non-narrative: here M. prefigures Christian Morgenstern. Wispel also has mannerisms of spelling and pronunciation: *Bansicht* (for *Ansicht* = "view"), *baichen* (for *eigen* = "own," translated as "boriginal"), and *wismen* (for *widmen* = "devote" or "dedicate"). The so-called *Wispeliaden* include a prose fragment in which Wispel, accompanied by his "brother," an "Uchdrucker" (for "Buchdrucker" = "book printer"), appears as a professor who challenges the categories of Linnaeus. He does so in terms which indicate that M. was basing this version of Wispel on the sayings of the prolific but obscure Gotha professor, Johann Georg Galletti (1750–1828), whose "Lectern Flowers" are now collected under the quotation title *Das größte Insekt ist der Elefant*, ("The Elephant is the Largest Insect") edited by H. Minkowski (Munich 1965).

JOHANN KEPLER: The "star" in question is the planet Mars. Kepler (1571–1630) was a Swabian astronomer in the great Platonic and Pythagorean tradition going back to Albertus Magnus. He inherited Tycho Brahe's collection of data on planetary motions; the three laws which he verified served as the foundation for

Newton's mechanics. He is also remarkable for his esthetic joy at the truth of the Copernican system: "I have attested it as true in my deepest soul and I contemplate its beauty with incredible and ravishing delight," also for his quest for "mathematical harmonies in the mind of the Creator," not merely for empirical rules (see W. C. Dampier, *A History of Science*, Cambridge [England]: 1961, 127).

The elegiac distichs of the poem show M.'s characteristic combination of intimacy and majesty, rare enough in German hexamaters of any period. Thus he says not that he "beheld" or "gazed upon" the star, but "als ich . . . den Stern mir . . . lang betrachtete," which is almost as idiomatic as "when I was taking me a good long look at the star." Another feature: here is a servant of the Württemberg consistory, a salaried clergyman, writing from Cleversulzbach in 1837 an almost atheistic poem; and yet M. with his compassion still does wonder at the mysteries of the stars.

Selig (*blithely*): this is one of the most pregnant words in M.'s vocabulary: an ordinary word charged with special meaning. See also "On a Lamp" and "Corinna." It has various senses, such as: aloof, blissful, transcendent, blithe, inscrutable, unruffled. The Greek noun εὐδαιμωνια (*eudaimonia*) is an ancestor of the word.

AN EINE ÄOLSHARFE / TO AN AEOLIAN HARP: An aeolian harp, or wind harp, consists of a wooden or metal frame holding several strings with varying lengths. The wind blows through and the strings vibrate. M. makes several references to wind harps in his letters, and evidently he regarded the instrument as a medium of elemental music.

The Latin quotation (Horace, *Odes* 2, 9, 9 ff.) says: "You keep besetting Mystes, who has been taken away, with tearful melodies: your loves do not leave you when Hesperus rises, nor when it flees before the fast-moving sun." The Latin poem advises against prolonged mourning for a dead beloved person. The "boy" in M.'s poem is his younger brother August, who died suddenly of a stroke on 25 August 1824 (thirteen years before the poem was written). Not long before his death, he and M. had been to a performance of Mozart's *Don Giovanni* together. There were wind harps on the Emichsburg (the *Schloßpark* at Ludwigsburg), near which August was buried.

Note the oxymorons denoting mixed feeling (torment and delight): "von wohllautender Wehmut," "ein holder Schrei," "mir zu süßem Erschrecken" ("sweetly startling me"), also the relation between these and the death-in-life and life-in-death imagery of nature (the full rose, the scattered petals). The dactylic-trochaic rhythms are a fusion of various Greek elements: lines 1–2 make a complete hexameter, lines 9–10 are in the adoneus measure (/∪∪/∪) employed in ancient laments for the god Adonis. The last line is a sequence of two adoneus measures. Syntactically the poem has a remarkable symmetry: see the middle stanza, lines 11–18, where present participles (= *a*), past participles (= *b*) and verbs (= *c*) are arranged in a perfect chiastic pattern: *a a b c c b a a*. These and other features can only be shadowy, if not eclipsed, in translation.

AN FRIEDR. VISCHER / TO FRIEDRICH THEODOR VISCHER: The first edition of M.'s poems, *Gedichte*, appeared in 1838. Friedrich Theodor Vischer (1807–87), whom M. had known since boyhood in Ludwigsburg, and who came to Tübingen during M.'s last year as a student there, was one of the most eminent literary critics of the century in Germany. In the preface to his *Kritische Gänge* (1844), he expressed the opinion that M. no longer had "roots in the age," and that he was "a great talent, but one that had ceased to develop." The second and enlarged edition of *Gedichte*, 1848, seems to have convinced him otherwise. In his masterly characterization of lyric poetry, dated 1853, Vischer often refers to M.'s poems as model versions of what he called "the point-by-point ignition of the world in [the poet's] subjectivity" ("das punktuelle Zünden der Welt im Subjekte") (F. T. Vischer, *Ästhetik oder Wissenschaft des Schönen*, part 3, sec. 2 [Stuttgart 1857], 1330–33). There is correspondence between the two men, who were good friends.

AN PHILOMELE / TO PHILOMEL: Unusual: comic Horatian alcaics. Philomel is the stock lyrical name for the nightingale.

WALDPLAGE / PLAGUE OF THE FOREST: The meter is senarius, a six-beat iambic line (Greek: trimeter—counting 3 × 2 iambic feet). Originally it is the line of the dialogues in Greek tragedy. Goethe used it, for its monumental dynamic effects, in the Helena Tragedy (act 3) of his *Faust II*. The line has been little used in English; its cousin, the alexandrine, hardly more (see G. S. Fraser, *Metre, Rhyme, and Free Verse*, London, 1970, 37–38). The difference between senarius and alexandrine (the latter first appears in French twelfth-century narrative poems) is that alexandrines are usually rhymed; also, at least in French practice from the mid-seventeenth century on, the alexandrine can modulate to include anapaests ($\cup\cup/$), reducing the number of beats to four. Thus Racine: "Je ne crains que le nom que je laisse après moi," is anapaestic; likewise Baudelaire: "Pour l'enfant amoureux de cartes et d'estampes," and Rimbaud: "Glaciers, soleils d'argent, flots nacreux, cieux de braises,"—syncopated anapaests, as compared with the regular iambic alexandrine, "Or moi, bateau perdu sous les cheveux des anses" (Rimbaud). M. brings to the senarius a conversational (*parlando*) élan, by varying the positions of grammatical pauses in the lines: note the positions of commas and semicolons in lines 1–12; also by giving the line a near-trochaic thrust. Other senarius poems: "To

Longus," "Divine Reminiscence," "On a Lamp," "Edifying Observation."

Klopstock (Friedrich Gottlieb, 1724–1803) was the most influential *enfant terrible* of German poetry in the 1750s, widely read at the beginning of the Goethe period, on account of his blendings of personal and religious passion and his devising of quasi-Greek stanzas. By M.'s time he was hardly read. The joke at the end rests not least on the general solemnity of Klopstock's poems. *Schnake* means both "gnat" and "joke."

An Longus / To Longus: H. W. Rath argued in 1919 that "Longus" was a pseudonym for the poetaster F. E. Ostertag, with whom M. was acquainted (*Deutsche Rundschau* 45 and 46). This widely accepted view was challenged in 1952 by G. F. Hartlaub, who proposed that Hermann Kurz was meant (*kurz* = short), a writer whom M. met in 1838 (*Euphorion* 46). More likely, it seems to me, M. meant Longus, the author of the Greek pastoral tale *Daphnis and Chloe* (second-third century). The passage alluded to would then possibly be in book 2, 12, where the young "gallants" (Thornley translation) from Methymna arrive on the island where Daphnis and Chloe live. The crucial word would be πλούσιοι (Νέοι Μηθυμναῖοι πλούσιοι): *plousios* = opulent, ample, wealthy. M. might have also read the word cross-linguistically, with the Latin *plus* in mind. One of the texts available to him was a Greek text with Latin translation: R. F. P. Brunck, G. H. Schaefer, F. Boissonade, E. E. Seiler, *Longi Pastoralia* (Leipzig 1835). He might well have also known the translation into German by F. Jacobs: *Longus Hirtengeschichten von Daphnis und Chloe* (Stuttgart: Metzler Verlag 1832). There were two earlier Greek texts with Latin translation: Jungermann (Hanau 1605) and Boden (Leipzig 1777). E. E. Seiler's own edition, with parallel Greek and Latin texts, did not appear until 1843.

Leier und Schwert ("Lyre and Sword"): patriotic poems by Theodor Körner (1791–1813), still widely read in the 1840s for their national-liberal sentiments.

The godlessness of the times disturbed M. In his narrative poem *Idylle vom Bodensee* (1846) he criticized comically another form of godlessness: avarice and acquisitiveness.

An Wilhelm Hartlaub / To Wilhelm Hartlaub: Hartlaub (1804–85) was M.'s friend at Urach (1818–22) and thereafter for the rest of his life. He was a clergyman's son, with both literary and musical talents, and took over his father's parish, Wermutshausen, when he was only twenty-six (while Mörike was still an itinerant curate). There is a lively correspondence between M. and him. On leaving Cleversulzbach and the clerical profession in September 1843, M. went with his sister Klara to live with the Hartlaubs for six months. It was on Hartlaub that M. played the trick of pretending to be a ghost: but he ended by frightening himself, while Hartlaub did not even wake up (letter of 27 October 1841 to Hartlaub).

BEI DER MARIEN-BERGKIRCHE / THE CHURCH OF MARY AMONG THE HILLS: Dedicated to Wilhelm Hartlaub on his birthday in 1842. The church was at Laudenbach, between Wermutshausen and Mergentheim.

GÖTTLICHE REMINISZENZ / DIVINE REMINISCENCE: The epigraph: "All things were made by him." The picture mentioned, if it ever existed, has not to my knowledge been identified. M. describes finding a marine fossil in the country near Schwäbisch-Hall in a letter to Hartlaub of 13 September 1844; he was a keen collector of fossils.

His insistence, unusual for a German poet, that playfulness and sublimity can be allied, is borne out by the relation between the word *Zeitvertreib* (*pass the time away*) and what follows (cf. letter to F. T. Vischer, 13 December 1857: "the sublime can be connected not only with naïveté but also with playfulness".)

VOM KIRCHHOF / FROM THE CHURCHYARD: An occasional poem, sent (probably) with a blade of grass to Margarethe von Speeth. In April 1845, M. and Klara had taken lodgings in her father's house at Mergentheim (he married Margarethe in 1851; she was a Catholic). There is a saying of the Elder Pliny's which delighted M. in 1841: "The nature of things is nowhere more whole than it is in small things" ("Rerum natura nusquam magis, quam in minimis, tota est").

AUF EINE LAMPE / ON A LAMP: *Lustgemach* (*pleasance*): there is no proper English equivalent. The word denotes a special room, found in grander eighteenth-century houses, for the entertainment of guests; it need not be large. "Still undisturbed" also indicates that the lamp is an eighteenth-century object, not yet discarded, though largely ignored. The poem is M.'s aesthetics in a nutshell, but there are observations in Schiller, Goethe, and Novalis, which show the basis of this aesthetic in a certain nexus of German Classical and Romantic thought:

Schiller: "The whole form (*Gestalt*) rests and dwells in itself, a completely closed creation" (*Briefe über die ästhetische Erziehung des Menschen*, 15). Likewise Goethe: "Das Schöne bleibt sich selber selig," and Novalis: "Alles Schöne ist ein selbsterleuchtetes vollendetes Individuum" ("Everything beautiful is a self-illuminated complete *individuum*"). See also Wordsworth's lines (in *The Recluse*): "A whole without dependence or defect, / Made for itself and happy in itself, / Perfect contentment, unity entire." M. would not have known Wordsworth's lines; both poets hark back to the same source: Plato's Pythagorean description of cosmogenesis—the perfect spherical cosmos—in the *Timaeus* (32d–34b). Also relevant is the Greek phrase εὐδαίμων καί αὐταρκίς (blessed-spirited and self-dependent).

Admiring Theocritus as he did, M. would also have been familiar with the description of the wooden cup in that poet's first idyll: "Along the lips above trails ivy, ivy dotted with its golden clusters, and along it winds the tendril glorying in its yellow fruit" (Gow's translation). I am inclined to think that the repetition of ". . .ivy, / ivy . . ." (". . .*Κίσσος*/*Κίσσος* . . .") in Theocritus is at the back of M.'s ". . . *Rand* / . . . Efeuk*ranz* . . ." Among other subtle structural features in this circle poem, one should observe the sequences of liquid consonants, *l* and *r*. The sounds are drawn in tight to give in line 6 the wreathlike sequence of "Schlingt fröhlich eine Kinderschar den Ringelreihn": *l-r-l-r-l-r* (with two muted *r*'s in *Kinderschar*). The sounds gestically enact the roundelay or ringdance. The last line is untranslatable to the extent that *selig* has special connotations (see note to "Johann Kepler") and *scheint* plays on the two meanings *seem* and *shine*, while echoing the classical aesthetic of art-play as revelation through "seeming" or "illusion" (Schiller).

ERBAULICHE BETRACHTUNG / EDIFYING OBSERVATION: The translation deviates from the senarius, into pentameters. The opening lines I read as a mock-Homeric simile, hence the English archaisms. The third paragraph alludes to M.'s friend Ludwig Bauer (1803–46). Fellow students at Tübingen, they were introduced in 1823 by the poet Wilhelm Waiblinger (1804–30), and the three of them would sometimes take the mad Hölderlin (then in his fifties) for a walk, or they would take him with them to the Chinese garden-house belonging to Archdeacon Pressel on the Österberg. Herman Hesse wrote a story about this (*Im Presselschen Gartenhaus*).

Der sichere Mann (*the Certain Man*): an imaginary giant invented by M., hero of his "Märchen vom sicheren Mann" (1837–38).

DENK' ES O SEELE / THINK NOW, O SOUL: The poem appears at the end of M.'s novella *Mozart auf der Reise nach Prag* (*Mozart on the Way to Prague*, 1855) as a "Bohemian folksong."

CORINNA: For circle imagery, see Introduction, and notes to "On a Lamp."

ERINNA AN SAPPHO / ERINNA TO SAPPHO: Metrically, the poem is a fantasia on various Greek measures: sapphics, hexameters, asclepiadics, glykonics. It begins and ends with near-sapphic measures (/ᵕ/ᵕ/ᵕᵕ/ᵕ/ᵕ).

Tochter Demeters (*Demeter's . . . daughter*): Persephone of the Underworld.

BILDER AUS BEBENHAUSEN / PICTURES FROM BEBENHAUSEN: M.'s own footnote (not included) says: "[Bebenhausen] a Cistercian abbey with a lake, one hour from Tübingen, now the regional forestry center. The former hospice of the abbey, where the writer spent a few weeks [in September 1863] is the birthplace of C. F. von

Kielmeyer, property and summer residence of the family of the same." M. had been there with his sister Klara at the invitation of Karl Wolff (1803–69), rector of the *Katharinenstift*, the girls' school in Stuttgart where M. had been giving weekly lectures on literature since November 1851. The poems, eleven of them, were written as a gesture of thanks to Wolff. The original architecture of Bebenhausen was twelfth-century Romanesque; Gothic additions were made in the fourteenth and fifteenth centuries— the tower has a Gothic steeple and flying buttresses, hence *gegliedert* (*jointed*).

Sommer-Refektorium, (*Summer-Refectory*), last 2 lines: an allusion to the Württemberg Counts Palatinate of the twelfth to fifteenth centuries.

IN GEDANKEN AN UNSERE DEUTSCHEN KRIEGER / THOUGHTS CON-CERNING OUR GERMAN WARRIORS: Refers to the Prussian victory over France in the Franco-Prussian War (1870).

SELECT BIBLIOGRAPHY

*(restricted to publications in English, excepting German
textual and iconographic sources)*

FRIEDRICH HÖLDERLIN (1770–1843)
Source:

Sämtliche Werke, ed. Friedrich Beissner. Stuttgart, 1943–61
(Grosse Stuttgarter Ausgabe).

Translations:

Burford, William, and Middleton, Christopher, eds. *The
Poet's Vocation.* Austin (Texas), 1966. (Letters by Hölder-
lin, Rimbaud, Hart Crane.)

Gascoyne, David. *Hölderlin's Madness.* London, 1938.
(Imitations.)

Hamburger, Michael. *Selected Verse,* Harmondsworth (Eng-
land), 1961; *Poems and Fragments,* Princeton and London,
1966.

Henderson, Elizabeth. *Friedrich Hölderlin: Alcaic Poems.*
New York, 1963. (Twenty-one metrical translations.)

Leishman, J. B. *Friedrich Hölderlin: Selected Poems.*
London, 1938.

Prokosch, Frederick. *Some Poems of Friedrich Hölderlin.*
Norfolk (Conn.), 1943.

Trask, Willard. *Friedrich Hölderlin: Hyperion.* New York
and London, 1965.

Books and Essays about Hölderlin:

Beck, Adolf, and Raabe, Paul. *Hölderlin: eine Chronik in
Text und Bild.* Frankfurt am Main, 1970.

Benn, M. B. *Hölderlin and Pindar.* The Hague, 1962.

Bowra, C. M. *Inspiration and Poetry.* London, 1955.

Butler, E. M. *Thè Tyranny of Greece over Germany.*
Cambridge (England), 1935.

Hamburger, Michael. *Contraries.* New York, 1970. (Contains a general essay, and an essay on Hölderlin and Milton.)

Hamburger, Michael. Introductions to Friedrich Hölderlin in *Selected Verse,* Harmondsworth (England), 1961, and *Poems and Fragments,* Princeton and London, 1966.

Häussermann, Ulrich. *Friedrich Hölderlin in Selbtszeugnissen und Bilddokumenten.* Hamburg, 1961.

Montgomery, Marshall. *Friedrich Hölderlin and the German Neo-Hellenic Movement.* Oxford, 1923.

Muir, Edwin. *Essays on Literature and Society.* London, 1949.

Peacock, Ronald. *Hölderlin.* London, 1938.

Friedrich Hölderlin: an Early Modern, ed. Emery George. Ann Arbor, 1972. (A digest also exists, dated June 1971.)

Quarterly Review of Literature 10, nos. 1–2, 1959. (Essays by Hellingrath, Heidegger, and others.)

Salzberger, L. S. *Hölderlin.* New Haven, 1952.

Silz, Walter. *Hölderlin's Hyperion: A Critical Reading.* Philadelphia, 1969.

Stahl, E. L. *Hölderlin's Symbolism.* Oxford, 1945.

Stansfield, Agnes. *Hölderlin.* Manchester, 1943.

EDUARD MÖRIKE (1804–75)

Source:

Sämtliche Werke, ed. H. G. Göpfert, 3d edition, revised and enlarged. Munich, 1964. The present text restores the apostrophes marking elided vowels, most of which Göpfert omits.

Translations:

Cruikshank, Norah K., and Cunningham, Gilbert F. *Poems by Eduard Mörike.* London, 1959.

Loewenstein-Wertheim, Leopold von. *Eduard Mörike: Mozart's Journey to Prague.* London, 1957.

Middleton, Christopher. "Theocritus through Morike." *Arion* 8, 1969. (Mörike's translation of Theocritus, "The Cyclops," translated into English, with postscript.)

Books and Essays about Mörike:

Browning, Robert. "Auf eine Christblume." *Germanic Review* 42, 1967.

Dieckmann, L. "Mörike's Presentation of the Creative Process." *Journal of English and Germanic Philology* 53, 1954.

Farrell, R. B. "The Art of Eduard Mörike." *Proceedings of the Australian Goethe Society*, 1952–53.

———. *Mörike: Mozart auf der Reise nach Prag.* London, 1960. (Commentary on Mörike's story.)

———. "Mörike's Classical Verse." *Publications of the English Goethe Society* 25, 1956.

Holthusen, H. E. *Mörike in Selbstzeugnissen und Bilddokumenten.* Hamburg, 1971.

Koschlig, M. *Mörike in seiner Welt.* Stuttgart, 1954.

Lange, Victor, "Eduard Mörike," In *On Romanticism and the Art of Translation: Studies in Honor of Edwin H. Zeydel.* Princeton, 1956.

Mare, Margaret, *Eduard Mörike: The Man and the Poet.* London, 1957.

Middleton, J. C. "Mörike's Moonchild: A Reading of the Poem 'Auf eine Christblume,'" *Publications of the English Goethe Society* 28, 1959.

Prawer, S. S. "Mörike's 'Mein Fluß.'" In his book *German Lyric Poetry.* London, 1952.

Slessarev, Helga. *Eduard Mörike.* New York, 1970.

Thomas, L. H. C. "Bilder aus Bebenhausen." *Modern Language Review* 55, 1960.

Williams, W. D. "Day and Night Symbolism in Some Poems of Eduard Mörike." In *The Era of Goethe: Studies Presented to James Boyd.* Oxford, 1959.

INDEX OF TITLES: HÖLDERLIN

GERMAN

ENGLISH

INDEX OF TITLES: MÖRIKE

GERMAN

ENGLISH

INDEX OF FIRST LINES